THINK LIKE A BREADWINNER

THINK LIKE
A BREADWINNER

A Wealth-Building Manifesto for
Women Who Want to Earn
More (and Worry Less)

JENNIFER BARRETT

G. P. PUTNAM'S SONS

New York

PUTNAM
—EST. 1838—

G. P. Putnam's Sons
Publishers Since 1838
An imprint of Penguin Random House LLC
penguinrandomhouse.com

Hardcover ISBN 9780593327890
E-book ISBN 9780593327906

Printed in the United States of America
1st Printing

Book design by Katy Riegel

*To my husband, Victor, a tireless supporter
and loving partner, and our two boys*

To my friend Simran, whose story inspired me and this book

*To my Mom and Nana, who blazed trails for my sister
and me and lit fires within us*

*To my Dad, who taught me the value of hard work,
perseverance, and dreaming big*

*To Bea and Andy, who generously opened their hearts
and home, offering solace and a quiet place to write*

*And to my sister and the dozens of other incredible women
who shared their stories, insights, and advice for this book*

Contents

Preface

UNTIL RECENTLY, FEMALE breadwinners in America were generally the outliers—not, as is increasingly the case, the norm. But the number of breadwinning women has risen sharply over the last few decades across all ethnic, income, and education groups, with the Great Recession accelerating that trend. This move toward female breadwinning has been significant and relatively recent.

With one exception. A significant percentage of Black mothers are the primary source of economic support for their families—and that has been the case for decades. While the total number of female breadwinners has reached record levels in recent years, it's important to acknowledge the hard work and lived experience of the millions of women (many of them women of color) who have been providing for themselves, and for their families, for years. And to recognize that there are many women from all backgrounds who have not had the luxury of counting on a partner to bring in most of the household income.

I am the granddaughter of a female breadwinner, who raised two girls on a secretary's salary after her husband left her. And my own mother stepped into the role for a time after my parents' divorce (and continued to manage the finances after she got remarried). I have witnessed firsthand both the challenges and the metamorphic effects of breadwinning. My mother and grandmother did not *choose* to be bread-winners, and each struggled initially, but over time they transformed into truly independent women capable of providing the lives they wanted for themselves and their daughters, confident in their money choices and investments, and secure in their futures. They showed me what was possible with a breadwinning mindset.

But I didn't recognize that right away. I was seduced by princess fantasies growing up and, like many women, viewed breadwinning warily—as daunting and burdensome and something hoisted upon you like a yoke. It took me years to realize that claiming financial responsibility for myself and my future meant having more power and agency over my life, and that learning how to manage, make, and grow money myself was the best way to ensure the future I wanted came to be. It may feel like the harder path in the short term, especially as many of us aren't taught how to manage our own money successfully, but, ultimately, it is the more rewarding and empowering path.

With this book, I hope to make that journey shorter, easier, and more joyful. I share my story and the hard-won lessons I've learned and unexpected benefits I've experienced. I also conducted lengthy inter-views with more than one hundred women from around the country and across a range of ages, income brackets, and ethnicities—including single, married, and divorced women. This book reflects their varied experiences and perspectives, as well as my own, and recognizes and celebrates those women who are already thinking like breadwinners (whether they're single or married). My intent is not just to encourage all women to embrace that mindset, but to provide the tools and tips and real-life lessons to allow all of us to feel confident in our money choices, to afford the lives we want now *and* in the future, and to experience the joy of being in a position to provide for ourselves and those we love—whether we have to or not.

THINK LIKE A BREADWINNER

The Breadwinner Revelation

The great courageous act that we must all do is to have the courage to step out of our history and past so that we can live our dreams.
—OPRAH WINFREY

MY WAKE-UP CALL came late one spring night when our son was about eighteen months old. My husband, Victor, and I had just fallen asleep in our one-bedroom apartment in Brooklyn when Zach started wailing. I leapt out of bed instinctively, as I'd done many nights before, lifting him from the crib a few feet away from our bed and nestling him against my chest.

As I paced back and forth across our bedroom, trying to rock Zach back to sleep, I gazed around bleary-eyed at the familiar furnishings that usually brought me comfort. The colorful curtains my mother-in-law had sewn for us, the indigo-print bedspread that was starting to fray at the edges, the IKEA set of drawers now doing double duty as a diaper-changing table. But this time as I looked around, I felt a growing sense of unease.

Victor and I had lived in this apartment for seven years now—through our engagement, a wedding, four jobs between us, and now a baby. As I crisscrossed the room that night, it dawned on me that we were in a totally unsustainable situation. We were sharing our only bedroom, which also doubled as a home office for Victor, with a son who was getting close to outgrowing his crib.

What would happen as he grew older? And what about that second child we'd always planned to have? That definitely was *not* going to happen if we were still sharing our bedroom with a toddler!

I'd always imagined that we'd be in a home of our own when we started a family, not renting a one-bedroom apartment and wondering if we'd be able to afford another child. But even with two paychecks coming in, we seemed to be making slow progress financially. And our expenses were growing. Now we had to pay for childcare, diapers, bottles, and an ever-changing assortment of toys and clothes. We'd have to buy a toddler bed soon. And the rent for our apartment had just gone up. Here I was in my thirties, an independent-minded woman with a successful career and a steady paycheck. How had I gotten to the point where some of the things that mattered most to me were now at stake?

A little voice inside my head said, *This isn't the way it was supposed to be.*

Confession time: When I'd imagined our future together, I'd assumed that Victor's salary would far surpass mine. But he'd been laid off a few years earlier, and it had taken him some time to find another job and regain his financial footing. I'd told myself this was a short-term setback, but his income still wasn't much higher than mine. We'd each already cut back on nights out with friends and had yet to hire a sitter to go out, just the two of us. Before the baby, we'd had dinner out at least once a week. Now we stayed home and often ate take-out pizza or canned soup with toast after our son finally fell asleep.

Although the gap in our earnings had shrunk significantly, I realized I was still clinging to the belief that Victor would be the one to get a raise or a better-paying job that would allow us to afford a bigger place. I'd been plodding along, paycheck to paycheck, happy in my job as a magazine writer and focused on our baby. I'd mostly resisted looking more than a few months into the future.

After I set Zach gently in his crib, I slipped back into bed and gazed at my husband, sound asleep and snoring softly beside me. I lay awake, my heart racing. Dozens of questions ran through my head. How much more would we need to save to have a second child? How much would we need to save to buy a home? What if Victor *didn't* get a better-paying job?

Then, the ultimate question, one I'd never asked myself before: Was I prepared to take on the main breadwinner role in order to afford the future we wanted?

Challenging Our Assumptions About Money

Looking back now, I wish someone had told me early on what I'm about to tell you. The choices you make with your money and career should be based on just one assumption: That you—and *only you*—are ultimately responsible for your future. They should be based on what *you* want for your life and what it will take to get there financially. On. Your. Own.

That doesn't mean you won't get (or stay) married, or even that you'll end up being the main earner in your relationship. It just means that you'll be in a position to afford the things you want in your life, regardless of whether you're single, married, or divorced. And that's a pretty sweet spot to be in. Plus, imagine: If you and a future partner are both thinking like breadwinners, you'll be well positioned to bring all your dreams to life.

Seems pretty logical, right? But many of us didn't get that message growing up. And that omission can have serious consequences later in life.

Technically, a lot of us are already breadwinners, responsible for at least ourselves. But we're not all *thinking* like breadwinners—looking at how to ensure the income we bring in and the money we're investing will be enough to support the future we want for ourselves and maybe a family, too. After all, many of us were conditioned to believe that we wouldn't have to take care of ourselves for very long, and we weren't brought up to prepare for that possibility. So the thought of actually taking full financial responsibility for ourselves and our future plans can be daunting. If we do end up in the main breadwinner role in our relationship, it's often not by choice.

But here's the good news. As I've discovered in the years since my midnight revelation, it's not that hard to shift your mindset and set yourself up for financial success. The toughest part may be getting comfortable claiming wealth for yourself, because we've been told for so long that wealth building, and the power that comes with it, is not for us. But I can tell you now, from hard-won experience, that nothing is more empowering than knowing you can take care of yourself and your future without needing to depend on anyone.

You may be aware of this on some level, and you've probably already made some good money choices in your life. But there may be forces holding you back from your full earning and wealth-building potential that you aren't even conscious of. I'm talking about those sneaky self-sabotaging beliefs that have been baked into you since childhood and reinforced through years of cultural conditioning. They may have you questioning deep down whether you *can* earn enough to support the life you want on your own. And whether you really know enough to invest your own money successfully. You may be unsure of how much to save or how to build wealth effectively (not surprising, since few of us were ever taught).

You may wonder whether you truly have the ambition and abilities to command a high six-figure salary or a senior management role—or to say buh-bye to your soul-sucking job and start your own successful venture. You may fear that you will not be able to have a high-powered, high-paying career and a family. You may worry that it could emasculate the guy you're with if you earn more than he does, or scare away potential partners if they believe you don't need them financially. If you're in a relationship, it may seem easier to let someone else do most of the moneymaking and financial planning for the future, so you don't have to think about it and you can feel taken care of—even if it means you have less control over how things turn out.

I felt all of those things, and often not consciously. It was only after I started to question why I hadn't made better money choices in my life that I uncovered the underlying beliefs that had guided my choices. I came to understand that many were a direct result of the messages I'd absorbed and then adopted growing up. This conditioning can seep into our subconscious and leave us settling for a life that's less than what we truly want. Once you start looking, you'll see those messages reinforced everywhere—from the ads, shows, and movies you see, to the headlines you read, to the advice you get from well-meaning family members and friends. In the coming chapters, we'll dismantle many of those disempowering beliefs that hold us back, taking a deeper look at where they came from, who they serve, and why they persist.

Shifting from Earner to Breadwinner

In all the long-overdue discussions that are happening these days around female empowerment, the concept of breadwinning has largely been missing. And it's a big one. When I finally started thinking like a breadwinner, it completely transformed my relationship with money and the choices I made in ways I couldn't have imagined that night more than a decade ago as I paced across our bedroom with our toddler.

In the years that followed, the entire trajectory of my life started to shift. I went from worrying about how to keep up with the rising rent to feeling exhilarated as I set aside enough for most of the down payment on our home. (I was five months pregnant with our youngest son when we moved in.) I went from feeling anxious about money to feeling a sense of satisfaction and security when I look at my bank and investment balances. I went from being underpaid for years to constructing a career path and negotiating the salaries that would allow me to start building real wealth. I went from living paycheck to paycheck to creating streams of investment income that will allow me to become less dependent on my paychecks. I went from being thousands of dollars in debt to helping us grow our household net worth to more than $1 million, something that makes me swell with pride. Money is no longer a constant source of anxiety but a means to create a life I love.

I want all of that for you, too.

This book is designed to be a road map to help you get there, no matter what your financial situation looks like today. And it starts with mindset. The chapters ahead are intended to help you expand your thinking about your capabilities and the possibilities for your life. We'll look at how to move beyond covering the bills and saving a little for retirement to truly taking care of yourself and having fun fulfilling your desires.

In this first section of the book, "The Breadwinner Evolution," we'll explore the often-unconscious beliefs and cultural conditioning that can keep us from having the life we truly want—and how to transcend or transform them so that you can take control of your future. We'll look at what having a breadwinner mindset means and why most women still aren't brought up to think like breadwinners. And at how shifting to that mindset is key to helping you earn more and build enough wealth to have what you want in life, without needing to depend on someone else for it.

In the second section of the book, "Breadwinning Basics," we'll get into the specific steps and strategies for saving more, building excellent credit, and investing successfully to create a strong financial foundation and set you on the path to the future you want.

In the third section, "The Breadwinner Mindset," we'll look at how to negotiate for better pay and opportunities and how to build a career that allows you to be financially and professionally fulfilled.

Finally, in the last section of the book, "The Breadwinning Life," we'll cover how to successfully navigate and overcome the systemic biases and barriers that still exist for women in and outside the workplace so that you can have the career *and* the life you desire. We'll also look at how we can work together (and are already!) to break down those barriers and help close the gender gaps—in wages, wealth, and leadership—for good.

When I shifted my mindset to start building wealth, I realized I'd been fed a fairy tale for years about what "independence" means. I'd been brought up believing that being independent meant bringing in your own income and being able to pay your bills. But true independence is being able to provide yourself with the kind of life you want, now and in the future—regardless of whether you're married, partnered, or single. Embracing a breadwinning mindset can help you become truly financially independent, reach your full potential, and experience the joy of having more choices in every area of your life.

The Benefits of a Breadwinning Mindset

Adopting a breadwinning mindset is rewarding and powerful. That's not to say it is always easy. There will be unforeseen obstacles and emotions to deal with along the way. But they can be overcome if you've got the right game plan and habits in place. In the coming chapters, I'll share the experiences of dozens of breadwinners from all walks of life—alongside my own sometimes cautionary story—to demonstrate the many different paths to financial freedom.

The benefits of thinking like a breadwinner and taking control of your financial future go well beyond having peace of mind and money in the bank. Having control of your finances means having control of your choices. It means:

- never being stuck in a bad job, relationship, or neighborhood because you're afraid you can't afford to leave;
- having the ability to say no when you want to—and to say yes to opportunities that excite you, even if they may take some time to pay off;

- knowing you can achieve the life you want—buying your dream home, having a baby, traveling the world, or retiring early—without having to depend on anyone else; and
- allowing money to bring you joy rather than stress.

In this book, we'll take a clear-eyed look at what we're really up against when it comes to confidently building our wealth and closing the persisting gender gaps. This book will help you successfully navigate around the beliefs, biases, and barriers that threaten to hold you back. It will show you how to use money as a tool to create the life you want, not some scary, complex thing that's difficult to manage or talk about.

Adopting a breadwinner mindset profoundly transformed my relationship with money and helped me experience real momentum toward my goals. It gave me the confidence to expand the possibilities I saw for myself and my future, and to feel a true sense of agency over my life. And I hope it will do the same for you.

PART I

The Breadwinner Evolution

How to transform our limiting beliefs and take control of our future.

CHAPTER 1

The Breadwinner Next Door

The New Face of Today's Primary Provider

If we can see past preconceived limitations, then the possibilities are endless. —AMY PURDY, PARALYMPIAN AND ENTREPRENEUR

HOLD UP. REWIND. So how did I get to that middle-of-the-night money epiphany that I described in the introduction? The same way most of us reach our financial breaking point: slowly, then all at once.

By the time I'd reached my late twenties, I was a staff writer at a national news magazine, living in a trendy Brooklyn neighborhood. I had a killer wardrobe and a full social calendar. From the outside, I looked like I had it all together.

But it was an illusion. The truth was, I was broke.

I'd cashed out my first 401(k) retirement account, racked up more than a thousand dollars in credit card debt, and had only a few hundred dollars to my name. I was focused mostly on keeping my head above water financially and getting from one paycheck to the next. I wasn't thinking about how much I needed to save or invest for my future because I assumed I'd be sharing it with someone else who *was* thinking about all that. I wasn't worrying about how to earn enough to provide for a family because I assumed my future spouse would be the main earner.

I remember feeling tangible relief when I moved in with the man who would become my husband. Victor was then a research analyst at a startup, earning quite a bit more than I was. He had no debt. He was investing—not just in a retirement plan at work but in an E*TRADE account. And as I saw his investment balance rise each month, I felt assured that things would be fine.

So for the first few years of our relationship, I coasted. Victor was the one who found the great deal on the one-bedroom apartment we shared in Brooklyn. When we got married, he planned and paid for most of our honeymoon to Greece. And it was fantastic. While we split the rent and the cost of groceries down the middle, he managed and paid most of our bills. And I knew if I hit a rough patch, he would cover the rent.

I tried to save some money from each check, but if an unplanned expense came up—a gift for a colleague's baby shower or an unexpected trip to urgent care—I often tapped that meager savings or used my credit card. When we moved in together, I had a new 401(k) plan through work, but I was contributing the 3 percent default amount my company had selected and not a penny more. I had no clue whether that would be enough to cover my retirement. It didn't seem all that important at the time. Like a lot of women my age, I figured I had decades of steadily growing paychecks ahead—plus a partner who was already investing for both of us.

Then something happened that I hadn't counted on. Victor started having financial challenges of his own. The startup went under and he took a series of lower-paying contract jobs. He eventually got a full-time offer from a magazine he loved, but not for the job or the salary he wanted. Suddenly it seemed like we were struggling to get by rather than getting ahead. The relief that I'd felt when we first moved in together was replaced by anxiety. How had I not planned for this possibility?

It hadn't occurred to me that the man I married, who had an MBA and a better-paying job when we got engaged, might not always be in a position to take the lead in our financial lives. Or maybe I didn't want to consider that possibility because I wasn't sure I could (or wanted to) fill that role.

Even after my midnight wake-up call, when I realized I'd need to step up financially, I still struggled emotionally with the fact that I hadn't prepared for this scenario. All my life, I'd gotten the message that I didn't need to worry too much about money as long as I could cover my bills and save a little for a rainy day. That I didn't need to think like a breadwinner because I would marry someone who did.

Now, for the first time, I began to grasp the hazards of that assumption.

The Accidental Breadwinners

Some women have a breadwinning mindset from the start and make the kinds of money choices that will set them up for life. (We'll meet a lot of them in this book!) But a lot of us still aren't raised that way, so we start thinking about how to support our future, or a family, only when it becomes necessary. And that can feel pretty jarring at first.

Around the same time I had my awakening, I started to notice other women around my age having similar revelations—finding themselves in situations they never expected to face.

One evening I was having cocktails downtown with a former magazine colleague, a bright blonde in her midthirties who was a successful editor, and single. When I asked her how work was going, she looked me in the eye. "I'm exhausted, Jenn. I have worked my butt off for nearly fifteen years without a break," she said, tears suddenly welling up in her eyes. "Am I going to have to do this for the rest of my life?"

The possibility that she might have to support herself for life had only recently occurred to her. By this point, she told me, she'd expected to be married with kids—not playing the dating game in New York City, an increasingly high-stakes exercise that often ended in frustration. I knew the long hours she worked and the effort she'd already put into her career to get where she was. But while her job came with prestige, plus the pressure to be well coiffed and well dressed, it did not come with a huge salary. She was largely still living paycheck to paycheck. She'd seen marriage as offering relief from that cycle, so she hadn't set aside much money for her future. Now when she looked ahead, she saw years of work and financial catch-up ahead of her. "I feel like I'm on a hamster wheel and I can't get off," she said. "I never expected it to be like this."

Not long after, over dinner one night at a French bistro in midtown Manhattan, my friend Jessica told me that the man she'd been dating didn't want to have kids. But she did. Initially, she'd thought she might convince him to change his mind. But she'd recently come to terms with the fact that if she wanted a baby, she might need to have and raise that child herself—something she had not prepared for financially. She was worried that she couldn't support a child on her own, but at thirty-eight, she didn't feel she had much more time to think about it.

Within months of our conversation, Jessica had broken up with her boyfriend and gone to a sperm bank. She left her job at a daily newspaper to take a public relations role at a hospital that paid more and offered better benefits and a more predictable work schedule. She had her son just before she turned forty. And—poof—just like that, she became a breadwinning single mom, a role she never expected to be in. She loved being a mom but confided later that she was still surprised at the way it had unfolded. "I never planned for this," she told me.

In the months that followed, I began to take note of other women I knew, not just in New York but around the country, faced with responsibilities and circumstances they hadn't expected. In the span of a year, two more friends in their late thirties became single moms, a transition that wasn't easy for either financially. Two other friends were in the midst of getting a divorce, each with young kids they would need to support. Another friend's husband lost his job, and her salary, which was considerably lower, became the only source of income for their family of four for several months—requiring the family to move to a smaller apartment and cut many of their expenses.

Even friends who weren't shouldering all the financial responsibilities were feeling like they should play a more active role in their household finances.

Diane, a senior manager at a telecom company, said her husband had initially taken the lead in managing their investments. "He said he was building wealth for our future, and I wanted to believe what he was saying. But I should have pushed him for more details earlier," she told me. She later learned that they weren't earning nearly as much as he'd implied from the investments and that their financial situation wasn't as secure as she'd thought. "I had a very different perception of our net worth than turned out to be the case," said Diane. "Had I known, I would have made some very different money decisions."

I soon discovered these sorts of conversations were happening among women all over the country as we realized that this narrative many of us were fed—that we don't have to take full financial responsibility for ourselves—had left us vulnerable and without real agency over our lives.

What Changed?

What was going on here? How was it that so many smart, ambitious, well-educated women were finding themselves in situations they hadn't prepared for? It was as if we'd all wandered blithely through our twenties and into our thirties, working hard in our careers, yes, but with the underlying assumption that at some point we'd be able to slow down. At some point we'd have a partner to help cover the bills and future plans.

We'd saved money, but mostly for short-term goals—like a new couch or a flight to visit family for the holidays. We weren't thinking about saving money for a retirement we might be primarily responsible for covering, or to pay all the bills if a spouse lost a job, or to be able to afford to have and raise a baby solo. We weren't thinking about preparing financially for the possibility of supporting ourselves for the long term—much less supporting anyone else.

And yet, as we entered our midthirties or forties, we found ourselves facing one of those scenarios. And we were left reeling. It felt as if someone had unexpectedly changed the plotline halfway through our story and left us wondering, *How did I end up here?*

As a financial journalist, my instinct was to take a deep dive into the data to look for clues. I spent hours poring over U.S. Census Bureau and Department of Labor reports, studying demographic trends. I started asking questions—of friends, coworkers, gender studies experts, and financial advisors—trying to determine where our assumptions had come from and what they were based on, if not reality.

What I discovered is that for many women raised in a middle-class household—whether we were born in the 1970s or the '90s—a lot of the ideas and expectations we picked up around money aren't just disempowering; they're outdated. Our parents may have passed along what they'd experienced or believed would be true for us. But many of the long-standing assumptions upon which their ideas were based no longer apply.

In 1960, nearly three-quarters of the U.S. adult population was married, and divorce rates were relatively low. So it made sense to count on getting and staying married. But since the 1980s, the marriage rate has been on the decline. By 2014, single Americans actually outnumbered married ones for the first time in history! More than half of Americans between eighteen and thirty-four today say they aren't in a relationship—a record high.

The average age of first-time mothers in the United States has also risen, from twenty-one years old in 1972 to twenty-seven today—and to thirty for women with a college degree. And more of us are raising those kids *by ourselves*. Nearly one in four kids in this country is growing up with a single mom—an unprecedented number. Data show there are actually more single millennial moms than married ones!

What's particularly telling is that the birth rate for unmarried teens and single moms without a college degree—historically the group with the highest rates of single motherhood—has actually decreased sharply over the last decade. Meanwhile, birth rates have grown among unmarried women thirty-five years or older. "I don't think people realize that there are a lot of older women now who are having babies deliberately, single mothers by choice," Isabel Sawhill, a senior fellow at the Brookings Institution, told the *New York Times* in 2015.

Of course, when we're fantasizing about our futures, we probably aren't picturing ourselves among those numbers. Jessica and my other friends certainly weren't. Who wants to believe that we may not find a partner as early as we hope or that we may end up raising kids on our own? Most of us are still trying to wrap our heads around the idea of being financially responsible for ourselves. This doesn't mean we're all destined to end up divorced or to stay single a lot longer than we'd planned. But it means we can't necessarily count on a partner picking up most of the expenses or the financial responsibility for our future—even if we were raised to believe we could.

Taking Charge of Our Own Destiny

It's not just that men are trained from a young age to be providers, but that women are actually *discouraged* from thinking of ourselves as breadwinners every step of the way—steered into lower-paying fields and urged to spend money on disposable items that make us more attractive rather than investing in assets that can grow in value and make us wealthy. Billions of marketing dollars and years of cultural conditioning are still aimed at keeping women in debt and focused on spending; thinking of ourselves as consumers, not providers; and equating dependency with security.

"But if I become the breadwinner, who will take care of *me*?" one thirty-five-year-old marketing manager asked me when we discussed the likely possibility that she would outearn a partner. And I get it. Millions of us have been brought up to believe that "being taken care of" by a man means he's carrying the bulk of the financial responsibilities.

The fantasy of being taken care of financially is seductive—on the surface anyway. That's one reason it's persisted for so long, even in the face of shifting data. A 2015 Georgetown study, "Who Should Bring Home the Bacon?," found that even with the rise of dual-income households, the majority of men *and* women still said they prefer the husband to be the primary earner.

At first, counting on a man to be the main earner can feel like a relief. It certainly did to me. In fact, it seemed perfectly natural. It's what my own mom did when I was young, when she'd stayed home to care for my sister and me, and what the moms of almost all my friends had done, too.

But here's the problem. That setup is not just unrealistic for many of us now; it's also precarious. Being dependent on a partner to fund your future means that you have less control over how that future turns out. And having a partner who outearns you and covers most expenses now doesn't guarantee it will be that way for good—or even for long.

For one thing, as you've probably heard, nearly half of all marriages end in divorce.

I know. That's a bummer to think about. But even if you feel certain your union is for life, it doesn't hurt to be prepared just in case. Most of the time if someone tells us there is a nearly 50 percent possibility of a certain outcome, we'll prepare for it. Fifty percent chance of rain today? We bring an umbrella. Fifty percent chance that the path of that hurricane is going to cut through our city? We stock up on flashlights, batteries, and other supplies. Fifty percent chance that a coin toss will end in our favor? We're not going to bet *all* our money on tails.

But none of us goes into marriage thinking about the probability that the union may not last. (Where's the romance in that?) In fact, we're discouraged from talking or even thinking about divorce. Almost every marriage entails some entangling of finances, but preparing for the possibility that we may need to disentangle them again someday isn't just depressing; it flies in the face of the "happily ever after" narrative and intense marketing that tells us true love—like a diamond—is forever.

Still, the fact is that there's a decent chance we'll end up single again, even if we tell ourselves it won't happen to us. And research shows that women usually get the short end of the stick in a divorce. One government study found that women's household income fell by 41 percent after a divorce, more than *twice* as much as men's did. A divorce isn't cheap: The legal costs alone can add up to tens of thousands of dollars. But having your own money means that if a marriage isn't working, you won't feel stuck in it for financial reasons—and if your spouse initiates the divorce, you'll be okay financially.

When Gloria got married in her twenties, she worked at a nonprofit organization in Washington, D.C., and her husband worked in technology. "He was making good money, so I didn't think I needed to make a lot," she said. "He made all the decisions. He picked the house. He chose the car. I just put my paycheck into our joint account, which seems silly now. But I didn't think there was anything wrong with it at the time."

Then in 2016, when their three sons ranged from five to thirteen years old, Gloria and her husband got divorced, and she got full custody. Even with the child support payments, she says she struggled financially after the split. "No way did I ever imagine being in this position," said Gloria, who eventually got a better-paying job as a budget analyst in Maryland and began picking up side jobs like event planning and freelance writing to earn extra income. "Now my focus is really on making more money. My mindset has changed since the divorce. I still love a good romance story. I still believe in all of that. But I also believe that things happen—and it doesn't just have to be a divorce. We need to be realistic and have our own money, and plan for those possibilities from the beginning."

Here's the other thing to consider: Even if you *do* stay married, the likelihood that your spouse will outearn you is slipping. A paradigm shift is underway in the breadwinning model.

Over the last half century, the percentage of families in which only a father works has fallen by half, to just one in five families. Not only are more women working, but in nearly 40 percent of heterosexual marriages, we are now bringing home the bigger paycheck. An estimated 15 million wives were the primary earners in their household pre-pandemic, more than 30 percent of them because their spouses were unemployed. And that didn't include the estimated 6.5 million unmarried women in cohabiting opposite- or same-sex couples who were the primary earners.

In one 2018 NBC News–*Wall Street Journal* poll, 49 percent of employed women in the United States said that they were their family's main breadwinner. Even in the midst of the coronavirus pandemic, as millions of Americans lost their jobs (and women were disproportionately affected), a 2020 report by the Institute for Women's Policy Research calculated that moms were still contributing at least 40 percent of household earnings in half of the more than 30 million U.S. families with kids under age eighteen.

You might think that means that we are getting more comfortable taking the lead when it comes to making and managing money. But when I started digging into the data and talking to women who were the primary providers for their households, it became clear that this was *not* necessarily the case. If it were, do you think we'd still accept being paid 82 cents (or less) for every dollar a man earns? Or that we'd still significantly outnumber men in the lowest-paying career fields while men continue to outnumber us in the highest-paying roles *across every sector*? And no matter how successful we are in our careers or in other areas of our lives, too many of us still manage our money begrudgingly, handing the financial reins over to the men in our lives as soon as we can.

The Changing Face of Today's Breadwinner

So if the assumptions haven't changed, how is it that so many women became the sole or primary breadwinner for their families?

The Great Recession of 2008 played a pivotal role. In the past dozen years, the main-earner role flipped within many marriages after millions of men lost their jobs. The recession created the largest jobless rate among American men since World War II. Men lost 5.4 million jobs between December 2007 and June 2009—more than double the number of jobs that women lost. Some of those jobs never came back.

So millions of women became the main earners by default.

Many men—like my husband—found themselves struggling to maintain the same income and lifestyle that their own fathers had. The average guy today is earning less in inflation-adjusted terms than his dad made at the same age. The percentage of men working today is actually lower than it was a decade ago and is expected to continue to decline.

Meanwhile, the number of women in the workforce has grown. In the 1950s, less than 40 percent of women between the ages of twenty-five and fifty-four worked. By 2019, more than *75 percent* of women in that age group did. At the end of 2019, for the first time, more women than men were in the workforce. While the coronavirus pandemic wiped out some of the job gains women have made, the number was expected to rebound as the economy did and as regular school schedules and childcare help resumed. Even in the pandemic, women's earnings continued to account for a significant percentage of many households' total income.

I wish I could say that my late-night wake-up call was immediately followed by a breakthrough in thinking about my money and my ability to grow it. But the sudden recognition that I shouldn't depend on my husband initially left me reeling.

When I spoke with other women in similar positions, they told me they'd experienced the same sort of vertiginous feelings as they confronted the voice inside that whispered, *This isn't the way it was supposed to be.*

Soon after she got married in her twenties, Akima, a thirty-eight-year-old who runs a production company in Georgia, began outearning her husband. Looking back, she can see there were plenty of signs that she would wind up as the breadwinner; when he was still finishing his bachelor's degree, she was already wrapping up her master's. Still, she said, she continued to tell herself he'd catch up soon. "The reality is that men usually make more than women, and I thought he had the potential to surpass me. I really didn't expect to be the breadwinner for long—I thought the gap would close. Instead, it got wider," said Akima, who eventually got divorced and is raising their son.

Susan, a healthcare consultant in Chicago and mother of two, knew she would be the main earner initially because she got a great-paying job straight out of school. "Ultimately, though, I thought our salaries would end up being comparable—in fact, I thought we would be this great power couple," she remembered. She didn't count on her husband being laid off early in his career. She never imagined that he would struggle for several months to find another job. Even after he found a new role, her earnings continued to far exceed his, and she carried most of the financial responsibilities. "It turned out to be the opposite of what I'd expected," she said.

The crux of the resistance so many women feel about becoming, or even identifying as, a breadwinner often comes back to that: We never *expected* to be in a position to have to provide for ourselves—much less anyone else—for the long term. So we feel unprepared to assume the role.

Women are more comfortable leaning into their careers, but still don't expect to be the main earner in the household, Marianne Cooper, Ph.D., a sociologist at the Women's Leadership Innovation Lab at Stanford University, told me. "Culturally there's been a huge transformation with women becoming breadwinners, but there has not been as much of a shift in identity and then, literally, in [learning] the skills that help you do it. There's this discourse that women need to be financially empowered, but then there's this competing discourse that someone will take care of you," Cooper said. "Traditional gender norms are really hard to upend."

I definitely felt that. But once I was finally able to let go of what I'd thought my role as a woman, wife, and mother "should" look like and embrace the breadwinner mindset, it profoundly changed my life—and even my marriage—for the better. It was as if I'd unlocked a whole new range of possibilities for my life. (That's why I'm writing this book!) And many of the breadwinner-minded women I interviewed told me they'd experienced a similar transformation. You'll meet some of them in the coming chapters.

What I've come to realize is that, whether it's planned for or not, women are increasingly likely to be the primary financial support for themselves, and maybe others, too. The reality is, we can't afford *not* to think like a breadwinner anymore.

And whether or not we do become the main earner in a relationship, adopting a breadwinning mindset can help us feel more empowered and confident about our capabilities and our futures.

So why aren't more of us being raised as breadwinners already? I set off to find out.

CHAPTER 2

What's Been Baked into Us

Questioning Our Assumptions About Money

*I believe had I been a boy, I wouldn't have had this incredibly slothful
attitude toward money—because I wouldn't have been allowed to.*

—FRAN LEBOWITZ

I REMEMBER LAUGHING with my sister a few years ago when her daughter, then in elementary school, declared that "only women are doctors." It was an understandable assumption: She had yet to meet a male physician. My sister is a doctor in a suburb of Washington, D.C., and her daughter's pediatrician was also a woman. Initially my niece wanted to follow in their footsteps. Then she decided she wanted to be an astronaut. And then a couple of years later, just as I was starting to wonder if things might be shifting for girls of her generation, my niece, newly adorned in pink dresses and sparkly headbands, informed us that she had scrapped her astronaut ambitions altogether. "I want to be a princess," she announced.

Even for Gen Z girls, it seems, the fairy-tale fantasy still holds sway. My niece would go on to dress up as different Disney princesses four years in a row on Halloween, a costume choice so popular among female trick-or-treaters that my sister says she was swept up annually in a sea of tulle and tiaras.

"Snow White, Belle, Aurora . . . What little girl wouldn't want to be a Disney princess? Wouldn't want long, flowy hair, and wouldn't want to make a wish in a well and have the perfect life?" asked Anya Dubner, a high school student and the teenage daughter of *Freakonomics* podcast host Stephen Dubner, in an October 2019 episode. "What you want is probably, because of Disney, this fantasy life where everything is so easy, and everything is perfect, and you find a prince. [But] having your ideal life be so easy to achieve is a really bad message to send to anybody . . . especially to girls."

True, we're mostly over the idea of being *saved* by Prince Charming, but vestiges of that narrative still stick stubbornly to our subconscious as girls—and even as fully grown women. While the princess stories have evolved, some elements never seem to change. The heroines are still conventionally beautiful, with flowing locks and the wide-eyed, dewy glow of youth. And it's still their looks, rather than their smarts, that tend to draw the attention of men (and often the envy of women). "Pretty" and "princess" are synonymous, and evil and ugly are almost inevitably linked in these fairy tales. And while our heroines may be smart, adventurous, and independent-minded, they never have to worry about their income and ultimately end up finding their prince.

Is it any wonder then that so many women spend years building up their hopes instead of building up their wealth?

It's not just Disney that has perpetuated this fantasy. The fact is, if you're a woman, you've probably been lied to about wealth, and the importance of building it, your whole life. *But wait,* you may be thinking, *hasn't there been a ton of attention paid in recent years to women and money?* Yes. And in particular, much has been made of the gender pay gap: that, overall, women in the United States still earn just 82 cents for every dollar men do, and Black, Latina, and Native American women earn even less.

But then there's the gender *wealth* gap. We don't spend nearly as much time talking about that. And it is much wider than the pay gap. On average, single women in this country have just one-third the net worth that single men do. ("Net worth" meaning the money you have built up in investments, savings, and your home versus the money you owe.)

Unless something changes, that wealth gap is unlikely to close anytime soon. Women are still earning less and setting aside far less for their future than men are. In one recent report from the Transamerica Center for Retirement Studies, nearly half of the women surveyed said they weren't confident they'd be able to retire comfortably. And with good reason: The center found that women's median retirement savings amounted to a third of men's. A 2018 study from Merrill Lynch and the research firm Age Wave estimated that, by the time they reach retirement age, a man will have made as much as $1 million more in cumulative earnings than a woman.

Maybe a gap like that was okay fifty years ago, when the vast majority of households were supported by male breadwinners, and one income was enough to provide a comfortable life for a family of four. Back then most Americans could also count on pensions and Social Security to support them in retirement. But that's not the case anymore. Yet we still aren't being told or taught to build our incomes and wealth in the same way men are. In fact, we're often *discouraged* from going after more money.

"Despite the numbers, we still believe—and it's infused in what we teach our children—that men are the breadwinners, and for women, it's optional," Marianne Cooper, the sociologist at Stanford's Women's Leadership Innovation Lab, told me. And this assumption that men bear most of the responsibility for earning and investing the money, while women are in charge of spending it, continues to inform the way parents talk to their sons and daughters about money.

Cooper said even she fell victim initially to the belief. "I considered myself to be financially independent because I was able to take care of myself—I didn't need a guy to pay the bills or to pick up the check. But I was missing the larger point," she told me. "Being able to take care of yourself today financially isn't the same thing as being financially independent or financially empowered. Being financially independent means being in a position to take care of yourself for life and to afford the life you want, independent of whether you end up sharing it with someone or not."

Girls Budget; Boys Invest

Still, survey after survey finds parents are more likely to teach their sons core breadwinning skills like how to build credit and invest their money. Girls, meanwhile, are more likely to be taught how to track their spending and budget.

A GiftCards.com survey found that girls even get less money from their parents, with boys in high school and elementary school receiving roughly twenty dollars more on Christmas, three dollars more for completing chores, and one dollar more for allowance. "Girls are paid less, and are taught that they need to save and budget, while boys are paid more and taught about investing and credit scores," Bri Godwin, a media relations associate for GiftCards.com, told *Fast Company* in 2019.

Is it any surprise then that the gender wage and wealth gaps persist? Or that women end up with less credit and less money invested than men do?

At the heart of this is the fact that even today many parents are still holding on to two deep-rooted beliefs: that their sons will become the main providers for their families and that their daughters will get married. While women are seen as financial *contributors* who are able to have their own careers, we're still expected to be the ones in charge of managing the household budget (and often the household)—not managing the investments. We're taught how to budget our money but not how to grow it.

More boys than girls also report that their parents talk with them about setting financial goals. And in an annual survey produced by T. Rowe Price, twice as many boys as girls reported having access to credit cards and accompanying lessons on how to use them. The same survey also found that, across the board, boys feel smarter about money and better prepared for their financial future.

Often this isn't the result of any conscious decision by parents to withhold credit- and wealth-building advice from their daughters. It's that we still haven't wrapped our heads around the idea that these will be essential skills for girls to master in order to succeed as adults.

Even financial advisor Judith Ward, who works at T. Rowe Price, worried that she might have talked more about money with her son than with her daughter. "I find myself looking back on the way I talked to them about money matters while they were growing up. Did I inadvertently favor my son over my daughter?" Ward asks in an essay she wrote about the results of her firm's survey, which found that parents are more likely to talk with their sons about financial goals, credit, and saving for college. "Should I have talked to both of them more?"

Couple that mixed messaging with the incessant pressure on women to maintain our wardrobes, our homes, and our appearances, and the billions of marketing dollars aimed at encouraging us to spend our hard-earned money to do it, and it's not hard to see why even women who move into higher-paying careers still lag behind men when it comes to saving and investing money for their futures.

Even media created by and for women tends to reinforce these old tropes about budgeting versus investing. A couple of years ago, the research firm Age Wave analyzed the money coverage in the most popular women's magazines. Out of nearly 1,600 editorial pages it analyzed, guess how many covered financial advice? *Five* pages. Five! Women's magazines are full of tips on how to shed ten pounds, look ten years younger, and pick the perfect little black dress, but not how to pick stocks or build an investment portfolio to fund our dreams and our retirement.

When publications that target women do offer money advice, the focus is typically on spending less money—not growing more of it. Anne Boden, CEO of the British bank Starling, commissioned a linguistic study a few years ago of three hundred money-related articles. She found that *90 percent* of money articles aimed at women suggested spending less, while the majority of those aimed at men focused on investing and building wealth. "Women are told to cut back on coffee to save up for a new pair of shoes," Boden told the *New York Times*. "With men, money is all about power suits and investing and long-term goals."

What *are* women encouraged to invest in? Our wardrobes. Google "women's investment fashion pieces" and you'll get more than 28 million results, including headlines like "30 Investment Pieces Every Working Woman Needs by 30" from *Vogue* (the first: a $3,260 "neutral wool coat") and Goop's "Invest Wisely: 10 Classic Pieces That Pay Dividends" (including a $1,264 shirt dress). What's an "investment piece"? It's basically an addition to your wardrobe that costs the equivalent of your paycheck or more. Outside of a handful of vintage designer bags— which can run anywhere from a couple thousand dollars to more than $40,000 (meaning they're out of budget for many of us)—most items in your wardrobe, even designer pieces, will typically lose value the longer you own them, especially if you're actually using them.

Men, meanwhile, get headlines like "How to Become a Property Millionaire" (*Esquire*), "How to Make a Million Dollars" (*GQ*), and "Investing in These Stocks Now Could Make You a Millionaire Retiree" (Fool.com).

It's worth pausing here for a quick lesson on investing. If you'd invested your paycheck in a stock fund that mirrors the Standard & Poor's 500 Index (we'll get into how to do that in Chapter 7) at the beginning of 2009, your investment would have been worth *more than triple* its initial value a decade later. Had you "invested" that money in a new designer coat instead and tried to resell it later, you'd be lucky to get anything close to the price you paid for it. I don't know about you, but if I'm going to invest in something, I want it to go *up* in value.

It's not just that women's magazines and websites don't offer a lot of advice on investing in stocks and bonds and real estate—assets that are expected to increase in value over time and can provide you with additional income. It's that the financial advice they do give tends to focus on being able to cover just the basics. Extra goes to little luxuries like new shoes or a girls' getaway, rather than to saving for a house with a walk-in closet to put those shoes in or saving for a future that allows you and your loved ones to travel regularly. We're encouraged to be ambitious when it comes to our careers. Why not when it comes to our money?

Understanding how millions of us have been conditioned to think about wealth differently than men have—and not in a good way—is key to creating a mindset that will empower you to build wealth like a breadwinner. The truth is, most of us need to overwrite a lot of programming we got encoded into us growing up (and even as adults) in order to confidently grow our money.

Work Optional?

"From the very beginning, we train children to have unconscious gender bias," actor Geena Davis told *The Guardian* in a 2016 interview. "Even in kids' movies there are fewer female characters, and the female characters that are there are very often valued for their looks, and don't have the same kind of aspirations and goals and dreams as the male characters."

Research funded by Davis's Institute on Gender in Media found that female characters are far less likely to even be *employed* than their male counterparts in family films, prime-time programming, and kids' shows. At a talk I went to in January 2020, she told the audience that her research found that *81 percent* of jobs depicted in family shows are held by men. And even when women are portrayed as having a career, they typically have low-level support jobs, while the majority of high-powered, high-paying jobs—like corporate executives, real estate developers, and doctors—go to men.

It's not hard to imagine why many women grow up thinking that work is optional when many of the female characters they see on-screen are unemployed or underemployed.

While women's actual career opportunities and aspirations have grown significantly, our on-screen portrayals have been much slower to evolve. One recent review of advertising and gender stereotypes noted that ads continue to promote sexism and distorted female body images as valid and acceptable. While there's been more of an awareness of the impact, with some advertisers choosing to embrace a more realistic image of women and display a "softer" side of men, such depictions remain the exception, not the norm. (Think of how much attention ads from Dove's "Real Beauty" and Always' #LikeAGirl campaigns got just for presenting authentic portrayals of women and girls.)

In another study funded by the Institute on Gender in Media, girls and young women around the world watched more than one hundred popular ads. Their top takeaways? That girls have to be pretty. That men are more intelligent than women. That leadership is for men. And that a woman's place is in the home.

"We have more women than ever in positions of power making huge strides and yet the images, characters and depictions of women in the media do not reflect that. How are young girls growing up today supposed to feel about being a leader or being strong, when they don't have much to look up to in this constant negative media barrage?" Sarah Moshman, director of the documentary *The Empowerment Project: Ordinary Women Doing Extraordinary Things*, asked in a recent *Forbes* interview.

Then there's Disney.

Sarah Coyne, a psychology professor at Brigham Young University, looked specifically at the correlation between exposure to Disney princess movies and products and behaviors and attitudes among girls. Her article, published in the journal *Child Development*, concluded that engagement with Disney princess products and movies is indeed associated with more female gender-stereotypical behavior over time.

"And what we find is that girls who are highly gender-stereotyped tend to limit themselves in a number of key ways," Coyne told *Freakonomics* host Stephen Dubner in late 2019. "They don't think that they can do well in math or science, for example. They're less likely to want to go on to college when they get older. It's really about limiting yourself and what you could become."

When I talked to my friend Sarah, who works in tech in New York City, about the princess messaging her five-year-old daughter has gotten, she laughed and told me, "She's wearing a tiara right now."

But then she took a more serious tone. "I think one of the main reasons why girls can be so passive is because they expect the guy to be the prince who will rescue them, and then they will live comfortably, and the guy will take care of them. They don't even realize that's why they're dropping the ball when it comes to making sure they succeed financially because it is so culturally ingrained in them. As a parent, you have to deliberately introduce other interests and perspectives to your girls," she said. "I told my daughter that I get that it's fun and glamorous to pretend to be a princess, and she loves the sparkles. But I was clear with her: 'It's not actually fun to be a princess, because you get told what to wear, how to act, where to live. You don't have any real control over your life.'"

We're still being fed a princess fantasy—not just by Disney—and it can seem seductive. But at its heart, as Sarah pointed out, being taken care of is just another way of saying "being dependent." It's easy to forget that a princess has no real agency over her life; that her crown was given to her, and it can be taken away.

"I was lulled by the 'forever after' fantasy."

When Amy first got married, she earned nearly twice as much as her spouse as a consultant in New York. But over time, her husband's salary grew to outpace hers. By the time their third child was born, she'd begun taking on fewer clients so she could care for their kids and work on a book idea. "I made these choices assuming we were in it together," she told me later. "Looking back, I realize that I was lulled by the `forever after' fantasy."

Then, just after their ninth anniversary, her marriage ended unexpectedly. "As it turned out, he had been cheating on me for years, spending our money on other women even as he was going on weekly date nights with me and actively planning our future together," she told me. "After that, my choices became much starker. Fortunately, I had always worked while having my family, but I hadn't prioritized my career advancement and my financial goals as much as I should have."

She'd always considered herself to be independent, but her definition of independence shifted after the divorce. "The shift I had to make was: It's not optional. I need to make money, and it has to be a priority to support myself and my kids. What's funny is that's what all the men I work with do unapologetically. I'm not sure why I felt guilty about that at first."

Amy also realized that the family's credit cards, which they'd used for almost all of their expenses and then paid off each month, had all been in her ex-husband's name. She was just an authorized user, which meant he reaped most of the credit-building benefits and rewards points. (We'll talk more about this in the chapter on building credit.) Now she had to work on building up her credit, too, so she could buy a house for herself and her kids.

"I think sometimes we confuse dependency with trust," she told me, reflecting back on her marriage. "But it really puts women at risk to not have equal income and not have the same opportunities for advancement with their career, and to not be on top of their financial picture."

Amy says her top goals now are taking care of her children, making more money each year and saving and investing for the long term. "I tell my married friends who will listen, It doesn't have to take a challenging divorce to start thinking like a breadwinner."

Shifting from Budgeting to Breadwinning

Even today we're still raising women to be budgeters, while men are taught to be breadwinners. That messaging makes a difference, and it starts young. Even teenage girls report feeling less confident than boys feel about money. One study by the Girl Scouts found that nearly half of girls between the ages of eleven and seventeen felt uncomfortable making their own financial decisions. Only 12 percent said they would feel "very confident" making decisions about money as adults.

The numbers don't change much when we do become adults. In the Merrill Lynch–Age Wave survey, nearly two-thirds of women between the ages of eighteen and twenty-nine said that financial planning "is too difficult to even think about."

Men generally report having more financial confidence, especially when it comes to investing decisions. A recent study from UBS Global Wealth Management found that 58 percent of women leave those crucial choices up to their male partners. And that doesn't seem to be changing with Gen Y or Z. Younger women between ages twenty and thirty-four were actually the *most* likely to defer to their significant others, at 60 percent.

Similarly, a BlackRock survey found that men as a group are more interested in investing than women and generally enjoy managing their money more. (Only 36 percent of millennial women say they enjoy managing their investments, compared with *70 percent* of millennial men.) According to Fidelity, single women are less likely than any other demographic group to say they're knowledgeable about investing, saving for retirement, or creating a financial plan.

All that plays out in the money choices we make as adults. The result is that, by almost every financial measure, men are in better shape than women.

Women earn less money. We have less money saved and invested. We carry more credit card debt, and we have worse credit scores—which means we pay more interest on that debt.

A study by BMO Harris found that, on average, men have nearly twice as much stashed in an emergency fund as women do. Over the course of their lifetimes, men save more than three times as much money, on average, than women, TurboTax found. A 2018 Federal Reserve analysis found single women have more debt, higher credit card usage, and more past-payment delinquencies on their credit reports than men.

It's as if we're still waiting for someone to rescue us.

Imagine instead if you'd been raised to believe you'd be responsible for taking care of yourself financially—and probably a family, too. That you'd been taught how to invest in stocks and bonds and encouraged from a young age to start investing as soon as you got your first paycheck. Imagine if you'd learned how to negotiate everything from a job offer to the best deal on a used car, and how to build good credit without sinking into debt. What if, by the time you were living on your own, you already had a sense of what you'd be earning and what your expenses would cost you? And managing money—and asking for more of it—felt perfectly natural. How would that have affected the choices you made?

Happily, it's never too late to retrain your brain. Whether you're twenty-two or fifty-two, single or married, shifting to a breadwinner mindset is one of the fastest, most effective ways to take charge of your finances and your future. This is about reprogramming the cultural sabotaging that has been baked into our subconscious early on. It starts with becoming aware of all the messages you've already absorbed about breadwinning and wealth-building, and then transforming them into beliefs that will propel you toward the life of your dreams. In the coming chapters, we'll look at how.

CHAPTER 3

The Joy of Breadwinning

The Underreported Upside of Making More Dough

There is no limit to what we, as women, can accomplish.
—MICHELLE OBAMA

IN 2013, TWO University of Chicago economics professors, Marianne Bertrand and Emir Kamenica, noticed something interesting when they examined income inequality within young heterosexual couples. Looking at U.S. Census data on couples in their twenties and early thirties, they found that while the overall number of female breadwinners had grown, many marriages exhibited an unusual pattern: the share of household income earned by the wife grew steadily—until it hit 50 percent. Then it dropped sharply.

Traditional economic theories couldn't explain the steep drop-off. If relative income didn't matter to either spouse, Bertrand and Kamenica reasoned, women with the potential to earn more would earn more.

Instead, in an article published in the *Quarterly Journal of Economics,* Bertrand and Kamenica noted that if a wife had the potential to outearn her husband, she was often *less* likely to be in the workforce once her income matched his. And if she was working, she earned less than she could. It seemed that many wives were *intentionally* cutting back work hours, choosing work that paid less, and dropping out of the workforce altogether. And this wasn't happening just in couples with children.

Why would so many women sabotage their ability to reach their full breadwinning potential?

A look at the headlines offered some clues. "Men with Breadwinning Wives More Likely to Cheat," warned CNN. "Men Stress Out if They're Not the Breadwinner," blared the *New York Post*. An article in *Inc.* asked "Can a Female Breadwinner Have a Happy Marriage?" It seemed, noted the University of Chicago researchers, that gains in women's earning potential and labor participation had outpaced "slow-moving social norms and concepts of gender."

Married or not, successful, high-earning women are still too often depicted in the media as lonely or stressed out, desperate to find love or struggling to balance work with family—if they have not given up on having a family altogether. "Super-Successful Women Struggle in Love," proclaimed the *Washington Examiner*. "Dating Successful Women Makes Men Uneasy," claimed *Business Insider*. "A Sociologist Explains Why Wealthy Women Are Doomed to Be Miserable," reported Quartz .com. Meanwhile, the *Huffington Post* declared, "Most Successful Women Are Childless." (Advised the writer in the first line: "If you want to be successful in your career, don't have children.") Even the *Harvard Business Review* warned, "For Women Leaders, Likability and Success Hardly Go Hand in Hand."

Even now, it can seem shocking for a woman to even admit she wants to make a lot of money. For the first few years after my mindset shifted and my career accelerated, I remember playing down my own earnings and financial aspirations, treating my jump in salary as an unexpected situation rather than owning the fact that I had worked hard and strategically to get a higher-paying job in management so that we could afford to raise our family in New York.

When best-selling author Jessica Knoll wrote the essay "I Want to Be Rich and I'm Not Sorry!" in the *New York Times* in 2018, it went viral, landing her on all the morning shows and drawing nearly 1,100 comments. "Women are not supposed to aspire to power for themselves—not for a cause or their families but for themselves. She does, and this openness is so rare and bold that as the comment thread shows, people can't handle it," wrote one reader. Sure enough, while some readers came to her defense and applauded her for saying what many of them felt, others called Knoll greedy, self-centered, self-serving, tasteless, and obnoxious, among other things.

When faced with such a barrage of negative headlines (or comments), is it any wonder that some women hold themselves back? If we're professionally or financially successful, we're told our personal lives will suffer. If we earn too much, we will pay for it in other ways. Or so goes the narrative that has been echoed across conservative and mainstream media outlets. Being a breadwinner—or even being ambitious in our careers—will take us away from our families and deprive us of being there for our kids. Earning too much will make us seem less desirable to men and less likable to women. Our husbands will cheat on us. Our marriages will fall apart. If that's the price of being a high-earning, successful woman, who wants that?

But is it really?

Reading *those* headlines, you might think that breadwinning wives are an exception—and not the norm in nearly four in ten marriages. And that women who earn more than their male spouse does will end up divorced, though there's plenty of evidence to suggest that husbands not being willing to do their fair share of household work is the bigger factor in determining such splits. You might assume that you can't have a family and a high-powered career, though literally millions of women do. And that high-earning women are miserable, lonely, and childless. Although I have yet to meet one of those sad unicorns.

In fact, if you take a closer look at the studies (or even the articles) behind many of those headlines, the story is not the same.

What the Research Really Says

Last year, *USA Today* ran a story headlined "More Women Are Now Outearning Their Husbands—and Emotions Can Be Big." But in the 2020 TD Ameritrade study it was based on, the majority of men seemed to be just fine with the arrangement. About 40 percent of men with higher-earning spouses or partners said, "It's great, I love it!" about their situation, and nearly as many said it made them feel proud—while 20 percent said they had neutral feelings about it. Meanwhile, female breadwinners used words like "secure," "proud," "independent," and "in control" to describe how they felt about being the main earner in their relationship. Just 4 percent expressed feeling embarrassed or guilty about it.

And those headlines warning that husbands are likely to cheat on their higher-earning wives? Christin Munsch, an associate professor of sociology at the University of Connecticut, actually found that it's not economic independence but rather *dependency* that's a recipe for relationship instability. "For both men and women, economic dependency is associated with a higher likelihood of engaging in infidelity," she wrote. In other words, if *either* partner is completely financially dependent on the other, he—or she—is more likely to cheat than spouses who aren't dependent. She did find that men who were 100 percent dependent on their working wives were more likely to have an affair than if the roles were reversed—15 percent compared with 5 percent. But this is not the norm for most marriages.

Researcher Alexandra Killewald, a professor of sociology at Harvard University who looked at 6,300 couples, did find that those in which the wives earned more were at a higher risk of divorce, but only when the husband was unemployed or just working part-time. Even more important, she found that splitting the division of housework equitably could counter this effect and lead to marital stability. This has been echoed by several other studies.

It isn't women earning more, it seems, but men doing less around the house that actually increases the risk of divorce. Maybe it's time we started focusing on changing that instead.

About half of women now say they outearn or make around the same amount as their husbands or partners, according to the TD Ameritrade study. That is a significant change in just a few generations: less than 4 percent of women earned more than their husbands in 1960, according to the Pew Research Center. And it's taking our culture, and our press coverage, a little while to catch up with that reality.

That was something I noticed as I shifted my own mindset around money and eventually moved into the main breadwinning role for my family. I didn't see myself or my experience reflected in the majority of articles I read or in the shows I watched. In fact, the more I embraced the breadwinning mindset, and enjoyed the benefits, the more I wondered if I was an exception.

My husband didn't cheat on me. He praised me and said he felt grateful for the lifestyle my income was able to help provide. Yes, we each had to confront some deep-seated beliefs about breadwinning and caregiving roles when I began to earn more, especially after we had two kids. (I'll get into that more later in the book.) But ultimately, we found an arrangement that worked for each of us. As my salary and work responsibilities grew, my husband picked up more of the caregiving and household responsibilities. Increasing my earnings and investment balances left me with a stronger sense of confidence and security and more choices for our future. And as I rose through the ranks of management and eventually into an executive role, I found my circle of female friends *grew*. My female peers were typically key supporters—not competition—and I was able to forge strong bonds and friendships with many of them.

But I didn't see many stories like mine being told.

I didn't see headlines about what women *gain* by thinking like a breadwinner and knowing we can create the lives we want for ourselves. I didn't see much about the satisfaction that comes with negotiating a better salary or a bigger job—in fact, almost all the coverage about negotiating focused on how women need to get better at it. Nor did I see much in the media that reflected the confidence that came with learning how to invest wisely and the joy of watching our money grow. Most of the investing coverage focused on women's lack of confidence in investing (despite growing evidence that we often perform better as investors) and the fact that we invest less. Even with the rise of breadwinning women, we still don't hear much about the upside of earning more, being ambitious, building our own wealth, and even providing for our families.

But those stories exist all around us. They're just not being told.

That's what I discovered when I started putting out the call for interviews for this book. Sure, I interviewed some breadwinning women whose marriages didn't last. But I spoke with even more breadwinner-minded women who were in happy unions—heterosexual and same-sex—whether they earned about the same as their partner or the majority of the household income. And with women who were happily single.

The Stories We Don't Hear

When my friend Ann Shoket, the former editor in chief of *Seventeen* and author of *The Big Life*, offered to host a dinner party in early 2020 with some breadwinner-minded women, I wasn't sure what to expect. I hadn't met any of the guests before the event. But as we munched on gourmet pizza and sipped wine in her downtown Manhattan town house, and the conversation turned to making money and building wealth, each of them had plenty to say. And their stories presented a stark contrast to the prevailing narrative about women and breadwinning. Here were women who were unabashedly ambitious; who expected to be fairly compensated for their talents and negotiated for what they wanted; and who each described happy, healthy, and balanced relationships with their partners.

"I want to achieve. I feel great when I do—and I deserve to be compensated for that value I bring," Christi, a forty-one-year-old brand strategist in New York, told me. She is the main earner in her marriage—her husband is a doorman at a high-end, high-rise residential building in Manhattan. "While it can be stressful to have that responsibility," she said, "it's also really rewarding when I succeed and we can all enjoy the fruits of those labors together."

While her husband's job provides less income, it does provide security—plus healthcare benefits for the couple and their two young children. "We never have to worry about that foundation getting pulled out from under us," said Christi, who dreams of one day starting her own beauty-products company. "It's easier to focus on lofty dreams when you have a safety net on the basics . . . Our family won't be homeless or unable to feed ourselves or get medical treatment. So I have the freedom to chase bigger dreams."

Her husband's job also allowed four months of paternity leave for each child. She took three months and he took a month in the beginning with her and then another three months after her, both times. "So both kids got to bond with both parents individually," she said. "He never shucked that responsibility, and he wasn't fearful that his company would penalize his career for taking this time off. He went right back when his leave was up as if nothing had changed. I didn't have to take everything on by myself or have a husband who had no clue what it takes to care for a child by himself. It's made our shared parenting so much more equitable starting from that place."

"The greatest benefit of being the breadwinner to me is that I feel solidly in the driver's seat of my life," Missy, a thirty-four-year-old program director at a New York software company and another dinner party guest, told me. "It gives me an incredible sense of liberation and autonomy."

Outside of when she was getting her MBA, her partner, who works at a nonprofit organization, has consistently earned less than she does. They've been together for over a decade and were expecting their second child together when I saw her. "He makes me happy, and our relationship gives me stability and fulfillment," she said. And that's most important to her.

Missy remembered when she was growing up "overhearing my mom's conversations with her friends about navigating unsatisfying marriages with too much to lose if they left." Her takeaway, she said, was that she wanted a relationship because it made her happy, not because she was dependent on him financially. "Being the breadwinner allows me to feel like my relationship is fulfilling a desire to be with him and to build a life with him, not because I can't sustain the life I'm building without him."

I met Heather, a sales director in New York City in her midthirties, at my hair salon when she overheard me talking to my stylist about this book and jumped in to ask if she could share her thoughts. "Personally, I've squirreled away a lot of savings, and I've focused on getting ahead in my career," she told me. "I love being able to create my own wealth."

Heather's married now and earns about the same income as her spouse. But when she was single, she dated several guys who earned a lot less than she did and remembers a specific conversation about it with her close friend, who told her, "You have to realize that's so empowering. You don't have to put up with a jerk."

My friend Sarah, who recently turned forty, told me that she was initially disappointed her husband, who worked in a lower-paying field, wasn't earning enough for them to afford some of the things she really wanted—like buying a home in their neighborhood instead of renting. "But at a certain point in our marriage, I realized that there's no justification for me to sit here and resent him for it," said Sarah, who recently got a senior-level role at a startup that pays well and includes equity (or shares in the company).

"I have a solid career and am well-educated," she added. "Why am I sitting around and waiting for him to make my dreams come true? Why should we give up on our desires simply because our husbands are not able to afford them?"

In fact, we may even be able to help our partners make *their* desires come true. When Dara met her husband sixteen years ago in New York, she was a credit risk analyst, and he was working as an assistant at a financial firm while pursuing his passion for photography in his spare time. "From the start, I was the primary breadwinner. That's just who we are, and I was perfectly comfortable with that," she told me. "So he was able to pursue photography completely because I could support us."

Her husband went on to work professionally as a photographer, and eventually would take on more consistent in-house roles. Then when she lost her job years later in a corporate reorganization and started building a consulting business, he took a full-time position with a private foundation that runs educational programs, which provided health insurance and other benefits for the couple and their daughter. "I thought initially I had to start looking for a job right away. But he said, 'I want you to be in a place where you don't feel the burden of this,'" she recalled.

"There are societal pressures that the man has to be the breadwinner, but I don't think he's ever been hung up as a man with earning less," said Dara, who eventually took an executive role at a media company. "I think it's more about being a good partner, about looking out for each other. I knew going in that he would not be a high-powered executive, but I was marrying someone who loves me, who shares my values, and who is creative and supportive. That is the kind of partnership we have."

Michelle, a thirty-eight-year-old entrepreneur in Brooklyn, recalled how her mom was married more than once and stopped working each time. "She would be working and liked her job, then married someone who didn't want her to work. Then I watched as the whole lifestyle got downgraded. She would have her own income and this great life, and she was traveling. Then she quit and was back to being frugal and cutting coupons," Michelle told me. "And every time she left her husband, she had nothing financially. She didn't have two nickels to rub together. That was so formative for me: I absolutely never wanted to be in that situation."

Michelle started her own business, a financial consulting firm, when she was just twenty-six. "I started from: How do I create a business to make money to have the lifestyle I want for myself? I wanted a certain income and reverse-engineered what skill set I needed to get there," she said.

Now married with a young daughter, she told me, "There's no interdependence in our household. Truly, my husband could walk out tomorrow and I would be very sad, but not much would change financially."

Mandi, a thirty-two-year-old content director who lives outside New York City, and her three siblings were raised by a single mom after their parents divorced. "I thought it was brave of her to leave my dad, because his income was so important, and she really struggled financially. I was in awe of my mother's resilience and capacity to weather a lot of financial and personal storms in her life, but I also had a deep drive to create a life for myself where I wouldn't be as vulnerable financially," she told me. "When I approached my career, it was very much in the spirit of finding my own success, because I needed to know that money wouldn't be the reason I stayed in a bad relationship or job. I wanted to set myself up in a way that I could be self-sufficient. And focus not just on growing a paycheck but growing my savings and assets."

Mandi's income surpassed her husband's not long after they began dating—something he's taken in stride. "When I bring up money, he says that I'm like a hot stock and he got in on the ground floor," she said, laughing.

Shellby, an ambitious and breadwinner-minded twenty-eight-year-old I met through a networking group, grew up in California with a single mom and helped put herself through college. "The ideas we have about breadwinners need to evolve," she told me. "There's this perception that comes from fragile masculinity, patriarchy, and archaic values that men have to earn more, do more . . . It's still ingrained in so many things we consume."

But Shellby said that she could definitely see herself earning more than her boyfriend. "And I have no qualms about that. We've talked about it, and I don't think he'd be upset," she said, "but it would be an adjustment."

I met Chris Peach, a firefighter and the founder of a popular money site, Money Peach, a few years ago at a financial conference. When the topic of earnings came up, he told me with pride that his wife, then a TV anchor in Phoenix, was the main breadwinner. So when I began work on the book, I reached out, and he and his wife, Andrea, agreed to a joint interview.

When I talked to them in spring 2020, their earnings had evened out. But he said that, until recently, she'd earned more than he did since their 2008 wedding. "She got a job at a TV station, and I got a job at a fire station, so she made more from the start," Chris told me. "She always was the main breadwinner."

Andrea jumped in: "I get that society still has a narrative that men are breadwinners, and women are not. But our relationship has never been the typical man going off to work and making the money and me staying home and tending to the kids," she said—even after their kids were born in 2010 and 2012. "I didn't think of myself as the breadwinner necessarily. I just really loved my job. I felt blessed that I got to do what I love."

Were there times when it was difficult for him, I wondered? Did Chris's friends at the firehouse know? "Oh yeah. The guys would say, 'It must be nice to have a sugar mama!'" said Chris, laughing. "But honestly, I think every guy there would rather their wives generated income than not. They had to work so much overtime to make the money, and I never had to do that."

Chris and Andrea insisted that the ribbing and occasional comments from friends—they couldn't think of any couples they knew in which the wife outearned her husband—didn't faze them. And I believed them. I remember clearly when Chris bragged about his wife at the conference. It was the first time I'd ever heard a man speaking of his higher-earning wife with such pride. But not the last.

"Rigid ideas of what men and women do"

Preeti, a Chicago doctor in her late thirties, has been the main breadwinner throughout her decade-long relationship with her boyfriend, John, who was in the U.S. Navy when she met him. Initially, she says, she was bringing in about 60 percent of their income, but he has since gone back to school to get an engineering degree. Although he has money coming in through the GI Bill, she still covers most of the expenses. And she admits that at first the disparity was hard. "A lot of early fights were about that," she told me. "When I was younger, I had read a lot of romance novels that were heteronormative, with the women not making much money, and the man making a lot. I think I carried some romantic notions around that."

Her parents also played a role. They'd assumed she would marry another doctor and actually signed her up for some matchmaking services. "They continued to send me men's profiles until four years into my relationship with John," she told me. "I never felt like my parents thought, 'Oh, you'll get married and your husband will take care of you.' But they have rigid ideas of what men and women do."

While she felt the financial pressure, John also felt self-conscious about not contributing more—even when it came to planning vacations. "There have been moments when he said, if you want a vacation, we'll do it," Preeti told me. "But he feels uncomfortable planning one himself because he says he can't pull his weight. I have to remind him, this is for me, too! And we try to talk it out."

After some early fights, Preeti says that they learned communication was critical so pent-up feelings don't boil over into resentments. "Fortunately, it's been relatively easy to talk things through," she says. They also had to adjust the division of household responsibilities until it felt fair for both. "We do divide the housework," she says. "But he does the cooking, most of the laundry, and he takes care of our two cats . . . vaccinations, cleaning the litter box, all of that. He had kitchen duty, and he made beds in the military, so he's not unfamiliar with those."

Preeti never expected a man to take care of her financially, but she says she's been surprised at how good it feels to be taken care of in other ways. Over the past few years, she says she's come to increasingly appreciate that in their relationship.

When I spoke to her by phone early one evening, she told me she was savoring the scent of the meal he was cooking in the next room. "I walk in from work some nights, and I smell the food, and it smells so lovely. And he says, 'It'll be twenty minutes.' And I can have a shower and just sit down and relax. And that is very satisfying," Preeti told me. "I wouldn't have thought of myself as a 'Honey, I'm home!' kind of person, but that has been a very nice thing."

If I'm Not My Mom or My Dad, Who Am I?

As I was doing research for the book, I wondered what I could learn from same-sex couples, as the roles in those partnerships would not be predetermined by gender assumptions. Indeed, a recent *New York Times* article ("How to Make Your Marriage Gayer") noted that same-sex couples "are far more likely to each take on some traditionally 'feminine' and some 'masculine' chores." And, researchers found, they're happier for it. Studies, including a 2016 report by the Treasury Department, have also found that lesbians tend to earn more than their heterosexual counterparts and that female same-sex couples report more total household income than heterosexual couples do (even if they have kids).

Jen, a thirty-eight-year-old lawyer who lives with her wife in New York City, had recently given birth to their son when I spoke to her. "I think I've identified more as the 'male' in the relationship, and there are some aspects of that that I carry with me," she told me. "I always thought I would take the job that paid so much more and my wife would be the one who stepped out of her traditional job once we had kids."

But then Jen decided to carry their baby. "And what does *that* mean about my identity?" she asked.

Being the one who was pregnant and gave birth, and who now got up most nights to nurse, had her questioning the role she'd initially assumed she'd have in their relationship. On a walk earlier that week with their baby and dog, her wife had questioned her assumptions, too. "She told me, you're considering new jobs that pay well that I don't think you really want to do," she recalled. "I told her, 'I want to contribute more money so that you can do what you want to do.' And she said, 'What if *I* got a job that pays twice as much as *yours*?'"

The more Jen thought about it, the more she began to question why she'd clung to the notion that she must be the primary provider for their family while assuming her partner would take the lead at home. "I'd always presumed I would be the one to support our family. But now I wondered why," she said. "I started thinking about masculinity and femininity, and the roles we equate each of them with."

Whether we're in same-sex or different-sex relationships, a lot of us are doing the same. The conventional breadwinner model—even the traditional makeup of households—is changing, and that ambiguity can feel uncomfortable. Most of us don't have a model to guide us.

Jen said she'd always identified more with her mom, a retired assistant school principal, growing up. But she recounted a recent conversation she'd had with her about a general counsel job she was up for that paid well and would make her the only attorney in-house at the company. "My mom said, 'But do you *want* to be in charge?' I was so baffled. I'd always thought, 'Isn't that the goal?' It seemed so obvious to me," she said. "Growing up, my dad was always clearly jealous that my mom made more money than he did. I knew I wasn't my dad—I didn't want to be in that position. But talking to my mom that day, I realized, 'I'm not you either. But then, *who am I?*'"

The fact is, we often can't look to our parents or to the past, because we're pioneering a new future. And as Jen expressed, it can be disorienting at first to realize that—whether you're in a same-sex or a heterosexual partnership—the rigid division of roles no longer applies for many of us. We're in uncharted territory when it comes to blending responsibilities. But this is also liberating. Because once you're free of the constraints of the past, you have the freedom to define your own role and to forge a future that's based on what *you* want, not what society tells you that you should be doing. Letting go of preconceived notions and prescribed gender roles lies at the heart of finding joy in breadwinning—whether you're the primary earner or not.

Farnoosh Torabi, the author of *When She Makes More*, told me that when her book came out in 2014, she still felt some apprehension about fully owning her role as the main breadwinner. "I think I wasn't thoroughly comfortable accepting that maybe I did this on purpose. I still had guilt about my circumstance," she said. "But I say it proudly now: Make no mistake, this was not by accident."

Torabi, who has two young kids with her husband and is still the family's main earner, calls taking on a breadwinner mindset "the most important decision" she ever made. "It has awarded me things like never feeling trapped or that I have to make a decision that is against my will. I can be a bigger giver. I can put my money toward the causes and movements I feel very strongly about. I can spend money on things that are meaningful to me," she told me. "There's no price you can put on feeling like you can make any choices for yourself. That is true freedom."

If you do end up being the main earner in a marriage, it can feel frustrating initially if this wasn't what you expected. But questioning social norms can also open up new possibilities. Ultimately, you can discover an arrangement that works for you—not one that you think *should* work, but one that actually works. A dynamic that allows each of you to find fulfillment at home and at work, to develop deep connections with each other and with your kids (if you have them), and to spend time doing activities that bring you joy and satisfaction.

What I've realized is that as breadwinner-minded women, we're pioneers, laying out new paths and creating new dynamics that support the lives we want. That allows us to ask: Who do we *want* to be in our relationships? What do we really want in a partner—if not financial support or status?

And whether we're alone or in a relationship, there's freedom in detaching ourselves from the "shoulds" that follow us around and instead focusing on what we want in our lives and what needs to be done to enable that.

Enjoying the Benefits of Breadwinning

There are things we cannot control, but we can control our mindset. We can stay true to our values and ambitions and make sure our needs are met. We can ensure that we make choices with our money that will allow us to feel less anxious, not more. It's true that spreading our wings and aiming for bigger goals can feel scary. Investing our money does require taking some risks. Growing is uncomfortable. And being financially responsible for yourself, and maybe for others, can feel particularly daunting for women. I know. I've felt all of that. (And it's likely most men have, too.) But it's also immensely rewarding.

For us to experience the joy of breadwinning, we've got to let go of any preconceived notions that have been baked into us about what breadwinning means. We can embrace a breadwinner mindset without feeling like we have to give up the other roles we enjoy.

Thinking like a breadwinner—whether or not you become the main earner in a relationship—doesn't mean you have to constantly prioritize your work over your life. You can find companies that respect boundaries and family, if you want one. (I did.) You can start your own business and make your own rules. And if you need to put up with some jobs in the meantime that aren't perfect but pay well, you will at least be doing it with the knowledge that you are working toward something better. You can have meaningful connections with the people you love and time to enjoy the fruits of your labor. You can have a deeply satisfying marriage and a happy family. You can feel good about the contributions you make professionally *and* personally. You're not a hamster on a wheel. And you're not bound by convention. You get to define what being a breadwinner means!

What I've discovered through my own experience, interviews, and research is that there are six important steps to building a breadwinner mindset and enjoying the benefits that come with it:

1. Dismantle and discard the beliefs that no longer serve you.
2. Get clear on what you desire—and allow yourself to dream big!
3. Build a strong financial foundation and investment plan.
4. Strategize your career and compensation to support the life you want.
5. Establish a strong partnership or support system.
6. Seek out other breadwinner-minded women who can encourage and inspire you.

So far we've focused largely on the first. Now let's dive into the rest.

CHAPTER 4

Dream Bigger

Visualizing the Financial Future You Deserve

The future belongs to those who believe in the beauty of their dreams.
—Eleanor Roosevelt

When I was living in that one-bedroom Brooklyn apartment, I used to dream about the home I wanted to move into next. I'd often find myself fantasizing about it as I lay in bed, my husband and son sleeping nearby. But it wasn't until the morning after my midnight wake-up call that I finally sat down and wrote out a description of it.

It was the first time I'd thought about everything I wanted in that home. I noted all the amenities as if I were writing my ideal listing: at least two bedrooms, two bathrooms, a washer and dryer (not a given in New York City), a balcony, rooftop access, an open kitchen, modern appliances, big windows, lots of light . . . As I started putting together the list in my notebook, I found my mind wandering. So I closed my eyes and imagined myself walking through this new home. How would it feel to run my hands over the smooth countertops and balcony railing? To look out at the city and nearby park I imagined? I visualized how it would feel to walk through big, light-filled empty rooms and realize this place was ours (umm . . . amazing!).

Writing out the list of amenities was a fun exercise, but I could also feel a knot of anxiety forming. At the time, I still had more than a thousand dollars of debt. I had a little less than that in savings. My husband was still getting back on his feet after being laid off. In other words, we were in no position financially to purchase a home like that in New York City. I wasn't even sure we could afford to rent a bigger place. It was difficult at the time to see how I would be able to bring that vision to life.

Still, I knew that I needed to have something tangible to work toward—a goal that mattered enough to me to endure any short-term sacrifices I'd have to make in order to save enough to make a change. Writing out the description itself helped me get a clearer picture, but it was only once I'd closed my eyes and imagined every evocative detail on my virtual tour of our potential home that I really began to connect with it emotionally. That was what ultimately provided the motivation I needed to start saving toward that future.

I didn't realize it at the time, but there's a lot of research behind that.

Academic researchers, neuroscientists, and psychologists have been studying the effects of mental imagery on the brain and on future outcomes for decades. In fact, it's become an increasingly accepted psychological technique to help accelerate learning and improve performance for students, athletes, employees—even U.S. Army soldiers. Army researchers found that adding a regimen of mental-skills training, including goal setting and visualization of task execution, dramatically improved soldiers' cognitive and physical abilities. The results were significant enough that the Army incorporated it into basic combat training across the organization.

Several studies have shown that even the simple act of visualizing positive future outcomes—like acing an exam, crushing a job interview, or nailing that presentation—can not only make them seem more likely, but can also help bring them about. One study found, for example, that students who simulated a successful performance on a midterm exam in their heads began studying earlier, studied longer, and got higher grades than those who hadn't. Olympic athletes from Lindsey Vonn to Michael Phelps have said they used visualization regularly to help improve their confidence and performance.

"The objective is to create such a lifelike experience that your body believes that it could be real," Dr. Michael Gervais, a sports psychologist who's worked with Super Bowl champions and Olympic gold medalists, told *Business Insider*. "It's a full sensory experience. So there's a switching on or an animation that happens within you when you create an image that is crisp and has color, and sound, and smell, and taste."

How does that translate to setting and reaching financial goals? The more clearly you can visualize what you want to achieve and connect with it emotionally, the more powerful the incentive to take the financial steps you need to reach it, which can in turn help increase your confidence in achieving it.

In one survey of more than 1,100 Americans, TD Bank found that those who visualize achieving their financial goals are less anxious about budgeting than those who don't; and that those who keep images, photos, or vision boards of their goals are almost twice as confident that they will achieve them as those who don't. One big reason for that: They are clear on their *why*. They know why they are saving money. They know that the future they're working toward is worth any small compromises they may have to make in the short run.

It's not just about confidence. The bank was also able to uncover a direct connection between visualizing a goal and achieving it. When it surveyed five hundred small-business owners, TD Bank found that one in five had used a vision board or engaged in other visual exercises when starting their business—and more than three-quarters of them said that today their business is where they envisioned it would be.

"There's so much power in audacious dreaming and visioning," Shoshanna Hecht, a New York–based executive coach and licensed clinical social worker who regularly does visualization exercises with her clients, told me. "It gives us language and vocabulary around it. You can't go after anything unless you're able to articulate what it is. That doesn't mean it won't evolve or that there aren't left and right turns along the way. But you need to start with the end in mind."

Visualize This

One way to get clearer on what you want is to do an enhanced version of my daydream: Imagine yourself one day in the future, experiencing the goals you've achieved. All you need are a notebook or loose paper, a pen, and about ten or fifteen minutes. You'll want to find a quiet space where you can close your eyes and spend some time visualizing what you want your life to look like in the future. Depending on the timeline you want, you can imagine yourself a year from now or go out a few years in the future.

Consider questions like these: Where do you live? What does your home look like? Do you share it with others? What are you doing for work? Do you work at home or at an office? What kind of people are around you? What activities are you doing? How do you feel? Imagine the kind of place you want to wake up in. How do you want to be spending your time and with whom?

Then write out as many details about your day as you can in the first person, thinking about the who, what, when, where, and how. *Who* are you spending time with during your ideal day? *What* are you doing? *When* do you wake up, go to sleep, eat, work, and play? *Where* do you live and work? *How* do you earn a living? *How* do you spend your time and energy? Then we'll look at the why.

At this point, don't let financial concerns factor too much into this future vision. This exercise is about more than just thinking of what you hope to be able to afford in the future—and may need to save and earn more to attain—but also considering other professional and personal aspirations. Basically, you're giving yourself time to think about what you *want* to have in your life. The goal is to create a detailed picture of an ideal day in your future that captures what is most important to you.

Once you've written this out in the first person, read it out loud to yourself. Notice how you feel as you envision your ideal day. Going through this can help you identify concrete goals that you want to work toward. For me, it was a new home with enough space for a second child and enough money in the bank (and in each paycheck) to feel confident that we could afford to have another child. I also knew I wanted to stay in Brooklyn and to find a neighborhood near friends with great schools and a park where we could put down roots. The next step was figuring out a timeline and a plan. In the coming chapters, I'll go deeper into that, and we'll look at what steps need to happen financially to bring you closer to the future you want.

Of course, writing about an ideal future day or creating a vision board isn't for everyone. If that doesn't resonate with you, you can also just think about what goals are important to you in both your personal and professional life and write out a list. You might want to do a digital version, compiling goals and screen-captured images in a Google Doc. Or even use a spreadsheet. Just take the time to consider why these goals are so meaningful to you. (It is also worth noting that researchers have found using visual images can help create more of an emotional connection, even if that just means cutting out a couple of images from a magazine that remind you of your future goals.)

It can help to do the exercise with a friend. "For me, it was critical to do it with another person and one who knows me really well," said author and journalist Jessica Bennett, who has been creating a new list of goals and a vision board each January for the last eight years with a close friend of hers. "Honestly, it can feel a little silly doing it by yourself, so it helps to do it together. We make it into a kind of ritual, and we can laugh about it. But it's also effective."

Over the course of a few days, Bennett and her friend dissect what they accomplished the year before professionally and personally, and then map out their aspirations for the coming year—in a notebook, a Google Doc or, once, all over the paper tablecloth at a local restaurant. They're often big goals, "but not insane things—they're in our line of vision," Bennett said. Then they pull out stacks of magazines and colored paper, scissors, and glue and start cutting out images. "You can't just flip through magazines shopping for your vision. You have to go in with purpose and find things you think support it," she said.

Bennett, a Brooklyn-based writer who wrote the best-selling book *Feminist Fight Club*, told me that book was an item on her vision board long before it became a reality—even before she'd written the book proposal and sold the idea to a publisher. "I don't think this process is magic, but it's a clarifier for me and provides self-motivation," she said. "And I believe in the power of stating a goal out loud and having some accountability. Once you say it out loud, you're committing."

Trying to come up with future goals, much less state them out loud, can also dredge up all sorts of self-doubt and self-sabotaging beliefs, making it challenging at times to create a vision or list of goals that feels real or attainable. That's one reason it helps to do the exercise with a trusted friend who can challenge any self-doubt or self-criticism, and also help hold you accountable.

But we can use other techniques, too, to help overcome the mental blockers like those below that can prevent us from fully envisioning the future we want and believing we'll actually achieve it.

1. Limiting Beliefs

This is an equal-opportunity offender, but women can be particularly susceptible, sometimes without even being conscious of it. If you concluded early on, for example, that you're not ambitious or that you're bad with math or money—whether from experiences you had growing up or from messages you absorbed from family, peers, or the media—those beliefs tend to stick around even when there's growing evidence to contradict them. This is known in psychological circles as belief perseverance or belief persistence.

"Once you believe something, you'll filter out evidence to the contrary. In addition, once you've developed a core belief, you'll pay close attention to any evidence that reinforces your belief," Amy Morin, a psychotherapist and the author of *13 Things Mentally Strong People Don't Do*, told *Forbes*. "Studies have shown it takes more compelling evidence to change beliefs than it took to create them."

To avoid letting them interfere with your dreams, you've first got to recognize them and identify them for what they are: limiting beliefs based on experiences or interpretations that are often years or even decades old—and not an accurate reflection of who you are or what you're capable of.

"Mistakenly, we think these stories are keeping us safe, protecting us from rejection and humiliation. The reality is, they're just stories we make up in our head by attaching made-up meanings to events. And they cost us dearly all our lives," Nina Cooke, a business coach certified in neuro-linguistic programming, told *Forbes*.

How to overcome them? First, be on the lookout for any critical thoughts that come up. For example: I can't ____. I'll never ____. I'm too ____. I'm terrible at ____. Those are classic conventions and often go way back to childhood. So when they pop up in your head, consider the source—and the facts. Look for evidence that contradicts the belief, and you're bound to find it. It can help to write down examples. Then look at how to transform each belief into one that supports you.

One limiting belief I had to face early on was that I'm not good with money. In my twenties, I'd had plenty of evidence to support that. And it got in the way every time I started thinking about how I wanted to change my life. I had a built-in bias that I would always be struggling, unless some windfall or savior came along to help—after all, I'd chosen a profession that I was passionate about but paid pretty badly, and I seemed to be trapped in a perpetual paycheck-to-paycheck cycle throughout my twenties. As I thought more about it, though, I realized I'd always been able to pick up a side hustle and earn more money when I really needed it. And I was surely smart enough to figure out a way to boost my earnings now and save more money. Plus, until I started writing about personal finance as a reporter in my late twenties, I hadn't gotten much of a financial education.

Maybe I'm not so bad with money, I thought. Maybe I've just never been taught how to be really good with my money, and I've formed some bad habits as a result that need to be changed. Once I'd reframed it like that, it was a lot easier to move forward and take the steps that would allow me to continue to prove that initial belief wrong. And as the evidence mounted in my favor, I was able to transform that earlier belief into a much more empowering one: I am really good with money. That's something I wholeheartedly believe today. And that belief has provided both comfort and confidence in the face of uncertainty and helped me stay committed to making the best financial choices for myself and my family.

2. Inner Critics

When I participated in a three-day retreat at the Hudson Institute of Coaching, I remember one of the instructors referring to inner critics as the "sh*tty committee." You know this group. They're like Statler and Waldorf, those two curmudgeonly old men known for heckling the other Muppets characters from their balcony seats in The Muppet movies. Only it's worse because we carry these voices around in our heads all the time, often without being fully aware of it.

They're the voices that tell you you're not good enough, smart enough, disciplined enough, pretty enough, thin enough . . . The stream of self-criticism can feel deafening at times, tuning out any external evidence to the contrary. It also functions to keep us small. If we think we're not enough, we'll inevitably scale back our dreams and expectations. We can also spend an inordinate amount of time and energy trying to become enough in whatever areas we feel we fall short—a Sisyphean task, of course, since we may never reach whatever ideal we've set in our heads as being "enough." And we often do this at the expense of putting our efforts toward attaining what we actually want in life.

I remember how distracted I was when I was dieting constantly in my twenties, trying to lose those last five pounds. I was consumed by counting calories when I could have been putting that considerable mental energy toward things that really mattered in creating the life *I* wanted. Obsessing about my weight also prevented me from being fully able to enjoy and celebrate myself, my accomplishments, and the love and friendships I already had in my life. If we're constantly telling ourselves we're not enough, we may never allow ourselves to fully appreciate what we have or go for all we want in the future.

It's not like men aren't self-critical, too. But thanks to the cultural conditioning many women get growing up, we can be particularly prone to comparing ourselves with others or holding ourselves to some unattainable ideal. A 2016 survey by Weight Watchers found that the average woman criticizes herself at least eight times a day. Not surprisingly, image-based self-criticisms were the most common. But those were closely followed by criticisms related to money and career—not earning enough money, for example, or not having the right job, or falling short in creative or other professional skills. Interestingly, 89 percent of the women surveyed said they compliment other women in ways they would never compliment themselves.

Tapping a friend can help to confront that self-criticism. It can also help to imagine talking to ourselves as we would to our closest friends. When I participated in some exercises around self-criticism at the coaching retreat, I was shocked at how harshly we judge and criticize ourselves in ways we never would others—especially those we care about. Coaches often talk about shutting down those self-criticisms by coming up with self-affirmations instead.

I know, it seems silly to stand in front of a mirror and compliment yourself. But there's research-backed evidence that practicing self-affirmations—especially out loud, as weird as that can feel—can improve our confidence and results. One study, published in *Personality and Social Psychology Bulletin*, found that participants boosted their performance at work through self-affirmations and were also able to calm their nerves. "Any time you have low expectations for your performance, you tend to sink down and meet those low expectations," concluded lead researcher Sonia Kang, Ph.D. "Self-affirmation is a way to neutralize that threat."

3. The "Shoulds"

Coach Shoshanna Hecht, who works primarily with women, says those insidious beliefs about what we "should" do or want can stymie our ability to tap into our true desires when we envision the future. "It's not just from the images we see on the Hallmark Channel or Instagram, but the early messages and expectations of our families, stated and unstated," she told me. "We get all caught up in the idea of how our lives *should* look. It is really hard to buck conventional norms and go after our wild and crazy dreams."

Her solution: Carve out quiet time alone so you can listen to your inner voice and get clear on what *you* want, rather than being influenced by what your peers have. "There's a tendency to compare our lives to others', to want to keep up," Hecht said. "But just because everyone is doing something doesn't make it right for you. You can't really assess that unless you spend some time getting quiet and thinking, 'What is the right path for *me*?'"

Think of it as consulting your inner sage. And who would you rather listen to: your inner critic or your inner sage?

Settle for More

All sorts of doubts and guilt and fear came up for me when I allowed myself to imagine the future I really wanted. And sorting through them was tough. In order to address them, I had to first recognize them for what they were: barriers trying to get between me and what I truly wanted. The future I imagined when I allowed myself to think big. The future I knew I wanted badly enough that I'd regret settling for less. And I had to get comfortable with acknowledging that wanting more for my life was okay. That it didn't mean I wasn't content with my life or unappreciative or selfish.

As women, we've been conditioned to compromise, to be accommodating and agreeable, and to prioritize others' needs and wants above our own—and it can be hard to undo that programming. How many times have you been asked to settle for less than what you truly wanted? One of the benefits of having a breadwinner mindset is that it allows you to think expansively. It's about building your own wealth and bringing your own dreams to life, however audacious they may seem.

Creating a plan would help ease some of the doubts that rose up in my mind. But deep down, I knew I was capable of saving and earning more, even though I was still uncertain about how exactly I would close that gap between where I was financially and where I'd need to be. In my vision, I tried to imagine what it would feel like to be financially secure. I walked around the new home confidently, joyful in the knowledge that I'd helped make it a reality. It was a powerful feeling.

Of course, it's not just about fantasizing your future, and then—poof!—you're on your way and all your desires are manifested.

To make our future vision a reality, we need to believe that it's possible, be realistic about what it will take to achieve it, and feel emotionally connected to the outcome. Our future goals also need to be informed by our deeper needs and desires—and reflect the values we hold dear—in order for us to have the momentum and motivation to persevere when obstacles arise.

Exercise: What Values Drive You?

Identifying the values that are most important to you allows you to ground your future vision in those values and create a plan that supports them. It's also a good test to see if that future vision you wrote out for yourself and your life truly aligns with your core values, or if it's been influenced by external ideas of what both *should* look like.

The challenge is that we can't prioritize all values all the time. Some may have to take priority over others. And some values can actually contradict others. If you value comfort or stability, for example, you may be less comfortable with risk taking. There's nothing inherently better or worse about any of those values. It's just a matter of personal preference.

That's why it's important to get clear on what values resonate the most with you and feel essential to who you are and the life you want. Sometimes it becomes clear when you do the visualization exercise, but you may still have trouble articulating why that vision is so compelling.

To help, here's a list of one hundred core values. As you scan the list, ask yourself which values resonate most with you. Which feel essential to who you are and how you want to live? Which values align most closely with your core identity? Circle them. (And no judgment!)

1.	Accountability	6.	Authenticity
2.	Achievement	7.	Autonomy
3.	Adventure	8.	Balance
4.	Altruism	9.	Boldness
5.	Ambition	10.	Brilliance

11. Calmness
12. Caring
13. Charity
14. Cheerfulness
15. Cleanliness
16. Collaboration
17. Commitment
18. Community
19. Compassion
20. Connection
21. Consciousness
22. Conviction
23. Creation
24. Creativity
25. Curiosity
26. Daring
27. Decisiveness
28. Dedication
29. Dependability
30. Dignity
31. Diversity
32. Drive
33. Empathy
34. Enthusiasm
35. Excellence
36. Fairness
37. Family
38. Friendships
39. Flexibility
40. Freedom
41. Fun
42. Generosity
43. Grace
44. Growth
45. Happiness
46. Harmony
47. Health (and well-being)
48. Honesty
49. Hope
50. Humor
51. Hustle
52. Imagination
53. Impact
54. Inclusiveness
55. Individuality
56. Innovation
57. Intelligence
58. Intuition
59. Irreverence
60. Joy
61. Kindness
62. Knowledge
63. Leadership
64. Learning
65. Love
66. Loyalty
67. Making a difference
68. Mindfulness
69. Open-mindedness
70. Optimism
71. Originality
72. Passion
73. Peace
74. Persistence

75. Playfulness	88. Spontaneity
76. Popularity	89. Stability
77. Power	90. Thoughtfulness
78. Proactiveness	91. Tradition
79. Purpose	92. Trustworthiness
80. Resilience	93. Understanding
81. Resourcefulness	94. Uniqueness
82. Risk taking	95. Usefulness
83. Safety	96. Versatility
84. Security	97. Vision
85. Serenity	98. Warmth
86. Sincerity	99. Wealth
87. Spirituality	100. Wisdom

It can help to group all the similar values you choose together in a way that makes sense and then to consider which word in each group is the most important to you—or best captures the group—and highlight that word. Ask yourself if the values you've selected feel consistent with who you are and how you want to be perceived. How does it make you feel when you read each word out loud? Do you see any that feel inconsistent with your identity— or that seem more like values you want to see in someone else (a boss, a partner, a leader) than in yourself? These lists may change over time, but doing this exercise can help you home in on what is most important to you at this stage in your life.

If you want to take it further, you can also put them into priority order: What value best reflects who you are day in and day out? Which is the most essential as a guiding force in your life right now? And then rank the others accordingly. After you've ranked your values, consider the role that they each play in the vision you've written up for your future self. You'll want to keep your vision and values in mind as you begin putting a personal plan together to reach your goals and to set yourself up for the future you want. You may also find that there are places where your vision feels out of line with the values you've prioritized. If so, ask yourself, Are there adjustments I could make to my ideal day that will allow for a better expression of my core values?

Living Your Values

In 2017, Alessandra Henderson was working with a career coach who assigned her the homework of writing a journal-like entry about a workday in her life nine months in the future. She was asked to describe in detail the people, experiences, and feelings that were part of that day. "I had to think about what excited me, what gave me energy," she recalled. "It sounds so simple, but sitting down with only oneself and a piece of paper to look inward and describe a day in the not-too-distant future brings so much clarity and focus to who you want to be, how you want to live your life, and helps define what's important to you."

As she read it aloud, though, she remembered her coach saying, "You don't really sound super excited about it."

And she realized, she wasn't. In her initial entry, she had envisioned herself as an investor. After all, she had founded the MIT NYC Startup Studio and at the time of the exercise was a VP at a venture capital fund. So it had seemed natural to imagine herself as an investor, helping to support female-founded startups—something she was passionate about. "It felt good, but it never felt right as my next step," she said. The more she thought about it, the more she realized that she actually wanted to start her own venture—that creation (of a team, mission, and product) was a top value for her and a compelling way for her to express many of her values, like her desire to have an impact. "So I went back to that day and redid the entry with an operator hat instead and wrote out what it would look like to build my own company," she remembers. "And it felt right."

She was admittedly daunted and wasn't sure yet what it was that she wanted to build, but she had some ideas. Within a year, she'd decided on one: building a company designed to serve women going through menopause. In December 2018, after saving money and continuing to flesh out her plan, she quit her job. She cofounded the healthcare company Elektra Health a month later. "And I have never doubted that this is what I am meant to be doing," she told me.

What Henderson learned in the process was to trust her gut and to pay attention to what felt right and made sense—both in her head and in her heart—and to stay flexible enough to refine the details as time passed. "Sometimes things feel good, but they don't feel right right now," she said. "It's important to continue to refine and then to map out a monthly plan."

Of course, launching a business is a big, audacious goal, and it's not for everyone. But the point is, it can take some tinkering to come up with goals that feel right.

The more time I spent honing the description of our future home that first morning, the more I was also able to uncover what was most important to me. I realized how much I valued being able to raise two kids in the diverse and vibrant city we loved and feeling connected to our neighbors and our community. Spending quality time with the people I cared about in a home that was inviting and warm was key, too. As was providing our kids with a good education and a stimulating environment that fostered curiosity and growth. And making sure that we had plenty of opportunities to exercise regularly, eat well, and stay healthy.

Visualizing my future also revealed what was less of a priority for me. Was it that worthwhile to spend money going out—or would I be just as content hanging out at a friend's place or having friends over so we had the chance to catch up and connect? I could justify spending money on organic produce and a health club membership, but we could definitely cut back on take-out meals and cappuccinos. Would I increase my commute by ten or fifteen minutes if it meant we could buy an apartment close to a five-hundred-acre park where I could go for regular runs and we could take our son to play? (The answer was yes.)

Your values will be different from mine, of course, but it's key to acknowledge them as you think about your future. Essentially, thinking hard about what you value and what you really want in your life makes it easier to identify and cut out the things that aren't as important to you. You'll get clear on where you are and aren't willing to compromise when it comes to your life and your money.

Those goals and values will help you determine something very concrete: your incentives for building wealth.

You want to be crystal clear on your purpose for building wealth. It doesn't necessarily mean getting rich in the way a lot of us think—living in a Drake-level luxury pad or traveling the globe in a hundred-foot yacht you've named after your cockapoo (though if that's what you want, no judgment). Wealth means having enough money to know you can afford all the things and experiences you want to have in your life. It's being able to live a full life that embodies the values that are most dear to you, regardless of whether you get married or can count on an inheritance or not. And here's the thing: You, right now at this very moment, have everything you need to have that kind of wealth and build that kind of life for yourself.

PART II

Breadwinning Basics

*How to build a financial foundation to
support the future you want.*

CHAPTER 5

More Savings = More Choices
Why Building a Safety Net Is Key

*When I look at my savings account, I don't see pounds and pence. I see
freedom.* —Merryn Somerset Webb, British journalist

In 2016, author Paulette Perhach wrote an essay for *The Billfold* called
"A Story of a Fuck Off Fund." It laid out the all-too-believable scenario
of a woman who ends up putting up with an abusive boyfriend and a
male boss who sexually harasses her because she has only $159 in the
bank, an overdue car payment, and maxed-out credit cards—and she
can't bear the thought of asking her dad for another loan.

When her boss calls for a one-on-one in his office, walks up behind
her, and puts his hand up her new dress, she just squirms away as he
apologizes, even though she knows she should tell him off or report
him. She hears herself saying instead, "It's okay. Just forget it." And after
she scurries out of the room, she surveys the office, half full of women,
and wonders to herself, "How many of them have secrets like the one
you're about to keep?"

I teared up when I read the essay. A friend had sent it to me in the
wake of the latest wave of #MeToo allegations, and that last line seemed
particularly germane. Not having enough money to cover even a month's
rent can leave you feeling powerless. If you can't afford to miss a single
paycheck, it's harder to speak up at work. If you're dependent on a partner to cover expenses, it's harder to walk away.

What I hadn't anticipated was that the article would dredge up memories from my own life that I'd brushed aside years earlier. Now I saw them through a different lens. I was nineteen and working as a hostess at a restaurant over the summer. The manager, a middle-aged man with a mustache and a belly that hung out over his jeans, followed me into the walk-in refrigerator, telling me how much he loved my lips and how he'd dreamed the night before of me going down on him. At the time, I remember brushing past him and mumbling, "Thanks, I guess." But at the end of my shift, I walked out the door of the restaurant, and I never came back. I was fortunate, I realize now, that I could walk out because I had some savings and the safety net of my parents to fall back on.

Years later, when I was in management, I had a notoriously sexist boss with a temper. By then I'd shored up my savings and knew I could walk away from a bad situation and be fine financially. It wasn't something I was conscious of most of the time. But I remember I didn't hesitate to speak up when he swore at an intern in front of the team, made dismissive and chauvinistic comments in a meeting, and later tried to move my desk away from the team in what felt like retaliation. I could raise my voice in large part because, if worse came to worst and he fired me, I had enough money saved and enough confidence in my ability to find another job to know I would be okay.

It hadn't dawned on me initially how fortunate I was that I had that safety net—and how different things might have been if I'd really needed each paycheck. It hit me that having savings isn't just for covering emergencies, upcoming trips, or things we want but can't afford right now. Savings provide security. Having savings is like having a protective shield, allowing you to deflect bad behavior, walk away from an abusive partner or a toxic workplace, and know that you'll be able to take care of yourself. If you're dependent on someone else financially, that person has the power in the relationship—whether it's a boss or a boyfriend. While you may tell yourself that you won't put up with any abuse or disrespect, if you don't have the ability to cover your expenses on your own if you leave your partner or job, you can feel trapped.

We talk about having an emergency savings fund to cover unexpected expenses like car repairs or a sick pet. But that's only part of it. Putting away money is really like building a boat that may one day carry you to safety—or wherever you want to go. That's what building wealth is about.

I didn't truly grasp that until after my midnight revelation. Before that, I had looked at saving as depriving me of the things I wanted now in my life. What I hadn't understood was that by limiting the amount of money I was saving and investing, I was just depriving myself of choices in the future. If I'd continued down the same road, tucking away a little here and there—but for the most part, spending much of each paycheck— I would have had to put off, or even give up, some of the things that meant the most to me, like a second child and a home we could grow into in the city we loved.

Until then, I hadn't acknowledged that just keeping my head above water financially meant that I could easily slip under at any time. If I'd lost my job then, or been hit with a big, unexpected expense, I would have been in serious financial trouble. And living with that knowledge (even if you try to ignore it) can create a lot of anxiety. The American Psychological Association surveys Americans each year about their top stressors, and money is consistently in the top three. In its 2020 survey, nearly two in three adults identified money as a "significant source of stress." And the research shows that women are more likely than men to report living paycheck to paycheck and to feel financial stress more acutely. The APA found that women consistently report higher stress levels from money worries than men do and are more likely to experience symptoms like feeling overwhelmed, anxious, and fatigued as well as having trouble sleeping.

Continuously treading water *is* exhausting. Yet we often keep it up, hoping that maybe someone will notice us flailing about and "save" us or that things will just improve over time. The better solution is to learn to take care of ourselves financially so that we can propel ourselves forward and stop moving in place. Saving is the antidote to the stress of living paycheck to paycheck.

More money = more choices. It's that simple.

It's Not How Much You're Making, But How Much You're Saving

One spring night, driving home from a friend's party, my friend Simran's husband was killed in a car crash. She was twenty-six at the time. Suddenly a single mom with a toddler, Simran was now forced to cover all the bills on her own. Without her husband's salary, their monthly household income fell by 60 percent. It would have been completely understandable if, when the five-figure life insurance check arrived, she deposited it in the bank and used it to subsidize their expenses while she figured out her next move. Instead, she cut her monthly expenses, buying groceries in bulk and packing her lunch—and putting off any purchases that weren't absolutely necessary. Parents and in-laws helped with childcare. She used the insurance check to buy a small apartment on the outskirts of the city and rented it out for regular income. That rental income helped supplement her salary until she could find a better-paying job.

When she first told me that story years later, I was stunned. Who would have the wherewithal at twenty-six to cut expenses and invest that insurance money—especially after being widowed with a small child? When I asked her why she hadn't thought to spend some of it to cover her bills as she adjusted to life as a single mom, she looked at me incredulously.

Her dad, she explained, had taught her early on to live on the regular income she brought in—and to save some of every single check for her future. And then to invest anything she got outside of that, whether it was a bonus, a birthday gift, or a check from the insurance company. If she was in a bind, she should tap her savings—not this insurance windfall—and then work to replenish them. As she saw it, this was a chance to invest for their future, not money to spend on everyday expenses.

Even as a young girl, Simran remembers putting money aside for her future—carefully dividing her allowance into four piles. "I had one for fun, one for clothes and other 'essential' expenses, one for short-term goals like a stereo system for my bedroom, and one for my future," she told me that night, as we were swapping childhood stories over margaritas. "My dad instilled early on the importance of saving money. He always asked me not what I was making but how much I was *saving*. He told me, 'When you get money, it's not about what you can buy. It's about what you can save.'"

This approach is key to the breadwinner mindset: thinking about how each check you get can help you build your wealth (and make you less dependent on future checks!) and bring you closer to the future you want.

One popular budgeting framework is the 50/30/20 rule. Half (or less) of your paycheck goes to needs: essential expenses like your rent or mortgage, utilities, insurance, and basic groceries. Another 30 percent can go to wants: everything from travel to take-out meals. And the remaining 20 percent goes to saving, investing, and paying off debt. However you split up your paycheck, financial advisors generally recommend trying to set aside at least 15 to 20 percent for saving and investing.

So did Simran's dad. And starting with her first job, she got in the habit of setting aside at least that much from each paycheck. Even after she got married, and especially when she gave birth to their son, Simran—who was one of three daughters raised by a middle-class couple in Delhi, India—continued to set aside some of each check for her future.

Years later, when she got a marketing job at the New York office of a big financial firm, Simran, who was still a single mom, would use the earnings from selling that first apartment to help purchase a two-bedroom condo in downtown Manhattan for herself and her son. Then she bought a second rental property. The money she would make from *that* investment and the earnings she'd saved from her jobs would eventually help her cover the bulk of her son's college tuition, buy a home in San Francisco, and pursue her dream of starting her own business in her late forties. She didn't get there overnight. But being in the practice of saving and investing early on not only helped her get by as a single mom but also gave her more choices and opportunities later in life.

Why We Don't Save

You may not have been raised the way Simran was. Most of us weren't. (I certainly wasn't.) The United States is a consumption-driven country, and saving isn't valued here—nor is debt reviled—as much as it is in other cultures. Much of what we're taught about saving is framed in terms of spending goals. Save money now for that designer bag or spa getaway.

Living paycheck to paycheck is perfectly acceptable, even normal, in America. And so are excuses like "I'll start saving and investing when I start making more." (I used that one myself.) But women disproportionately feel the effects of it because we're more likely to carry student debt, we earn less, and most of us aren't making money choices based on the assumption that we may need to provide for ourselves and a family in the future.

In fact, research shows that women consistently lag behind men when it comes to saving and investing—both for short-term goals and emergencies and for longer-term goals like retirement. A 2016 survey by the nonprofit group America Saves found that fewer than half of women were regularly saving even 5 percent or more of their income. Another survey found that nearly one in four women had less than $100 saved to cover unexpected expenses. In a 2020 survey by Bankrate, nearly one-third of women said they had more credit card debt than savings.

As a country, we've normalized debt. And we've framed saving as something to aspire to—not a habit to put into practice with every paycheck. What if instead we were conditioned to set aside 20 percent of every single paycheck from *day one*, saving some for short-term goals and investing the rest for mid- to long-term ones? Imagine how much money we would already have by the time we were in our thirties or forties.

Actually, you don't have to imagine it, because we can run some calculations. For simplicity's sake, let's say, hypothetically, that over the next ten years, your annual income averages $48,000 after taxes (the equivalent to a salary of around $60,000) and you put 20 percent of that aside for saving and investing. That'd be $800 a month. If you put one-quarter of that amount into savings, you'd have $2,400 after one year, not including any interest you earn. And after a decade, if you had it in what's considered a "high yield" savings account with an interest rate of 1 percent, and you left it alone, you'd have more than $25,000!

Not bad. But let's say you put the remaining 75 percent ($600 a month) into the stock market and invested in an index fund that mirrored the S&P 500-stock index, which returns about 7 percent on average per year after inflation. You could have more than $100,000 in that account a decade later! (Although, keep in mind, that the amount could fluctuate year by year, as 7 percent is an average.) I'm not saying that's the ideal allocation for you—we'll talk more about investing in Chapter 7—but getting in the habit of saving and investing money from each check early on means you'll benefit big-time from compounding. That's when the returns on your investment earn returns and so on and so on. And that can help your money grow exponentially. That $100,000 could be a down payment on a home or enough to kick-start a business. Or a big head start on a retirement fund. And if your earnings went up more over that period (as I'd hope they would!), your investment balance would be even bigger.

Of course, many of us may feel that we can't put quite that much aside, especially early in our careers. (And not all of us are making $60,000.) And that's okay. What's critical is to start regularly saving and investing *something* so that your money has the chance to grow. Then you can increase the percentage you set aside incrementally over time. Even $50 a month auto-deposited into a high-yield savings account could net you more than $3,000 after five years. Put another $50 a month into a brokerage account and invest in a fund that mirrors the S&P 500-stock index, and it could grow to more than $8,500 over a decade and to more than $25,000 over twenty years (using the same 7 percent annual-return assumption).

Saving Gives You More Flexibility When You Need It

Saving and investing some of your income now helps that money grow over time. And that can give you more options later.

For Samira, a forty-four-year-old endocrinologist in California, having savings allowed her to take five months off after giving birth to her twins in 2013 and then come back to a three-day-a-week work schedule, knowing that she and her husband would still have enough money to cover their expenses with ease. "If we hadn't saved a significant amount of money, there's no way we could have considered that—or me even being off those five months," Samira told me.

Samira's parents always lived frugally, making purchases with cash and saving as much as they could, and their habits rubbed off on her. "I have saved since I first got paid," she said, anywhere from 30 to 50 percent of her income. "There's a lot in life that's unpredictable. Saving gives you so much more flexibility when things come up."

"My husband used to think someone was wealthy because they drove a BMW or lived in a big mansion. But it's really about having the money to have the flexibility you want," she added. "My husband was able to leave his job and try working on his own startup. I was able to go part-time after we had kids. And if I don't like my job now, I can quit and know that we'll be okay financially. If you don't have savings, you don't have choices like that."

Laura, who runs a PR consultancy in New York City, started saving early in her career, too. Was it easy? Not at first. Laura remembers sharing a four-hundred-square-foot apartment and a foldout couch with a roommate when she first moved to the city. "It was so uncomfortable that after a month we put a mattress on the floor, and I woke up with round welts because the springs came out. My roommate ended up buying a sleeping bag, and I slept on the couch," she remembered. "We were just scraping by."

Eventually, she rented her own place. "It was an itty-bitty apartment. But I didn't try to go bigger, because I wanted to save money," she said. "I didn't have a number in my head, but I was saving as much as I could with the idea that I would eventually buy an apartment."

Her savings mentality helped her out when the unexpected happened early in her career: emergency back surgery at twenty-five. At the time, Laura was working as an assistant for a soap opera. It was her first year, and health benefits didn't kick in until her second, so she'd purchased a high-deductible emergency insurance plan. Eight months into her job, she started having severe back pain. It turned out she had a cyst on her tailbone. Her doctor said she needed surgery immediately, and her insurance only partially covered the cost. "I ended up having to put in ten thousand dollars. I cleaned out my bank account," she told me. "That experience convinced me of the importance of having savings and good health insurance. I immediately started saving again."

Less than seven years after she'd rented the tiny studio apartment, Laura had saved enough to buy herself an apartment nearly twice as big.

"Without savings, I wouldn't have been able to do that," she told me. "And I love this apartment."

Saving money enables you to have more of what you want in your future and, just as importantly, to be able to avoid situations you don't want to be in. That could include going back to work before you want to after giving birth. Or staying in a relationship with a partner who treats you badly because you don't think you can afford the rent or mortgage on your own. It could be staying at a soul-sucking job way longer than you know you should because you can't afford to miss even one pay-check. It may mean wondering if you can afford to see that specialist when you get sick. Or if you can afford to visit your mom or someone else you care about who lives far away, when you know how much it would mean to both of you. I don't want you to be stuck in a terrible situation or to miss out on time spent with the people you care most about—or any of the things that really matter to you in your life—because you didn't save and invest enough money. That's how you'll be able to afford the goals you came up with in the last chapter.

The night I was up, pacing back and forth with my infant son, real-izing I had to start putting money toward a life that reflected my values and dreams because no one else cared more about my future than I did, I knew I might have to take some pretty dramatic steps to get on track financially.

The next morning, when I first wrote out a description of my future life, I felt invigorated and motivated. But when I opened my laptop and started researching what making this vision a reality would actually cost, I had a total breakdown. I sat hunched over the desk my husband and I shared in our bedroom, sobbing as the numbers sank in. Until I'd actually looked at the costs, I'd been able to fool myself into thinking it wouldn't be *that* much of a stretch to get a bigger place in New York City and afford another kid. But now it was as if every bad choice I'd made with my money for the past decade was suddenly catching up to me. There was no denying that I had to make some changes.

In the days and weeks and months that followed, I made a series of choices about my money that were guided by a completely new set of motivations. Now every single decision I made with my money was in service to the future I wanted to create. That meant no more mindless spending or impulsive purchases. And it required me to budget my money so I knew exactly what I could afford to spend in order to save what I needed.

Pricing Out Your Goals

In Chapter 4, you determined the values that really matter to you in your life and the financial incentives you want to put in place to keep up the momentum on your journey. Now it's time to think about how much you'll be able to put away in order to get on track to both reach those wealth goals and be able to address short-term incentives as well as un-expected expenses that pop up along the way (because they will).

Everyone's goals are different, so there's no one approach to figuring out the right number for you right now. It's really a matter of pricing out what you want in the future, calculating how much you need to save to get there, and then figuring out how long it will realistically take you to save that money—and what you may be willing to do to speed up that process.

When I did my calculations, we had very little money saved up, so we were saving the down payment almost from scratch. That meant checking out homes in neighborhoods we liked, figuring out what the minimum down payment and monthly mortgage and insurance payments would be, and then looking at how much my husband and I could each set aside for them. Since I felt more urgency than he did and had my sights set on certain neighborhoods—and I had more catching up to do financially—I set myself a big savings goal.

When I'd had my midnight revelation, things looked pretty bleak. I was still carrying over a thousand dollars in credit card debt. I was living paycheck to paycheck. The thought of planning for our future still made me anxious. I felt unprepared to be in charge of making financial choices that could affect not only my future but now my family's future, too.

But I put my initial concerns to the side temporarily and started to create a spending plan that I could actually follow—one that cut back sharply on things that were less important to me and allowed me to continue to indulge in some of what I loved—so that I could put more money against my debt and start saving more. That meant more cooking at home and less going out to dinner with friends, though I still met them for drinks and happy-hour menu specials. It meant skipping vacations and taking the bus to visit my in-laws rather than flying. It meant cutting back on new clothes unless it was absolutely essential and shopping secondhand or sales for our son's clothes. It meant skipping pricey Pilates classes and making better use of my discount gym membership. And picking more family activities that were free or close to it, like picnics in the park, readings at the local bookstore, and free concerts and other events around the city.

When I first looked closely at where my money was going, I realized a lot of what I spent was out of obligation, guilt, convenience, or habit. I was spending money to attend social functions that I really wouldn't have minded skipping. I often picked up take-out meals when I didn't feel like cooking or got groceries at the expensive food store down the block when I didn't feel like walking another three blocks to the cheaper supermarket. I bought a coffee and a snack most days on the way to the subway out of habit, even though we had a coffee maker and plenty of snacks at home and at the office.

I hadn't thought much about it until I realized that each of those choices meant that I would have less money to spend in ways that were more meaningful. The bottom line was this: I often did *not* spend my money in ways that brought me real satisfaction or fulfillment. So what would it look like if I did?

Once I started earmarking more of my money for the things that would really benefit me—leaving me feeling satisfied and fulfilled, confident in the knowledge that I was taking care of myself and my hopes and needs—I found that there was less money left to put toward purchases that weren't as satisfying. It's like the old adage of paying yourself first: Allocate money toward your future goals *first*, and then budget what's left for spending.

It also helps to share your goals with friends and loved ones so that they can help support you. Around the same time I started spending more mindfully, a good friend of mine left her corporate job and was trying to get her consulting business off the ground. For the first few years, she wasn't making much money, and what she did earn went to her mortgage and other essential expenses and toward building her business. So we decided that when we met up—and we usually got together once every week or two—we would either eat dinner at her place, and I'd bring a cheap bottle of wine, or she'd find a happy-hour or Groupon special somewhere if we went out. Rather than feeling like we were depriving ourselves, I discovered that I had just as much fun. And I felt better afterward when I looked at what I had spent. While I was ostensibly helping her keep her expenses down, I was grateful to spend less, too, and still share quality time with her. Even after she was earning more, we continued to stick to the same plan.

Whether we realize it or not, our spending is largely guided by the values we've prioritized. But whether those values are truly ours, or simply family or societal values we've adopted, is an important distinction. If we're spending money in order to conform or to please or impress others—values that we may have picked up from social conditioning but which may not reflect our true desires—we may end up spending in ways that leave us feeling dissatisfied and frustrated. Because our spending is out of line with what we truly value.

"Societal values are often incompatible with personal values," Jessica Dore, a licensed social worker and trained psychotherapist, writes on

Psych Central. "The things we are taught to value through television, movies, and magazines may not resonate with what feels truly important or supportive of our values as individuals. As a result, we have all found ourselves stuck—at one point or another—chasing something that we don't even want."

The antidote to that is to be clear about *your* values and goals. And to spend mindfully. It can even help to ask yourself what value something brings before you spend money on it. Is your spending bringing you closer to the life you want or taking you further away?

"Whatever seemingly small money decisions I am making now, I ask myself, How is that going to influence the future we want to have?" said Sargi, a thirty-nine-year-old executive VP at a global advertising company who's married with a newborn son. "Whether it is about saving or purchasing decisions, I try to look at the cumulative effect. Every day it's about re-grounding myself in what is truly important."

That means building enough savings to provide a "substantial cushion" for their growing family and being able to take advantage of investment opportunities that can pay off in the future. Ultimately, she told me, "It's to have the financial freedom to make choices."

I wasn't sure that changing the way I spent and saved my money would be quite as simple as changing my mindset. But in some ways, it *was* that simple. Because once I truly understood how much the everyday decisions I made affected my future and my family's future, I made different choices.

I slowly built up my savings account. And I taught myself to invest and began to put as much as I could into my retirement and other investment accounts. Those early days weren't easy. There were periods of self-doubt and some real sacrifices. But the desire to create that future I'd imagined outweighed all that. So I kept at it.

Just when I was starting to look around for a better-paying job, I had the chance to volunteer to take a severance package at the now-struggling magazine where I worked. There was no question I would sign up. I invested almost all the money I got, then hustled to bring in freelance income, surprising myself when I increased my earnings substantially. About a year and a half later, I was hired by a former colleague for my first management role. The salary was almost double what I'd been earning at the magazine. (More on that in Chapter 8.)

In less than three years, my debt was gone and I had enough in my savings and regular investment accounts to start house hunting. I began to feel a stronger sense of confidence, grounded in the newfound recognition of my own capabilities. Soon after, I put down most of the down payment on an airy two-bedroom home in Brooklyn with all the amenities I'd written down on my imagined ideal listing. And it was less than three blocks away from a beautiful park with running paths and a playground. I was five months pregnant with our younger son, Sebastian, when we moved in. It's hard to describe the feeling of pride and joy that came over me when I took my pregnant self on a tour of our beautiful, brand-new apartment and reminded myself that I'd helped make it ours.

Whatever the results of your calculations, the most important lesson is recognizing the value of saving or investing some of *every single* paycheck, bonus, birthday check, and any other money that comes in. In fact, any additional money that comes in is an opportunity to boost those saving and investment accounts that are quietly chugging along, growing larger over time as you go about your daily life. (In other words, if you can afford it, put anything you get outside your regular income straight into your savings or investment accounts before you have a chance to spend it.) That's how you'll no longer have to depend on those paychecks, or a partner, down the road to afford the things that matter to you. That's how you'll be able to reach your goals even faster.

For me, it was incredibly reassuring to have more control over my ability to achieve the future I wanted. This newfound sense of agency felt good. As I further educated myself about personal finance, I became more active in managing our money. And as our net worth grew, so did my confidence and sense of security. Even now, I often remind myself what I am earning and saving money for. I still regularly check in with myself to make sure I never lose sight of what matters most. When I look around at my life, it feels good to say, I *chose* to create this.

That's the power of saving and investing money for your future. The more money and thought you put toward your future, the better the chances it'll be the one you want. In the next few chapters, we'll look at ways to free up more cash and increase your earnings, so you can save even more, and how to invest to grow your money faster. But first, let's look at how to pay down any debt you have more quickly and how to transform your relationship with credit, so it can help you build wealth—not hold you back from it.

CHAPTER 6

Give Yourself Some Credit

How to Leverage It Responsibly to Your Advantage

Some of us just accept debt as a part of adult life and trod on, shackled by consequences we don't fully understand.
—Vicki Robin, writer and social innovator

Google "women and credit cards," and you'll be bombarded with images of pretty women of all ethnicities smiling as they hold up a credit card in one hand and brightly colored shopping bags in the other. Look up articles about women and credit, and they almost inevitably include an image of a woman merrily swiping a card at a store or holding a credit card and her phone as if she's about to click "buy" online. Women wielding their credit cards like VIP passes at stores, restaurants, and even car dealerships show up regularly in music videos, movies, and magazines.

When I Googled "men and credit cards," though, up popped an image of a well-groomed man in a tailored suit, brandishing a gold card. And this is not surprising. Men are encouraged to build credit, presumably so they can buy a home one day and provide for their families—and to view acquiring a gold card, which requires a high income and credit score, as a sign of stature. Meanwhile, ever since the Equal Credit Opportunity Act passed in 1974, when women were (finally!) allowed to apply for credit in their own name, credit card companies have been urging women to use that credit to shop—to close the gap between the lifestyle we can actually afford and the one we aspire to. And apparently we've been listening.

In 2020, credit card debt in the United States topped *$1 trillion*, according to the Federal Reserve (the U.S. central bank). And guess who's shouldering most of that burden? Surveys show that more women than men tend to owe money on their credit cards, especially those in their twenties—one survey found nearly twice as many women as men between eighteen and twenty-four have credit card debt! We also carry higher balances.

One reason is that it takes us longer to pay down our balances. A study by the Financial Industry Regulation Authority Investor Education Foundation (established by the agency that regulates the financial services industry) found that women are more likely than men to make only minimum monthly payments and to be assessed late fees. Similarly, a Federal Reserve analysis found that single women tend to use their credit cards more and have higher total debt outstanding and more past delinquencies than single guys. And in several surveys, including one in 2019 by CompareCards (a division of LendingTree), men are much more likely than women to say they pay their bill on time and in full.

This costs us—and in more ways than we might realize.

- **Credit card debt is really expensive.** It's not just the higher debt balances. Compared with student and car loans and other forms of debt, credit card debt also tends to come with the highest interest rates. That means paying a lot more over time. How much? If you're making minimum payments, you could end up paying nearly as much in interest *as you borrowed*. Seriously. Let's say you owe $10,000 on a credit card with an 18 percent interest rate, and you're paying the minimum of about 3 percent of your balance. It would take you more than *20 years* to pay that off, and you'd end up paying nearly $10,000 in interest alone. In other words, you'd end up paying about double what you borrowed. (And you'd also be missing out on twenty years of interest you could have been *earning* on that money instead if it weren't going toward debt!) That may seem like an extreme example, but an analysis of 309 U.S. credit cards in mid-2020 found the *average* interest rate was over 20 percent. Even new card offers carried more than 16 percent in interest, according to Creditcards.com. An 18 percent interest rate isn't uncommon. And guess what? The FINRA Foundation study found that women pay a half point more in interest on credit cards than men do, on average. (I'll explain how to lower your interest rate later in the chapter.)

- **We file for bankruptcy more often.** Data from the Federal Reserve and the Institute for Financial Literacy show more women than men end up filing for bankruptcy—a process that helps wipe out most debts but will negatively affect your credit score *for years*. The most common type of bankruptcy is chapter 7, in which you pay what you can and erase most of your debt (with the exception of back taxes, child support, and often student loans). While it can provide debt relief, it can also take more than a decade for your credit to recover, since credit reporting agencies can leave that bankruptcy on your credit report for ten years after your filing date. According to data from FICO, the most-used credit scoring model, filing for bankruptcy can send a good credit score of 700 or higher down by 200 points or more to a "fair" or "very poor" one. That makes it much tougher to qualify for loans, credit cards, and even an apartment rental. (Landlords can legally check a potential tenant's credit report.) And if you do get credit, the rates can be significantly higher—subprime credit cards can carry interest rates of more than 25 percent.

- **We have lower average credit scores.** The Federal Reserve analysis found that single men had higher credit scores than women, on average, with the widest gap among those in their thirties. Other research by Credit Sesame found similar trends among men and women generally (although the gap is closing). Even if you're not stuck in subprime territory, a lower credit score still makes a difference. The higher the score, the lower the interest rates and the better the repayment terms. That can mean a difference of hundreds, thousands, or even tens of thousands of dollars in interest paid on a credit card, car loan, or mortgage over time.

All this boils down to one thing: If we're putting more money toward debt, that leaves less for us to save and invest for our future. Higher debt levels—whether from credit cards or car and student loans—make it harder for us to start building wealth. That's yet one more reason for the gaping gender wealth gap.

So how did we end up here? For one, most of us haven't been taught how to use credit to our advantage. As we mentioned in Chapter 2, research shows that parents are more likely to teach their sons how to build credit and to teach their daughters how to budget and shop. And several surveys have found that women generally have lower levels of financial literacy, which can affect the way we approach credit. Combine this lack of education about credit with aggressive credit card marketing, and it's a recipe for disaster. By the time we've figured out the risks of carrying balances, we're often paying for it already. Carrying debt—especially credit card debt—makes it difficult to get ahead. I should know. I did it for much of my twenties.

But, let's back up . . . There's nothing wrong with using credit cards—as long as you pay off the balance quickly, ideally before the next statement arrives. (In fact, you can use credit cards to your advantage, which we'll dive into later in the chapter.) I learned the hard way that credit cards aren't meant to close the gap between your income and the things you want, even if that's the way they're often packaged and presented to us.

Used strategically, credit cards can help you build credit and even earn extra money. And building credit is a critical step to building wealth. The better your credit, the lower the rate a lender will charge you to borrow money. That can mean a difference of tens of thousands of dollars if you take out a mortgage. Literally. A recent study by LendingTree found that going from a "fair" credit score to a "very good" score (740 or higher) could save someone up to $41,416 in total interest paid over the lifetime of an average mortgage. And that difference makes it a lot easier to build wealth. A high credit score can even help you save money on your car and homeowners' insurance.

I'm no stranger to the lure (and pitfalls) of easy credit. For the first decade of my working life, I found myself caught in a destructive cycle: playing a perpetual game of catch-up with my credit cards. I'd rack up large debts over several months before implementing harsh austerity measures to pay down my balances. And then I'd slip up and overspend and have to hustle even harder to pay down my debt the next time. Along the way, I was paying hundreds of dollars in interest—essentially throwing money away. Plus, I could feel my blood pressure rise every time a new statement arrived in the mail. The stress of carrying around that credit card debt was starting to weigh on me. It felt like I would never get ahead. Rather than saving for my future, I was still paying for my past.

After that midnight wake-up call, when I realized how much I wanted a second child and a bigger apartment, something shifted in my mindset. I finally got how much my credit card debt was really costing me. It wasn't just the money I was paying in interest but the opportunity cost. Every dollar that went toward the interest I owed on my debt was a dollar that could have been *earning* interest instead to help me reach my future goals faster.

I stopped using my credit cards as a default payment method. I actually cut the card with the highest balance into tiny little pieces (that was fun) and sprinkled them like confetti into the garbage. And I made a commitment to pay off that debt. In the following months, I did—and I figured out how to start using debt in my favor. By the end of this chapter, you'll know how, too.

Build Credit Like a Breadwinner

Building wealth is one thing. But a true measure of your financial health is your net worth. That's a snapshot of what you have in assets (meaning anything you have of value) minus your liabilities (the debts you owe). You could have $20,000 in your 401(k), but if you have $20,000 in credit card and student loan debt, too, you net out at zero. In fact, if you owe a lot of debt, your net worth can be negative even if you've got money saved and invested. Ultimately, you want the balance to tip waaaaay over into the positive (assets) column. The less you owe, the freer you are, and the easier it is to build wealth and set yourself up financially. The goal is to be net-worth positive—and to grow that number as much as you can.

That doesn't mean you shouldn't ever have any debt though. If a low-interest mortgage allows you to buy a home that increases in value, netting you more money when you sell it than what you paid for it, that's worth it. But it requires thinking about debt strategically—going after the lowest interest rates possible and ensuring you use that debt toward something that you are confident will grow in value. Not just because you've got a gut feeling, but because you've researched the heck out of it and all signs are pointing up. That's essentially the calculated bet you make when you take out a student loan to get a degree (or it should be, anyway): that the amount you will be able to earn from having this degree will be a lot bigger than the amount of money you borrowed, and must repay with interest, to get it.

Got Student Debt?

While most of this chapter focuses on credit card debt, it's worth addressing student debt, too, especially since women carry most of it. There are about 44 million borrowers in the United States now with nearly $1.7 trillion in outstanding student loan debt—and women owe about *two-thirds* of that, according to the American Association of University Women (AAUW). That translates to almost $1.1 trillion in student debt that women owe, while men hold nearly $600 billion.

Why such a gap? For one, women now earn the majority of degrees at all levels—from associate to doctoral degrees. In fact, women earn about 57 percent of bachelor's degrees from U.S. colleges and universities. And a college education has become increasingly expensive. Although median household incomes in the United States have grown about 20 percent (in inflation-adjusted terms) since 1976, the median price of college attendance has *more than doubled* in that time period, according to the AAUW. That gap between household incomes and the cost of going to college is largely being filled by student loans. And the organization found that, on average, women take on more debt than men at almost every degree level and type and across all different kinds of institutions. In recent years, women's initial student loan balances have been about 14 percent greater than men's.

And because of the gender pay gap, we have less disposable income with which to repay those loans after graduating from college, so we typically need more time to pay back that student debt. In the time period between one and four years after graduation, men paid off an average of 38 percent of their outstanding debt, while women paid off 31 percent, according to the AAUW.

And female borrowers are most likely to experience financial difficulties: 34 percent of all women (and *57 percent* of Black women) who were repaying student loans reported that they had been unable to meet essential expenses within the past year. All this can impede us from getting ahead.

A general guideline is that you don't want to owe more than what you can make that first year out of college. "If total debt is less than annual income, you should be able to repay your student loans in 10 years or less," Mark Kantrowitz, publisher and vice president of research for Savingforcollege.com, told the *Detroit Free-Press*.

But that's not feasible for many borrowers, thanks to soaring college tuition costs. One report by a research institute in Wisconsin found that, on average, it can take student borrowers with a bachelor's degree just over *twenty-one years* to pay off their loans. While the standard repayment plan for federal student loans consists of fixed monthly payments for ten years, federal income-based repayment options assume a twenty-year time period.

The AAUW estimates that, on average, women take about 1.9 years longer than men to repay their undergraduate student loans. If we're paying off student loans more slowly than men are, that means we're also paying more in interest on our loans since it accrues over time.

If you're still struggling to pay off your student debt, that makes it tougher to get ahead. Here are some strategies to shorten the repayment time period or ease the monthly burden:

1. **Enroll in an income-driven repayment plan.** If you have federal student loans, you can qualify for a long-term income-driven repayment plan. Under these plans, your monthly payment is

generally capped at 10 percent of your discretionary income. And any remaining loan balance is forgiven if your federal student loans aren't fully repaid at the end of the repayment period (which is either twenty or twenty-five years, depending on the repayment plan). This can help lower your monthly payments and free up extra cash each month, but it may also mean you end up paying more over the long term, as the plan simply extends the life of your loan. It doesn't decrease the amount you owe; in fact, you could end up paying more in interest over time. Unless you . . .

2. **Enroll in a Public Service Loan Forgiveness (PSLF) program.** This is available to government and qualifying nonprofit employees who have federal student loans. Eligible borrowers can have their remaining loan balance forgiven tax-free after making 120 qualifying loan payments (so, after about ten years). In order to benefit from a PSLF, you'll want to make payments while enrolled in an income-driven repayment plan. Otherwise, on a standard repayment plan, the loan would essentially be paid off just as you're eligible to benefit from forgiveness. There are also student loan forgiveness programs for teachers in low-income schools, nurses, and members of the military, as well as some state-sponsored repayment assistance programs. So it's worth checking to see what your options are. Just note that the requirements for continued eligibility can be very particular, so it's important to read the fine print and ensure each employer you work for qualifies.

3. **Refinance your student loan(s).** By refinancing your student loans, you could lower the interest rate you pay and save hundreds or even thousands on your student debt over time. To qualify for the best rates, you'll typically need a FICO credit score that is at least in the high 600s (more on credit scores soon). If

you're refinancing private loans, this can be a great chance to lower your monthly payments and the total amount you pay over time. You can also consolidate loans into one payment. If you're thinking of refinancing federal loans with a private lender, though, keep in mind that doing so means you will no longer have access to federal programs and protections, including forgiveness programs. So it's important to weigh the pros and cons.

Generally, if you have a great credit score—and we'll get into that next—you can qualify for the lowest interest rates on any money you want to borrow. And that works in your favor when it comes to leveraging credit to build wealth.

Low interest rates mean you can borrow money for less to buy that home, for example. In the fall of 2020, interest rates on a thirty-year, fixed-rate mortgage were as low as 3 percent (*if* you have great credit). With a mortgage, part of each payment you make goes to the principal, so you gain an increasingly larger share of ownership in the home. The goal is that the home will increase in value, too, so that when you eventually sell it, you can earn a tidy profit.

If you're paying a low interest rate on your mortgage and your home is gaining in value, you are well positioned to increase your net worth. And your home is often one of your greatest sources of wealth. Researchers at the Federal Reserve Bank of St. Louis found that 68 percent of the median U.S. household's wealth comes from its primary residence. And a 2019 Census Bureau analysis found that homeowners' median net worth was *eighty times* larger than renters' median net worth. That makes sense: When you rent, you're just paying for the privilege of living in that space. When you buy a home, you own more of that home outright as you pay down the mortgage, so you're increasing your net worth with each payment.

But in order to qualify for the lowest mortgage rates, you need to have great credit. And that often starts by getting a credit card in your name and using it responsibly. Diana, a twenty-eight-year-old magazine editor in New York, told me she feels very fortunate that her parents—who both work in finance—talked to her a lot about money while she was growing up, helped her get her first credit card when she was nineteen, and instructed her on how to use it responsibly. She knows that's not the norm—a well-educated coworker of hers had recently admitted to her that she knew nothing about credit and had just gotten her first card at twenty-six at her parents' insistence. By then, Diana had already been building her credit for years. She pays off her balance each month and checks her credit score at least every other month.

When I spoke to her, Diana said she was consciously working to build up her credit—and her savings—so that she could afford to buy an apartment, among other goals. "I want to own property," she told me, "I want to build wealth—I don't want to live paycheck to paycheck. You need to think about your future, not just the now."

Thinking like a breadwinner means thinking about credit in a whole different way. It's thinking about how to *build* credit to get the best terms in order to minimize your debt and maximize your wealth-building potential. It's thinking about how to leverage debt to actually earn money and grow wealth.

How Does Credit Work?

If you're already well versed in how credit works and your credit score is high, skip ahead. But if not, here's a quick refresher on how credit scores are calculated and what credit score to target. Then we'll look at the most effective ways to get it.

FICO, or the Fair Isaac Corporation, is the OG of credit scoring. It was founded by engineer Bill Fair and mathematician Earl Isaac, who developed and sold their first credit-scoring system in 1958. Today, the company's scoring model (essentially, software that analyzes your credit report to generate a credit score) is used by about 90 percent of lenders. FICO isn't the only scoring model—VantageScore, a joint venture among the nation's three biggest credit-reporting firms (Experian, Equifax, and TransUnion), which launched in 2006, is also used by some lenders—but it's the most well known.

FICO scores range from 300 to 850. Here's how it breaks down:

- **Poor:** 300 to 579
- **Fair:** 580 to 669
- **Good:** 670 to 739
- **Very good:** 740 to 799
- **Exceptional:** 800 to 850

Anyone with a score below 670 is generally considered a subprime borrower, meaning lenders consider them likelier than most borrowers to have trouble repaying their debts. About 30 percent of borrowers fall into this category, meaning they'll have a tougher time getting loans or credit and have to pay a (sometimes significantly) higher interest rate if they do. When I owed thousands on my credit cards and was paying the minimum most months, I teetered right on the edge of this group with my score. I had some late payments on my credit history. And the amount of debt I owed then compared with my credit limit was above 30 percent—not so much because I owed a lot of money, but because my credit limits just weren't that high in my twenties.

Turns out that isn't unusual. Federal Reserve researchers found that, on average, men between twenty-one and thirty years old had credit limits that were nearly *$4,500 higher* than women in the same age group. Why? Who knows. Maybe it's because men have higher earnings generally. Or maybe they asked for higher limits. But whatever the reason, a lower limit means that carrying the exact same credit card balance would hurt my credit score (or any woman's, generally) more than it would a man's, since credit rating agencies look at how much debt you have outstanding compared with your total credit available. This disparity puts women at a disadvantage from the get-go, and has a circular effect: a higher credit-use-to-total-credit ratio means a lower credit score, which can mean you end up paying higher interest rates and more overall, which makes it harder to pay down that balance.

Nearly 57 percent of Americans have a FICO score of 700 or higher now. But only one in five Americans has an exceptional score, of 800 or more—the type of score that unlocks the best rates and credit card rewards.

So, What Goes into Your Credit Score?

FICO scores are calculated using different pieces of data in your credit report. Your payment history, or how often you've made credit card or loan payments on time, counts the most, at 35 percent. (Late payments can stay on your report and affect your score for up to seven years.) That's followed by the amount of debt you owe, which counts for 30 percent of your score. FICO isn't looking only at the total amount of debt you owe but also at what percentage it represents of the total credit available to you, as well as the different amounts you owe on various accounts. Your score can get dinged if you're using a lot of your available credit. The general advice is to owe less than 30 percent of your available credit at any given time, whether it's on a particular credit card or from the total amount of credit available to you. But FICO research shows that the highest-scoring 25 percent of Americans—those with scores above 795—use an average of just 7 percent of their credit limits. (Mortgages are treated differently.)

Another factor that figures into your credit score is the length of your credit history, which counts toward 15 percent of your score. Generally, the longer, the better. FICO also looks at the mix of credit you have available, including credit cards, retail accounts, and installment loans. Those last ones can include car, mortgage, or school loans in which regularly scheduled payments are made until the amount you borrowed is paid in full. Demonstrating the ability to consistently pay down loans as well as credit card debt helps, and counts for about 10 percent of your score.

The final 10 percent of your FICO score is determined by looking at how many new accounts you have applied for or opened. FICO considers both the type of accounts and the time frame in which you applied. Basically, applying for a lot of credit in a short period of time can hurt your score. The exception is if you're shopping around for the best rate on, say, a mortgage or car loan. If you apply to three different lenders to compare rates, for example, it will usually count as just one inquiry on your report. Generally, you want to submit all the applications in a two-week period to make clear that you're rate shopping.

You can take steps in each of these areas to improve your credit. But if you're just starting out, the simplest way to start building credit is to apply for a credit card with no annual fee, use it regularly, and pay it off in full every month.

Of course, many of us don't start that way though. We overdo it and then end up paying for it—both in interest and with a lower credit score. So it's more a matter of repairing our credit than starting from scratch.

How Can You Improve Your Credit Score Quickly?

Diligently paying down your balances can help improve your score over time. But there are a few ways to jump-start the process and give your score a boost.

1. **Ask for an increase in your credit limit.** Since credit usage accounts for 30 percent of your score, improving that number can have a big impact. One way to do that, of course, is to pay down

your debt quicker or pay it off altogether. Another is to increase your credit limits so that the credit-utilization ratio—the amount of credit you're using as a percentage of the total credit available to you—goes down. You can call credit card issuers directly (if you've been making on-time payments) and ask them to increase your credit limit, at least enough to ensure that whatever outstanding balance you have will count for less than 30 percent of your total credit. When you ask for the increase, it's worth requesting that they *not* do a hard inquiry on your credit before raising it. Too many hard inquiries can pull down your credit, though just temporarily.

2. **Make frequent payments.** If you are able to make two or more payments throughout the month, that can help keep your credit card balances down. This is important because credit reporting agencies check your credit usage at various times during the month—not necessarily when your payment is due. So paying down your balance during the month instead of waiting till your due date will keep your credit utilization rates lower, which can give your score a boost.

3. **Get credit for making on-time utility and cell phone payments.** Typically, these aren't reported to the major credit bureaus. But if you've been making utility and cell phone payments on time and want those to count toward your score, there are options. One is Experian Boost, a free product launched by the credit agency in early 2019. It does require you to connect your bank accounts so that it can pull utility and telecom payment history, but once you confirm you want the data added to your Experian credit report, the agency will share an updated FICO score in real time. Experian says that among those with a score below 680—who are most likely to benefit from this—75 percent saw their credit score improve after adding the info. Another option is to use a third-party service like PayYourRent or RentTrack, which will report your rental payments to all three major credit bureaus.

4. Become an authorized user. If your partner or parent has better credit than you, becoming an authorized user on his or her credit card can help give your score a boost. Assuming, of course, that everyone is using the card responsibly and, better yet, paying it off each month. Just keep in mind that being an authorized user does not carry the same weight as being a cosigner on a joint credit card account.

One way to help accelerate the debt-payoff process (and improve your score overall) is to take advantage of a balance-transfer offer that will give you better terms than the card you have does. That's what I did after I'd paid off one card balance, and my credit score improved. Banks are always trying to get and keep your business. So you can use a balance-transfer offer to move your balance to a new card with a lower interest rate, or as leverage to ask your existing credit card issuer to lower your interest rate. Once my credit score improved, I was able to qualify for some decent balance-transfer options. (You'll usually need a score of at least 690 for the best offers.)

If your credit score is very good, meaning it's above 740 (which mine was not at the time), you can qualify for even better deals. As of mid-2020, some card issuers were offering zero-percent introductory interest (for up to thirty-six months!), no annual fee, and no transfer fee if you transferred money within sixty days of opening a credit card. You can check out the best current balance-transfer offers on comparison sites like NerdWallet, Bankrate, WalletHub, and Creditcards.com. Just be sure you can pay off the balance before any introductory period ends. And keep the card open that you transferred the money from if your payment history was good. This way, your total credit limit is higher, your credit history is intact, and you can pay off your balance faster since you'll be paying less in interest, so less overall—all of which helps your score.

Seems like a no brainer, right? But research finds that men are much more likely than women to request a balance transfer, or even to ask a credit card issuer to lower a rate. In one survey by CompareCards, 54 percent of men said they'd used a balance-transfer card at least once, compared with just 31 percent of women. Other surveys by the same company have found that women are also less likely to ask their credit card company to lower their interest rate or even to waive a late-payment fee. "But the *success rate* in getting what they asked for isn't all that different between genders," Matt Schulz, chief industry analyst at Lending-Tree, told me. His point: Ask for it.

While a very good credit score can give you more leverage, he said, they've also seen high success rates among those with lower scores. "Banks view people as being valuable over the course of a lifetime. They don't want to lose you," Schulz told me. "Once you realize you are valuable to that bank, it should give you the confidence to wield that power that you have."

I used most of the tactics above to improve my score, outside of reporting utility and rent payments, which wasn't widely available then. And once I'd paid off my credit card debt, I started using the card with the best terms for a few purchases a month that I'd normally put on a debit card or pay for with cash. Then I'd check my account every couple of weeks and pay off the balance. In less than two years, my score had improved by more than one hundred points, and I started scouting out cards with the best rewards and other benefits, so I could start leveraging my good credit to make money from my card instead of paying for the privilege of carrying debt. It was a good feeling.

Using Credit Cards Like a Breadwinner

Once you've got a handle on your spending, credit cards become a way to actually *earn* money rather than costing you money. It's probably not going to be a major income stream, but if you play your cards right (sorry, couldn't help that), you can benefit from just about every purchase you make. And that should be the goal.

If you're disciplined enough to pay off your credit cards each month, there's usually no reason to use a debit card. Ever. With a few exceptions, you're not getting anything back when you use it. (By early 2020, only seven debit cards offered any kind of rewards, and the benefits aren't as generous as those offered by the best rewards credit cards.) And if you are still trying to get control of your spending, research shows that you're better off using cash than a debit card. Why? The less friction, the easier it is to spend. Using a debit card doesn't elicit the same feelings of loss as peeling off bills does. (Neither do credit cards, of course, or Apple Pay, so it's important to be aware of what you're actually spending when you use them, too.)

With good credit, you can get a great credit card that allows you to earn cash back or to earn points with each purchase that you can later cash in for airline trips, hotel stays, gift cards, or other perks. You also have access to other benefits you don't get with debit cards, like purchase protection: With a credit card dispute, you often have the option to withhold payment, but when you dispute a debit card purchase, your bank must decide whether or not to restore money that's already gone from your account (meaning you often have to wait until the investigation is over to get any money back).

When you're trying to choose a card, consider whether you just want cash back or whether you want to use the card to grow the number of points you have with a travel- or hotel-rewards program faster. Going with a cash-back card allows you the flexibility to use that money however you choose—including saving or investing it so that it can grow even more—but the amount you earn back may be less than you could have saved with a rewards card if you travel a lot. You may also choose to divide your expenses between both card types.

When I traveled a lot between our California and New York offices for work, I chose one airline I liked, which also flew to our family's regular travel destinations, and I applied for the credit card associated with its program. I earned a 40,000-point introductory bonus for signing up and spending $1,000 in the first ninety days. (That alone was worth $520 based on valuations by rewards-card expert the Points Guy, which more than offset the $99 annual fee.) I also got free checked bags, discounts on in-flight purchases, and trip delay and cancellation protection. And I earned six times the points per dollar on purchases related to the airline, twice the points at restaurants and grocery stores, and one point per dollar on all other purchases. Based on the Points Guy valuations, that is equal to a 7.8 percent return on airline-related spending, 2.6 percent on dining and groceries, and 1.3 percent on everything else. Given I was flying about once a month, that was a pretty good deal.

Of course, that card wouldn't make sense for everyone—or even for me, probably, if I wasn't then taking cross-country flights multiple times a year on the airline. But because I loved the airline and used it for personal travel, too, it made a lot of sense. The points I earned already covered one pre-pandemic family trip—and I still have plenty of points left to use. I've used that card in tandem with a cash-back card offering 2 percent back on all purchases.

Generally speaking, you want to look for an airline card with a point valuation of at least one cent, and hotel-program credit cards with point valuations of at least half a cent. And don't forget to factor in any annual fee, introductory bonus points, and other benefits like free in-flight purchases and upgrades. You can compare the fees and benefits of travel rewards cards on sites like the Points Guy, NerdWallet, Bankrate, CompareCards, and WalletHub.

For cash-back cards, the best cards with flat rates were offering up to 2 percent back on all purchases in 2020. Others offer higher rates on purchases in predetermined spending categories, like dining out or travel. Many cash-back cards also offer a sign-up bonus of $150 or more for opening the account, which you'll generally get after you meet a minimum spending requirement in a specific time frame.

Depending on how much you spend and what percent you get back (plus any sign-up bonuses), you can earn literally thousands. Or save that much on airfare and other rewards with a rewards-points card over time.

If I charged (and paid off) at least $1,000 a month in purchases with the card I got, with a 2 percent cash-back rate on all purchases and no annual fee, I'd earn a minimum of $240 a year in cash.

When we needed to do home repairs and renovations in 2019, I considered getting a home equity loan. But even with excellent credit, I learned the interest rate would be around 4 percent, and the process would require time and a lot of paperwork. So I looked for a credit card instead with a zero percent interest rate. I found one with a zero percent introductory interest rate and a cash-back rewards program. We ended up spending about $10,000 for the renovations the first month I had the card, which triggered an introductory cash bonus. I paid off the card over twelve months, before the regular interest rate kicked in. And I earned more than $350 in the process. So rather than taking out a loan and paying 4 percent on it, I paid no interest and actually *made* $350 by thinking like a breadwinner.

Of course, it's also worth making sure that the rewards you get aren't outweighed by the money you're spending on your cards. In other words, that you're not spending more than you would have otherwise just because you're using a credit card. There's plenty of social science research out there that suggests we tend to spend more using cards than we ever would with actual cash. The point is to make every essential purchase count—not to make more purchases. Do that, and you can start earning a steady stream of passive income and perks from your purchases that can help you grow your net worth.

CHAPTER 7

Invest in Your Future

How to Make Your Money Work for You

Being rich is having money; being wealthy is having time.
—MARGARET BONNANO, AUTHOR

MY FRIEND JESSICA vividly remembers the beautiful bracelet she got from her parents when she had her bat mitzvah at twelve. And she remembers clearly a couple of years later when, for her brother's bar mitzvah gift, their dad opened an investment account for him and started teaching him how to invest so that he'd have enough to help support his own family one day.

Of course, neither she nor her parents ever imagined that twenty-seven years later, Jessica—who became a single mom at age thirty-nine—would be the one supporting a family herself. "I could have used that investment account," she told me.

Women—much more than men—are rarely taught how to invest when growing up. As I mentioned earlier, surveys find parents are more likely to teach girls how to track their spending and budget and to teach their boys about building credit and investing. And while few Americans get much of a financial education in school, men are much more likely to take finance and business courses in college and tend to outperform women on financial literacy tests overall. So it shouldn't be surprising that, as women, we tend to feel less knowledgeable, less confident, and less comfortable talking about investing.

I still remember a party I went to when I was in my twenties with some friends from the newspaper where I worked. When the men started comparing the performance of their stock market investments and trading tips, trying to one-up each other with their investing acumen, the women fell silent. Lost, and a little embarrassed, my female friends and I turned to one another to discuss our weekend plans instead. When we did talk about money, it was usually related to the amazing deal we got on a pair of shoes or how to split up a restaurant bill. At the time, I was hardly putting anything into my 401(k) retirement account, and I had little idea of how the money was being invested. I'd literally just ticked off the portfolio that had been recommended to me.

From the data, it seems like things haven't changed much for women since. In a recent survey by Fidelity Investments, eight in ten women said they've refrained from talking about their finances with the people they're close to, and less than half of the women surveyed said they'd even feel confident discussing money and investing with a financial professional on their own. While women are almost equally as confident as men when it comes to financial tasks like paying bills and budgeting, men continue to be much more confident about managing investments— with only about one in four women saying they're comfortable with how much they know about investing. The result is that many of us end up waiting too long to put our money to work by investing it.

This is a critical mistake. And it is probably the single greatest reason why we lag so far behind men when it comes to building wealth and having enough money for retirement.

That's because time is often *the single greatest factor* in our ability to grow our money. More important even than the amount of money we invest. The earlier you start investing, with any amount, the better off you'll be. Wealth building, financial freedom, the ability to make the choices you want to make, the postwork life of your dreams—it all comes down to investing. Right now. Today. No matter what amount you start with, the most important thing you can do is to start. Because the moment you invest your money, it can start growing—faster than it would sitting in the bank, and certainly faster than sitting in your wallet.

Men have already figured out that investing money in the stock market can be one of the most efficient ways to build wealth. Yes, the market can go down. But over time, it has consistently recovered from every downturn and gone on to new highs. In the last fifty years, the stock market has grown more than sixfold. It's hard to find that kind of growth anywhere else.

Yet many women are still making the same mistake I did—and waiting. Well, actually, my mistake was worse, because I started investing in a 401(k) retirement account in my midtwenties but then *cashed it out* when I switched jobs, erasing all the hard work I'd done and years of potential gains. (Had I left it alone, instead of emptying it to pay off a car loan, it would have easily tripled in value in the years since.) I learned my lesson and quickly began investing again—for retirement, at least—but by then I was nearly thirty, so I'd already missed out on almost a decade of growth.

I thought I was an exception. But it turns out that a lot more women than men tap their retirement funds early, even though it means paying a 10 percent penalty on top of taxes. A 2015 survey by Boston Research Technologies revealed that, among those with 401(k) balances below $5,000, women tend to cash out at significantly higher levels than their male counterparts. As balances grow, that gap starts to shrink. But if you're cashing out early and then starting all over, as I did, it can leave you scrambling to make up for lost time.

And looking at the data, it seems like a *lot* of us are scrambling. Some of us start early and then tap our retirement savings, setting ourselves back. Many others don't start saving at all for retirement until they're already years into their careers. In a 2017 study by Financial Finesse, only a quarter of women said they felt they were on track for saving for retirement. (In fact, one in five women has *nothing* at all saved for retirement, according to a recent CNBC–SurveyMonkey poll!) And even when women contribute, we are less likely than men to put enough money into our employer-sponsored retirement plan to even capture a full match in contributions from employers that offer one, which means many of us are basically leaving money on the table.

Outside of retirement accounts, the investing gap is even wider, in part because women are much more likely to leave our money in savings instead of investing some of it. Yes, saving money is important, but once we've got enough money stashed away in a high-yield savings account for emergencies and short-term goals, continuing to funnel money into savings instead of investing it can actually hold us back. Yet many of us continue to do that.

In fact, the Fidelity survey found that more than half of women were not investing *anything* outside of their retirement accounts. Instead they were leaving nearly all their money in cash or in bank accounts—which, by the way, are paying out less than 0.05 percent annually in interest now, on average. (Yeah, that's a *nickel* for every one hundred dollars you deposit.) Meanwhile, the Standard & Poor's 500 Index, which tracks five hundred of the largest stocks and is used as a gauge for the overall stock market, has averaged annual returns of nearly 10 percent (or about 7 percent, adjusted for inflation). That's nearly *200 times* as much. That can be a difference of literally tens of thousands of dollars in potential earnings over time.

Preeti, the Chicago doctor in her late thirties who is the main provider in her relationship, used to be among them. She says she'd always been diligent about saving some of her income, but it took her years to get comfortable putting it anywhere other than a bank account. "I've generally been pretty conservative when it comes to money," she told me. "I would keep all of my money in my bank. I'm not sure why. Maybe because I felt like I could see it, and then I felt safe."

But after talking to her older sister, who was participating in her company's retirement plan, she started maxing out her own 403(b) plan (a retirement plan offered to employees of tax-exempt organizations and certain other workers). That was it, initially, since she felt uncomfortable investing on her own. But then she was talking about her finances with an older female colleague "who is excellent with money" and who encouraged her to invest in a regular brokerage account, too. Her guidance and prodding prompted Preeti to start looking at online brokerages. Had it not been for her colleague, though, Preeti's not sure she would have considered moving some of her money from a high-yield savings account—that still pays less than 1 percent a year in interest (so, not even enough to beat inflation)—into an investment account, which has the potential to earn exponentially more than that.

Why are so many of us still leaving most of our money in the bank? Probably because that's where we were told to put it! For decades, after all, men have been conditioned to look to the stock market as a means of supercharging their wealth-building efforts, while we have been encouraged to save our pennies. For a long time, that's how the financial responsibilities broke down in heterosexual couples: The men invested, and the women saved. The assumption was that men would earn more, so they had more to invest, and they were encouraged to focus on long-term planning. Meanwhile, women were encouraged to save for short-term goals like new furniture or vacations.

Wall Street was (and still is) dominated by men, and investing in stocks was portrayed in popular culture as a testosterone-fueled endeavor with mobs of red-faced men in blue jackets waving papers and yelling over each other on the floor of the stock exchange. (The first female trader wasn't allowed on the floor until 1967 and, more than fifty years later, women still make up just 9 percent of traders at the New York Stock Exchange. Even when I shot some episodes with Cheddar TV on the floor of the NYSE a few years ago, the female cohost and I were among only a handful of women on the floor.)

While all that is changing—the first female president of the New York Stock Exchange took office in 2018—there's still a perception that investing in the stock market is a man's game. And that men are more adept at investing (despite growing evidence that women actually have better results, but more on that in a minute). So, many women—even young women—still end up deferring to their male partners on invest-ing and financial planning decisions. A recent UBS survey found this to be true for nearly *60 percent* of women in their twenties and early thir-ties! Or they simply stash away their money in a bank.

We also tend to prioritize more immediate financial goals and needs over long-term ones. In a survey by insurance brokerage Willis Towers Watson, women ranked investing for retirement as their fifth most im-portant financial priority, after managing daily living and housing costs, paying down debt obligations, and building up savings. For men, invest-ing for retirement was number one. Sure, you can explain some of that because we earn less than men, on average, so we need to pay more atten-tion to daily expenses, and we tend to owe more student and credit card debt. But we also aren't brought up to believe we *need* to start investing for retirement—or for other goals in the decades before—right away.

"Investing is often just not as high a priority in the moment as what-ever urgent situation is right in front of us that day," said Bobbi Rebell, a certified financial planner and author of *How to Be a Financial Grown-Up*, when we were commiserating on how much money women miss out on by putting off investing. Why isn't planning financially for our future on our "self-care" list, too, she wondered, along with—or even ahead of—a manicure or spa day? "There's been a great movement recently, in large part because of marketing, to put ourselves first," she said. "But it is often focused on something we need to *buy*: a candle, a solo trip, or even a membership to a networking group."

Yet one of the best ways to care for ourselves is to take the time to make sure we're investing enough to set ourselves up for the future we want.

Battling a Scarcity Mindset

What a lot of this comes down to is mindset, and many of us are still operating from a scarcity mindset. Think about this for a moment.

While men are comfortable trading stock tips and trying to one-up each other with the returns on their investments, women are more comfortable comparing bargains and trying to one-up each other with the money we saved. Browse the bookstore aisles, and you'll see plenty of books about bargain hunting, budgeting, and couponing with titles like *Extreme Couponing* and *Never Pay Full Price!* and *Meal Planning on a Budget*—all of them written by women. But wander over to the investing section, and the majority of books on investing and building wealth—from *The Intelligent Investor* and *The Little Book of Investing Like the Pros* to *The Secrets of Getting Rich* and *I Will Teach You to Be Rich*—are written by men.

"Women will have five times the emergency fund they need, sitting in the bank, not doing anything," Cary Carbonaro, managing director of United Capital Financial Advisors of New York, lamented to NBC. "Women are afraid of losing money, while men seem to be afraid of losing out by *not* playing the market."

But here's the thing: By waiting, we do lose out.

Because the earlier you start investing, the more your money works *for you*—and the less time you'll end up having to work for your money. Think of it this way: Every year you're investing now could be a year less you have to work later. That's thanks to the power of compounding, or when the returns you've earned on the money you invest start earning money, too.

Kameka Dempsey, an executive coach and founder of KD Leadership Strategies, learned this firsthand. The first in her family to go to college, she grew up without much money and had little firsthand knowledge of how to build wealth. But her parents did instill in her a voracious love of learning, she says. "They convinced me that education was the way out."

Then a high school classmate encouraged her to apply to a program called INROADS, which targets talented minority students, through which she was able to take courses on business etiquette, acumen, writing, presentations, and even dress codes—"all of these things that are so important in how you show up in corporate America," she says. It also helped her to start working in paid internships just after she graduated from high school and throughout her time at Yale (which she also helped pay for through scholarships and a work-study program).

The program also gave her the opportunity to take a financial literacy course, and she paid close attention. "I wanted to make sure that once I started making money, it was not here today and gone tomorrow," she told me. "First, it was about getting paid the most I could get at that point in time. And then investing it."

She started investing in a 401(k) as soon as she had access to one. "I remember when I was presented with my first 401(k), and someone said, 'The company will match your contributions one hundred percent. You *have* to contribute the max you can!'" she recalled. "So I did."

More than twenty years later, she looked recently at the projections for her combined 401(k) accounts and realized she'll be a millionaire in retirement *even if she doesn't invest anything more.* "It's not that I'm going to be rolling in dough, but it's comforting to know that I will have enough money to live on even if I didn't invest another dollar," she told me. "I bought myself that flexibility, unknowingly, by investing early."

The breadwinner mindset is a growth mindset. It's thinking about how you can put as much of the money you earn to work *for you* so that you are not stuck working for your money for the rest of your life. A million dollars in retirement may seem like a faraway goal. But the more your money works to earn money, the less you'll have to work for it. And the earlier you start, the harder those dollars will work—they can grow exponentially over time. "A lot of times women wait because they think they've got time . . . but then you miss out on all those earlier years and compounding returns," certified financial planner Stacy Francis, the CEO of Francis Financial and founder of the nonprofit Savvy Ladies, which provides financial education to women, told me. "Had you started earlier, those dollars would have been the hardest-working dollars you invested."

Debunking Common Investing Myths

What you earn is important, but what you do with each paycheck is even more important. One thing I noticed among all the breadwinner-minded women I interviewed is that they diligently put a double-digit percentage of every paycheck straight into savings and investing.

Some of that should go toward retirement—enough, eventually, to max out any employer-sponsored retirement plan, but at least enough right away to capture any employer match money. (If you don't have access to one, you can use an individual retirement account, which we'll get into later in this chapter.) Some money should also go toward saving for short-term goals—like an upcoming vacation or summer camp for kids, if you have them—and building up an emergency savings fund. You'll want enough, eventually, in a high-yield savings account to cover at least three months of basic expenses. (Basically, enough savings to cover your expenses in case you lose a job while you look for new income.) And once you've got enough savings to feel comfortable, you can put money into a regular investment account, too, for other mid- or long-term goals. By investing, you stand to reach them much faster because your money will be earning more money, too.

More so than any other area of personal finance, investing is plagued by myths that tend to hold us back though. So let's get some of the big ones out of the way.

Myth #1: Investing is hard.

Given how many books, podcasts, shows, and "pros" there are when it comes to investing, it's easy to understand why it's gotten a reputation for being something complex that requires a lot of expertise. But nothing could be further from the truth. Investing successfully is not hard. You don't need to day-trade (in fact, you probably shouldn't). You don't even need to pay that much attention to your investments on a day-to-day or even a month-to-month basis. I learned this when I started investing, and I'll share the simple, successful approach I took with you later in this chapter.

Myth #2: Investing in stocks is risky.

I grew up believing that investing in stocks was risky—their value could go up, sure, but it could also go down, or maybe even disappear altogether. (Remember Enron and Lehman Brothers?) But the reality is that just a small fraction of the thousands of companies that trade publicly have filed for chapter 7 bankruptcy (the kind that can wipe out any stock value). So if you invest in a broad and diverse mix of stocks, you can substantially lower your risk of losing money and increase your chances of picking winners.

Myth #3: Investing is something you can't do until you're wealthy.

I'd gotten it all wrong: The truth is, you usually don't get wealthy *until* you invest. Which is why it costs us so much when we don't do it. Sallie Krawcheck, founder of the investing platform Ellevest, estimates the gender investing gap can leave women with about $300,000 to $1 million *less* than men at retirement after a thirty-five-year career. That difference can make it much harder to fund the post-work lives we want and ensure we have enough to cover healthcare and other expenses.

Myth #4: You need to hire someone to help you invest.

Nope. Wall Street has done its best to perpetuate this myth. Financial advisors, who are still predominantly older white guys, act as if investing is so complicated that it's best left to the professionals—that you wouldn't understand. Of course: Their business depends on that. But as I've learned from personal experience, the truth is that investing is not hard. And while you may choose to work with a financial advisor, you don't *need* someone to do it for you.

Myth #5: Men are better at investing than women are.

In a 2017 survey in which Fidelity asked men and women who they believed made better investors, just 9 percent of women thought they'd outperform men. But here's the twist: A growing body of evidence, including an analysis of more than 8 million Fidelity clients, shows that women actually *do* tend to outperform men in the returns they generate on their investments. That's partly because men tend to be, shall we say, *overconfident?* And that results in a lot of churning (e.g., buying and selling and buying again) of stocks. So they end up paying more in trading fees. And they are more likely to buy when prices are high and sell when they are low. If you're a woman who was raised to be risk-averse, you can use that to your advantage in investing.

The challenge is that we've been fed these myths for years. So it shouldn't be surprising that a whole lot of us are afraid to even get started. And that leaves us lagging later in life. Women today have retirement balances that are about half the size of men's on average, according to the Vanguard Center for Investor Research. That's a big reason why women are 80 percent more likely than men to end their lives in poverty. I know, that's a pretty scary stat. But we have the power to change those odds. And doing so doesn't require a lot of effort, know-how, time, or money.

Whether you're making $30,000 or $300,000 a year, all you need to do is get started and follow some basic guidelines. Take it from my grandmother.

Nana's Guide to Stock Market Success

My maternal grandmother, born in 1912 in Perth Amboy, New Jersey, didn't fit anyone's stereotype of a wealthy person. She worked as a secretary, with the modest salary that accompanied it. In her thirties, she married my grandfather, had two daughters, and stopped working. Then, when she was in her forties, my grandfather returned from a business trip and told her he was leaving her for a woman he'd met in Florida, and she suddenly found herself a single mom of two adolescent girls. At the time, she had been out of the workforce for more than a decade.

My grandmother, or Nana, as I called her, had no paycheck and very little savings. And now she was responsible for a twelve and a fourteen year old and herself—possibly for the rest of her life. (In fact, she never did remarry.) At the time, there weren't 401(k) retirement plans or individual retirement accounts. And the lawyers' office where Nana went back to work as a secretary, like many private employers, didn't offer a pension. If she was going to save enough money to support her family and herself in old age, she realized, she was going to have to figure out how to do it largely on her own. So Nana hired a broker to make trades on her behalf and opened an investment account. She spent most of her lunch hours at her broker's office, staring at the ticker tape that showed the ever-changing stock prices and asking him questions. She continued putting some of each paycheck into her investment account. And she left that money alone to grow until she needed it.

In other words, she thought like a breadwinner. She wanted to have enough money in retirement that she wouldn't burden her daughters with having to take care of her. She wanted to have enough to help them cover the costs of college. And she wanted to remain independent and to live on her own terms. And she did. Her financial habits were guided by her values, and she used those values to incentivize herself to save and spend wisely. Even in her seventies, she was living the dream she'd imagined for herself. She lived on her own, played jazz standards on her piano, drove a bright-red sports car, and regularly broke swimming records in competitions for her age group. And by the time she passed away in her early eighties, she had amassed an investment portfolio that was worth nearly half a million dollars. On a secretary's salary.

What was her secret? Her strategy was simple, and it reinforces the fact that you don't need to do a lot of research, or trading, to earn a lot in the stock market. Nana invested in every company she either wrote a check to or whose products she bought on a regular basis. That included a wide range of publicly traded companies—from her electric and phone companies to her favorite department store chains to Coca-Cola (my aunt's favorite drink). Without even realizing it, Nana ended up following four basic principles for successfully investing in the stock market.

Invest in a diverse mix of stocks.

Rather than bet on a few stocks, spreading your money across a diverse mix—large and small companies across different sectors—can help you lower the risk of losing money on one bad bet. It also increases the chances that you'll find some winners and that if stocks in some sectors are down, others will be up. Back in Nana's day, that required multiple buy orders as you snapped up shares of different companies. Now you can simply buy shares in one or more funds that invest in a range of stocks to get the same kind of exposure (more about that below).

Buy what you know.

You don't need to be familiar with all the intricacies of a company you're interested in investing in, but it helps to have a basic understanding of the business (or to understand what types of companies are in a fund if that's the route you want to go). Nana's approach was to invest in the companies she wrote checks to, whose products she bought, or that operated stores where she shopped. She didn't invest in currencies or pork-belly futures or precious metals. She invested in companies she understood. Her approach allowed her to be not just a customer but an investor in the companies she supported. A bonus was that if her electric utility rates went up, for example, she would pay more as a customer, but she would gain as an investor because the stock's value could increase as a result.

Use dollar-cost averaging.

This sounds like a complex term, but all it means is that you're investing regularly—like a small portion out of every paycheck—instead of waiting to invest a large sum once or twice a year, for example. By doing so, you'll buy more shares when stock prices are down and fewer when they're up, and you can lower the average price per share you pay over time. You can also invest earlier than if you'd waited until you had more money to invest, so your money can start growing sooner.

Stick with it.

Stock prices fluctuate every day, and there are periods when the value of many stocks goes down—sometimes by a lot (as in March 2020). But every stock market downturn in history has ended in an upturn. And the market has gone on to hit new highs. Buying and holding is usually a better strategy than trying to time the market, because timing the market's ups and downs is nearly impossible. But over time, the stock market's value has grown exponentially.

"Investing is not trading, or buying the hot stock and selling it at just the right time. If you're watching one of those business channels, you may think that's what investing is and wonder: How will I choose the right stock among thousands? How will I choose the right day to buy or to sell?" financial advisor Stacy Francis told me. "But that's not really what it's about. Investing can be really boring, but that's not a bad thing. You pick a broad basket of stocks in a fund, and you stay with it. The better investors are the ones not watching it on a daily basis. The better investors have a life and look at their portfolios once a month or a quarter."

And by the way, while it's never too early to start investing—time (and the compounding returns it allows for) is a powerful tool in growing wealth—it's also never too late. Nana was forty-six when she started investing.

How to Start Investing Today

The first place to invest is in a tax-advantaged retirement account, then consider a regular brokerage account for medium-term goals (after building up some savings). It's a pretty simple process.

Step 1: Sign up for your employer-sponsored retirement plan.

Usually, this is either a 401(k) or a 403(b) plan.

Step 2: Contribute the maximum you can afford.

Eventually, you want to contribute the max allowed under law—$19,500 plus another $6,500 if you're fifty or older, in 2021. But in the meantime, make sure you are at least contributing enough to get any employer match money (do not leave free money on the table!) and try to stretch yourself to contribute more. You can always adjust your contribution rate back down, but behavioral science says you probably won't—and future you will thank you for that.

If you don't have access to an employer-sponsored plan, open up an individual retirement account (IRA) and try to max it out. Even if you do have an employer-sponsored plan, you might consider opening an IRA, too—if you're in the enviable situation of already maxing out the plan—so that you can save more for retirement or even some earlier goals. (More on IRAs below.)

Step 3: Open a regular brokerage account for mid-term goals.

Those could include buying a home down the road or starting a business or a family. Prioritize your retirement accounts. They've got tax advantages, and you don't want to miss out on any employer matches or end up short when you're ready for retirement. But investing even a little at a time in a regular investment account, too, can help you grow that money to reach goals you've got in the decades before retirement (more on what to look for in a brokerage below).

What's an IRA Anyway?

Individual retirement accounts (IRAs) are a great way to invest for retirement, especially if you don't have access to an employer-sponsored retirement plan like a 401(k). Anyone with earned income can open one.

The two main choices are Roth and traditional IRAs, although Simplified Employee Pension (SEP) IRAs are also a good option if you're self-employed or run a small business. All IRAs offer tax benefits, including the fact that your earnings grow tax-free. So, for example, if you sell stocks in your retirement account for a gain before retirement, you don't pay taxes on that. You won't pay taxes on any gains in your account until you withdraw money from your account in retirement—and maybe not even then. Let me explain.

With a traditional IRA, you may be able to deduct your contributions and lower your tax bill now, but you will have to pay taxes on the money you withdraw in retirement. With a Roth IRA, though, the opposite is true: You have to contribute money that's already been taxed, but your withdrawals—including earnings—come out tax-free in retirement (as long as you've had the account for at least five years and are fifty-nine and a half or older).

The one catch is that there are income restrictions on who can invest in a Roth IRA. To max out a Roth IRA contribution, you must have earned less than $125,000 in 2021, or $198,000 if you're married and filing jointly. Above that, the amount you can contribute starts to drop. And if you earned $140,000 or more (after adjusting for deductions), or $208,000 if you're married and filing jointly in 2021, you can't contribute at all to a Roth.

There are no income limitations to contribute to a traditional IRA, but to claim the full tax deduction for 2021, your adjusted gross income must be less than $66,000 if you're single or $105,000 for married couples filing jointly, if you're also covered by a retirement plan at work. If neither you nor your spouse has access to a work plan, there are no income limits.

Another benefit of the Roth IRA is that you can withdraw your contributions at any time without paying taxes. Just remember that withdrawing any money early means you can miss out on long-term growth.

A SEP IRA allows those who are self-employed (like freelancers or anyone with side gigs) and small business owners to contribute to their own retirement as well as any employees' retirement savings. Just keep in mind that if you have employees who are eligible to participate in their SEP IRA plan, you'll have to contribute on their behalf, too—not just your own. Although you should get a tax deduction for it. (If you have others working for you, they may be eligible for a SEP IRA if they're at least twenty-one, earn at least $650 a year, and have worked for your company for any three of the last five years.)

One big plus of a SEP IRA, especially if you're self-employed: It allows you to contribute a pretty hefty chunk of your income. In 2021, you can contribute up to $58,000 or 25 percent of your salary, whichever is less. That's likely to be substantially more than the contribution limit of $6,000 (or $7,000 if you're fifty or older) for a traditional or Roth IRA. And you can deduct your contributions (up to the maximum allowed).

If you're just starting to invest on your own outside of picking a plan for your employer-sponsored retirement account, you don't need to do a lot of research. It's a remarkably straightforward process:

- **Open a brokerage account.** Look for one that offers zero commissions, meaning you won't be charged for your trades (e.g., when you buy stocks, bonds, or shares of funds). Those include Ally Invest, E*Trade, TD Ameritrade, Merrill Edge, Vanguard, Charles Schwab, Fidelity, SoFi, and Acorns (where I work).
- **Connect it with your bank account and transfer money to get started.** I'd also recommend setting up an automatic monthly or biweekly transfer so that you get in the habit of investing regularly. (I do it the day after my paycheck is deposited.) But don't forget that when you transfer money, it is typically *not automatically*

invested. So you need to then go in and invest the money you deposited. (Some, like Acorns, will invest it for you in a preselected portfolio.)

■ **Invest the money in one or more exchange-traded funds.** Look for funds that provide exposure to dozens or hundreds of stocks, like those that track the S&P 500 Index, and that have low expense ratios (more on both below). You can also balance those with funds that invest in bonds.

In Nana's time, having a diverse mix of stocks or bonds meant buying shares in, or bonds issued by, a lot of different companies. But today, you can accomplish the same thing just by buying shares in a fund that does that for you, and it's as easy as buying a stock. Exchange-traded funds (ETFs) trade just like stocks. But they save you time, and money if you're paying any trading fees, because you can just buy shares in that fund, rather than buying shares in (or bonds from) every company it's investing in.

Of course, you can invest in individual stocks and bonds, too. But generally, I keep most of my money in funds, so I know I've got a broad and diverse mix, and I'm not too concerned about (or dependent on) how one particular company does.

I started years ago by investing in an index fund that mirrors the S&P 500. That's the Standard and Poor's index that tracks five hundred of the largest stocks, representing roughly 80 percent of the stock market's total value, and is often used as a gauge for how the overall market is doing. When you hear that the "stock market" has returned about 10 percent annually on average (or about 7 to 7.5 percent adjusted for inflation), reporters and analysts are usually talking about how much the S&P 500 Index has grown each year, on average. You can't invest in the index directly, but you can invest in an S&P 500 Index fund that tries to match, or even beat, its performance.

I've found it to be one of the best ways to capture much of the stock market's growth over time. There are several different S&P 500 Index funds from which to choose, including:

- Vanguard S&P 500 ETF (VOO is the ticker)
- iShares Core S&P 500 ETF (IVV)
- Schwab S&P 500 Index Fund (SWPPX)
- SPDR S&P 500 ETF Trust (SPY)
- iShares S&P 500 Growth ETF (IVW)

Each of the funds tracks the S&P 500 Index and seeks to mirror or beat its gains. But when you're investigating any funds, it's smart to check something called the "expense ratio"—basically the cost of holding the fund. A fund's expense ratio is another term for the percent of assets that a fund takes to cover costs like management fees and other expenses associated with operating the fund. These come right out of your returns, so you may not even realize it's being taken out. Simply put, a bigger expense ratio means you get to keep less of your earnings.

A big plus of index funds is that they don't require a whole lot of management, so the fees are generally pretty low. Among the S&P 500 Index funds above, SWPPX and VOO had the smallest expense ratios in late 2020: 0.02 percent and 0.03 percent, respectively. That means that for every $1,000 you invest, you're paying just twenty or thirty cents! That's a very good deal. The IVW fund had an expense ratio of 0.18 percent. That means you pay $1.80 for every $1,000 you invest. On the other hand, this fund seeks to match the performance of the S&P 500 Growth index, which focuses on the "growth" stocks within the S&P 500, so its returns can be higher.

You can check out a fund's expense ratio on sites like Morningstar or Yahoo Finance, or just look up the fund itself online. Generally, you want to stick with funds that have below-average expense ratios. In 2019, the average expense ratio of an actively managed stock mutual fund was about 0.74 percent, while the average index fund had an expense ratio of just 0.07 percent, according to the Investment Company Institute.

Bottom line: If you don't want to spend a lot of time managing your portfolio, investing your money in an exchange-traded fund that tracks the S&P 500 Index is one of the simplest, most cost-effective ways to spread your money out over a diverse mix of stocks. If you'd invested $500 in a fund that tracks the performance of the S&P 500 Index back in December 2009, it would have been worth more than $1,700 by December 2019. That works out to a total return of more than 240 percent over a decade. Obviously, the share prices of companies in the S&P 500 can go down, too, as we saw in the spring of 2020. But over time, the S&P 500 has grown significantly.

You can also open an account with a brokerage firm that offers and recommends preselected portfolios based on your goals, timeline, and tolerance for risk. (Acorns, where I'm the chief education officer, is an example of that.)

Want a Boost? Use Dividends

Dividends are sums of money that some companies and funds regularly pay to their shareholders—no joke!—to incentivize you to start or continue to invest in them. Not all companies or funds offer dividends. Those that do tend to be more established, so they're in a position to offer a sliver of their revenues or reserves back to investors, usually on a quarterly basis. Generally, they figure that providing a dividend can make their stock or fund more desirable, driving up demand (and therefore the price) of shares. So ultimately, it benefits them, too.

How do dividends work? Say you own ten shares of a stock at $50, or $500 worth of the stock. If the stock goes up to $55 per share after a year, your investment value rises to $550 in total ($5 times the ten shares you own). If you earn an additional 2 percent dividend on top of that, you'd earn up to another $20, or $570 altogether (though the exact amount could vary depending on what the share price was when the quarterly dividends were paid out). That may not seem like much, but these dividends can really add up when you have more money invested. If you have enough invested by the time you stop working, you could earn a decent income from dividends and earnings alone. In the meantime, reinvesting dividends can help you grow the amount you'll have waiting for you later.

How much? My mom inherited 700 shares of Middlesex Water Company from Nana in 1992. They were worth around $17,000 at the time. By not touching them and reinvesting the regular dividends into additional shares of stock, her investment had grown to 1,400 shares by 2020, worth about $110,000. She hadn't put in another cent herself, and her investment grew *by more than sixfold* in less than three decades just by reinvesting the dividends. That's the kind of exponential growth you might experience with reinvested dividends plus compounding returns. (Middlesex Water also had some stock splits, which increased the number of her shares.)

Even small dividends can dramatically improve your investment performance over time. And if the market goes down, you typically still get dividends. So it's worth checking if a company stock or fund you're interested in offers them, or even Googling "dividend-paying companies" or "dividend-paying funds" and researching ones that look like they may be worth investing in as part of your portfolio—meaning they've got a good track record, solid financials, and low expense ratios if they're funds.

Your brokerage firm will typically offer you the option to reinvest those dividends. (Some automatically reinvest them for you.) And that's a smart thing to do. Because when you reinvest dividends, you are putting someone else's money to work for you. You're buying additional shares with the dividend rather than using your own money. That allows you to own more shares for less money, which earns you even more over time.

The Benefits of Bonds

Financial advisors generally recommend putting most of your money into stocks when you're young and then shifting more money into bonds as you grow older. That's because the stock market can have very good years—and it can also have some not-so-good years. And you don't want to be in a position where you need to access your money at a time when the market is down. On the other hand, stocks tend to have significantly better returns than bonds over time. So that's why you want a mix.

One general rule of thumb: Subtract your age from 110 and the result is the percentage of your retirement portfolio that should be in stocks. So if you're thirty-five, you'd put about 75 percent of your portfolio (another term for the money you've got invested) in stocks. The other 25 percent could go into bonds. If you're investing for a goal you want to reach sooner, like in less than ten years, you may want to put more of your invested money into bonds, just in case stocks start sliding as you near your goal. Bonds generally yield less, but they provide pretty reliable returns.

Buying shares of stock means you're buying a little piece of that company or fund, but buying a bond is a little different. Basically it's an IOU, or a loan that you give to the issuer. When you buy bonds, you do so with the expectation that you will get that money paid back to you—and with interest—in a certain amount of time. Yeah, it's kind of boring, at least compared with watching a stock you invested in shoot up 10 percent in a day. But it's also pretty predictable, which can be comforting when your stocks have a down day.

Companies issue corporate bonds. The U.S. government issues Treasuries. States and municipalities (which are cities or towns with a local government) issue municipal bonds, nicknamed "munis." They each differ in the level of risk and returns.

Generally, we consider Uncle Sam a pretty trustworthy lender. (The federal government can print its own money, after all.) So the risks of buying Treasuries are pretty small. But so are the returns. In mid-2020, the yield on the ten-year Treasury bond was just 0.75 percent. That means the bond would pay $7.50 each year for every $1,000 in face value you own until you get your $1,000 back a decade later—for a grand total of just $75.

Corporate bonds typically offer greater returns, though they also come with greater risk. You can keep that risk low, though, by investing in highly rated companies. Generally, if you invest in corporate bonds, you want to look for those that are "investment grade." That means they got relatively high ratings from the credit ratings agencies—a Baa3 or better by Moody's Investors Service, or a BBB or better by S&P Global Ratings and Fitch Ratings. In mid-2020, investment-grade bond funds, which allow you to buy into several companies' bonds by buying shares in the fund, were up year to date by about 3 to 5 percent. Some big ones include the Fidelity Investment Grade Bond Fund, which trades as FBNDX; Goldman Sachs Access Investment Grade Corporate Bond ETF, which trades as GIGB; and iShares Intermediate-Term Corporate Bond ETF, with the ticker IGIB.

Munis fall somewhere in the middle on the risk-and-return scale. A big benefit of municipal bonds, though, is that the interest on them is typically exempt from federal income tax and may also be exempt from state and local taxes if you reside in the state where the bond is issued. Moody's, S&P Global Ratings, and Fitch also rate munis, so look for those with high ratings if you choose to invest in these. As with corporate bonds, there are muni bond funds, too, that you can invest in. Some exchange-traded funds (which you can buy on the stock exchange) that invest in a broad mix of municipal bonds include IQ MacKay Municipal Insured ETF (MMIN), an actively managed fund that invests in investment-grade munis; the Vanguard Tax-Exempt Bond ETF (VTEB), which tracks the performance of a benchmark index of investment-grade munis; and iShares National Muni Bond ETF (MUB), a large ETF with holdings in more than 1,200 securities.

How you divvy up your money among bonds is up to you. But as with stocks, it's smart to spread your money among a mix of bonds (though be careful with any high-yield bonds that have low ratings). One efficient way to do that is to invest in bond funds that have purchased several bonds.

Of course, there are investment options beyond stocks and bonds, too. But if you do nothing but put at least 10 percent of your paychecks into a mix of stocks and bonds—prioritizing your retirement accounts, with their tax benefits, and investing largely in funds with high ratings, decent returns, and low fees—you can set yourself up pretty nicely to afford the future you want.

The More You Invest, the Less You Depend on Each Paycheck

A transformative moment for me came when I met a woman named Alia through a close friend. A self-taught real estate investor living in San Diego, Alia had used some of her initial earnings from investing to co-create a fund that invested in storage units. By pooling money with other investors, she'd been able to invest in over a dozen self-storage complexes. The properties generated a steady cash flow from the monthly rental fees. And, eventually, the team would refinance or sell the storage properties that had significantly increased their occupancy rates and overall value to help pay back the investors' principal contribution plus remaining interest earned.

As a real estate investor, Alia eventually made enough money to leave her full-time job as a director of nonprofit programs. She spent far fewer hours managing her investments and had more flexibility, which allowed her to spend more time with her family. That was particularly important because she was expecting twins when we talked and already had two kids. She could also work on the causes she was passionate about, like teaching financial literacy. Although I had no burning desire to invest in storage units at the time, meeting Alia was a game changer for me in the way I thought about investing and income.

For a long time, I'd looked at investing as something you do to make sure you've got enough money to retire. And maybe you put a little extra money into a brokerage account to save for goals that are at least a few years out, like saving to buy a home in my case. But I hadn't thought about creating enough income through investing to supplement—or possibly even one day replace—my paycheck. I hadn't really thought about earning passive income: money you make that requires little to no effort outside of your paycheck. Alia was making enough money from passive income that she didn't have to take on any work outside of managing those investments.

I looked at her lifestyle and the control she had over her daily schedule and I thought, *I want that! And before I'm old enough to retire.*

Of course, it takes time to get to the point where you might make enough passive income from investments to cover your bills. Alia spent years building up her knowledge and her savings, and it took time to find the right partners, properties, and investors to build a system that would generate steady income and profits. Not everyone has access to enough money or people with money with whom they can pool funds to invest in properties either. I didn't have any plans to invest in storage units. But talking with Alia did get me thinking about how investing my money smartly might provide me with enough income down the road that I could depend on some of it to cover expenses. Then I'd be less reliant on my paychecks and could have more freedom to choose the work I took on and the hours I worked. That is the real joy of investing.

Ultimately, we want to use some of each paycheck to invest so that we can become less and less dependent on each check over time. That is how you find true financial freedom. Sure, you can continue to collect a paycheck. But having enough income to cover the basics from investments means you only have to take the work you really want. It also gives you the freedom to cut back on work if you need to care for a loved one, or if you want to start building your own business, and know that you'll be okay financially.

The Perks of Passive Income

Interest from bonds—and even dividends from stocks and funds—are examples of passive income. They're regular payments that can be used as income above and beyond a paycheck. And they require very little effort to get. Once you've purchased shares in the dividend-yielding company or fund, or bought a bond, you can basically sit back and make that money in your sleep. When you're younger, reinvesting dividends is a smart growth strategy. But retirees often look at interest and dividends as one source of steady income to live off once they've stopped working, allowing them to leave their principal (the amount they've invested) alone, so they know their money won't run out.

There are plenty of other potential sources of passive income, too.

Renting Out Unused Space and Stuff

One friend in California who was preparing to get her startup off the ground decided to rent out her second bedroom and bathroom through Airbnb, and to rent her parking spot to a neighbor. She earned enough from the two to cover most of her mortgage, which meant she had more money from her paycheck to put toward bills and toward the business she was starting to build on the side. It required some effort on her part to set it up, and to prepare for new guests, but not a lot.

As her business grew, she also decided to convert a section of her living area into a small office nook with a couple of employees, rather than paying rent for office space. While she wasn't bringing in income, she was saving money. Basically, she told me, "I looked at every dead asset I had—anything I wasn't really using and that wasn't making me money—and I tried to figure out how to monetize it."

There are other creative ways to make money from your unused stuff or space beyond renting out your home to vacationers or your parking spot to neighbors. These days you can make money renting out everything from your car (through sites like Turo and Getaround) to camera equipment (through sites like ShareGrid and KitSplit) to space in your home or yard for commercial video or photo shoots or events (through sites like Peerspace, Splacer, or Thisopenspace). Of course you want to balance that with the time and effort required (and any other concerns, as arose during the pandemic). But it is possible to bring in regular income by thinking creatively about what you already have.

I didn't have a car or high-end camera equipment, and we were usually in our space, since my husband worked from home and I started working remotely in the spring of 2020 (and sharing our space in a pandemic didn't seem prudent). But I did start to think about how to set myself up so that I could earn more money outside my regular paycheck. One of those strategies is something you may already be doing.

Using Cash-Back Credit Cards

This is not a strategy to pursue unless you are able to pay off your bill *in full* every month. If you do, rewards credit cards can provide easy income, thanks to perks like cash-back bonuses.

Once I got wise to credit, as I mentioned earlier, I started spending strategically on my credit cards (while paying them off each month) so that I could earn as much rewards money as possible from each. It wasn't a huge amount, but it added up to hundreds of dollars in extra income outside my paycheck that required very little effort on my part. It was passive income. And that was the goal.

Investing in Rental Properties

Rental properties can be another way to get regular passive income (rent) while also building wealth (equity)—the goal being to get enough to cover more than the mortgage payment. Over time, the hope is that the property also increases in value, so you can sell it later for a profit.

So before you purchase any rental property, make sure that you can cover all the costs—which typically include insurance, taxes, and maintenance, on top of the mortgage payment—and still turn a profit on top of that. You want a property that will have both continued interest from renters and a strong potential to grow in value.

How Hannah Did It

Hannah and her husband, who's in the military, invested in a duplex property in 2019. The couple, who are in their late twenties, had lived frugally and saved up the money for a down payment on their own home in Washington state a few years earlier. They'd gotten a good deal since it needed some work, and they saved up nearly $20,000 to renovate it. Once they'd lived there for three years and fixed it up, they were able to sell it for enough of a profit that they began thinking about investing in a property for rental income. They used their earnings, plus some money they'd saved during that time, to buy a $140,000 duplex on the Virginia coast near Hannah's mom. "I had family there, and I knew the area, and the prices were much lower than where we lived," she told me.

They'd looked for a place that needed minor renovations, figuring they'd get a better deal. And they'd done their research, discovering that the asking price was lower than that of other waterfront properties in the area. They also checked rents on nearby properties to get a sense of how much rent they could charge.

Once they'd completed the renovations, which cost them about $10,000 (taken from the profit they'd made on their first home), they were able to increase the previous monthly rent by nearly $500 per unit. In the end, the rent they collected was significantly higher than the mortgage payment—which is exactly what you want. That means you're earning money each month, and then you can (ideally) make back at least what you paid for the property when you eventually sell it.

Hannah, a former assistant property manager of a large complex in Washington, said she and her husband came up with some general rules when looking for the right rental property: (1) It's in a city and neighborhood they know, where prices are likely to rise. (2) They're either close by or someone they trust is nearby who can check on the property. (3) It's one of the least expensive properties in a nice neighborhood. (4) The property can need some minor work *if* the price discount (versus other properties in the area) is more than enough to cover repairs and they won't be too time-consuming. (5) The rent they can get must be at least 1 percent of the asking price. (That's known as the 1 percent rule among real estate investors.)

Eventually, as my money grew, I expanded my investments, too. I divided my portfolio among stocks and bonds that would generate regular returns, but I also put money into investments that might take longer to pay off. I invested in a friend's startup after doing a good amount of due diligence, and I bought vested options in my own company's stock with the hope that we will be acquired or go public one day in the not-so-distant future and those shares will be worth a whole lot more than I paid for them. Those are longer-term plays—it could be years before I have a chance to cash in—and riskier than investing in an S&P 500 fund, but they also offer the chance for higher returns.

My point is, there are a lot of different ways to bring in income outside of your paycheck and any side gigs. You can often leverage stuff you already have to earn more income. And you can find the investments that feel right for you, based on the money you have, the time you have to invest, and your tolerance for risk. But you don't *have* to do all these things to build your wealth. I hit $1 million in net worth within a decade primarily by investing in stocks (mostly) and bonds, and through buying our home, which has nearly doubled in value.

Yes, increased earnings played a part in it, as that allowed me to invest more each year. And timing played a part in it, too. I was fortunate that I invested a lot of money in the stock market right at the onset of the Great Recession, when I got my severance package from the struggling magazine and advances on two books I coauthored. Of course, I didn't feel fortunate at first as I watched the value of my stock portfolio drop by nearly half, but I left my money alone (and even invested more), and the market has grown exponentially since then. A decade later, my initial investments had more than tripled in value. We also purchased our home in 2010, when the housing market was still recovering and housing values in New York City had dropped. But we bought it in a neighborhood that had great schools and a huge park and public transportation nearby, and also had building restrictions in place—meaning there was a limit to the amount and height of new housing that could be built—so we felt confident that our home was likely to increase in value. I never imagined it would nearly double in value in a decade, but I was pretty sure we'd be able to sell it for more than we paid for it when the time came.

You may not experience the same growth in the same amount of time that I did. But ultimately, if you do nothing else but invest in stocks and bonds and buy a home that you plan to stay in for a while before selling, you can generally build more than enough wealth to support your postwork life. (When that life starts, of course, depends on when and how much you invest.)

At its essence, thinking like a breadwinner comes down to looking at each paycheck as an opportunity to grow your wealth. That's what changed for me. I realized that the end goal isn't increasing my paycheck. The end goal is to become *less dependent* on each paycheck entirely by building enough wealth to sustain me one day. Once that clicked, I was incentivized to put as much of each check as I could to work for my future and my family's. And I would try to stretch that percentage a little bit more each year.

The more I invested and the more I spoke with other women who were building their wealth, the more I realized how smartly investing my money—rather than working harder just to earn a bigger paycheck—could help me get to a place where I could work *less*, have more time for my family, and be able to focus on the kind of work that really lit me up. One day I might actually be able to cover the basics with the income from my investments. Think of the freedom that would allow! I could take whatever work I wanted, whenever I wanted, rather than feeling so reliant on my paychecks. It wasn't even about retiring early (though that would be nice) but about having enough money invested that I could have more control over the work I did or didn't do. And have more time to enjoy this life I was creating!

Until I started thinking like a breadwinner, I'd never experienced the comfort and sense of possibility that came with having money that was invested and growing. It changed the way I looked at money—and the possibilities for my life—entirely. And it can do the same for you. Now let's look at how to maximize your earning potential so that you have even more to invest for your future.

PART III

The Breadwinner Mindset

*How to craft a career path that's professionally
and financially fulfilling.*

CHAPTER 8

Getting the Dough You Deserve

How to Negotiate for More

Never apologize for advocating for yourself.
—KATIA BEAUCHAMP, BIRCHBOX COFOUNDER AND CEO

ONE DAY, NOT long after I'd returned from maternity leave to my magazine job, a friend came rushing into my office. "You will not believe this," she said. A new colleague had just been hired in a similar position to ours but had negotiated a much higher salary. It turned out that this new hire, who had just a couple of years' more experience than I did, was making nearly *50 percent* more than I was. When I heard the number, I paled. I don't think I said anything but "wow." But when my friend left, I closed the door and leaned against it, tears welling up in my eyes.

Not only had I missed out on money in my paycheck, but, I realized, a smaller salary had meant smaller contributions to my 401(k) and less money to put toward savings. When I started to add it up, I realized I'd probably given up *tens of thousands of dollars* in potential earnings by not negotiating my salary at the magazine where I'd been working for nearly seven years.

Why hadn't I asked for more? I could say it's because I'd dreamed of working at that magazine since I'd first read it as a teenager, and the offer only came after months of interviews, phone calls, and waiting. So I was grateful to get the job at all. And I'd convinced myself that if I worked hard, I'd be rewarded for it. (Although, in reality, my salary wouldn't grow much despite two promotions and half-hearted negotiating attempts—increasing less than $10,000 over seven years.)

I could say, too, that I didn't ask for more money because I was naive enough to think that I'd been offered as much as they were willing to pay. And because the thought of asking for more money made me feel uncomfortable. But the deeper reason I didn't ask for more—why it didn't even occur to me to push for a higher salary or to consider how important that extra income could be over time—is because I hadn't been thinking like a breadwinner. I didn't think I'd be responsible for taking care of myself financially for the long term. I was in my late twenties and living with my boyfriend. I figured I'd get married soon enough and his earnings would exceed mine. At the time, I felt fortunate just to have landed a job I loved. I didn't consider how much my complacency would cost me.

The fact is, if you're a woman, you are probably being underpaid. Most of us are. As women, we make up nearly half the workforce but continue to earn significantly less than men who do the same jobs. That nearly 20 percent wage gap has barely budged in years. The Institute for Women's Policy Research found that we earn less than men in nearly *every, single occupation* where there's enough data to calculate a gender ratio. Even the fact that we're better educated than at any other time in history, and getting undergrad and advanced degrees in greater numbers than men are, hasn't made a difference. The Georgetown University Center on Education and the Workforce found that men outearn women at every level of educational attainment. And the gender wage gap is often *even wider* among those with higher levels of education, according to the American Association of University Women.

So, yes, that means the burden is on us to ask for more. We're probably not going to get paid equally otherwise. And it's not just about asking for it, but developing an airtight, quantifiable case for the value we bring to our employer. Because there's plenty of evidence to suggest that even when women do ask, we are not rewarded as men are. It's understandable that many of us are still reluctant to ask for more and feel like we need to do more to prove we deserve it. But sometimes we don't even think to *question* the dollar values of our salaries, or to negotiate a job offer, especially when we're early in our careers. We may not be regularly checking the market value for what we do and the skills we bring. I know I wasn't. I was underpaid for years—and didn't even realize by how much.

It wasn't until I took a severance package from that magazine and started freelancing with the goal of earning more money to save for a home that I started paying close attention to market rates. Pretty quickly I learned that I was able to make more on my own than I had in the full-time job I'd had for seven years. In fact, by hustling and taking on different types of projects, I made nearly 50 percent more through freelancing in twelve months than I had the year before at the magazine.

Leaving Money on the Table

The truth is, if your boss thinks you're happy to continue doing the great work you're doing at the same salary, he or she has no reason to pay you more. If an employer makes you an offer and you don't counter it, there's no reason to offer you more. You *have* to ask for it. Learn from my mistakes, and don't wait for someone else to notice and reward the value you bring. Asking for more doesn't just increase your paycheck; it has a ripple effect on your future earnings and your ability to build wealth.

Even a $5,000 salary difference can have an exponential impact over time. Start a job at $50,000 a year instead of $55,000 a year, and if your raises are percentage-based and your salary at any new job is partly based on your previous salary, the cumulative lost earnings can add up to between *$1 million* and *$1.5 million* over the course of a career, estimates economics professor Linda Babcock of Carnegie Mellon University. And that doesn't include all you've missed out on in company retirement contributions that are based on a percentage of your salary.

These aren't just hypothetical calculations. In 2019, researchers at Johns Hopkins University School of Medicine put an actual price tag on the gender pay gap's lasting effects at its own institution by applying wealth accumulation models to the medical school faculty's salary and gender data. They found that male staff in 2005 made 2.6 percent more than female faculty members, on average. Using that as a starting point, they estimated that a woman hired in 2005 who consistently worked under even a 2.6 percent pay differential lost out on more than half a million dollars in salary and retirement-plan investment returns over thirty years!

Think about that for a minute. When you negotiate a raise of a few thousand dollars, or a raise that's another percent or two higher, you are setting yourself up to earn tens or hundreds of thousands of dollars more over your career. You are ensuring that you have enough money to support your postwork life. You are able to build the kind of wealth that will allow you to become less dependent on those paychecks one day and to have more freedom to choose how you spend your time. Remember that when you're negotiating.

And here's another thing to consider—something I learned only when I moved into management and was the one doing the hiring. Open positions typically have a budgeted salary range. And you can bet that the first salary offer you get for any job is going to be on the range's low end. This is in part because there's an expectation that many job candidates will counter the first offer. What I noticed when I moved into a hiring manager role, though, is that male candidates were way more likely to negotiate a job offer than female candidates were. I can recall an instance when I made an offer to a talented female candidate that was about $10,000 below the top end of the range that had been budgeted. She accepted immediately, and I had to resist the urge to tell her to ask for more. As managers, we are generally incentivized to try to bring in the best talent for the least amount of money. So most offers start low, and it's up to the candidate to ask for more. But it is not uncommon to up an offer if it looks like we might lose a great candidate, especially for mid- to senior-level roles. I remember actually asking for an increase in the budgeted range itself, and getting it, for a standout candidate who'd said she was hoping for a higher offer. In another instance, when I'd hit the budget ceiling, I was able to get a candidate extra vacation time as an added incentive.

What happens when you don't negotiate your starting salary? Stephanie, a forty-six-year-old doctor in Maryland, remembers when she learned a few years ago that her colleague, who was in the same position at a health agency but had more years of experience, was making $25,000 *less* than she was. They were driving to see a talk about burnout on the job and the topic of cost of living came up. "I remember I said something about how I was glad that this job pays more than the last job I had to cover the difference. She said, 'Really? I am making less than I used to make,'" Stephanie recalled. Turns out Stephanie had negotiated while her friend had not. When they realized how big the difference was between their salaries, her friend went straight to their boss to discuss it.

Their boss admitted she'd been hired at a lower salary than she was qualified for, but told her he couldn't get her a raise now. Instead, he would try to get her promoted faster. "The trouble was, her promotion was based on a percentage of her salary," Stephanie told me. "She and two other colleagues got promoted at the same time, but the other two were earning more. So she was still making less, and now the gap was even wider. I realized then how a difference like that ends up following you throughout your career there."

Not surprisingly, Stephanie told me, her friend ended up leaving for another job.

Switching jobs can be a lucrative strategy for regular salary boosts, especially if it looks like you won't get the raise you want from your current employer. CPA Cameron Keng calculates that staying at a company for longer than two years can actually decrease your lifetime earnings by as much as 50 percent (assuming you don't nail a big raise or promotion in that period). That's because employees who stick with the same company can generally expect a 3 percent annual raise (based on industry benchmark studies) on average, while changing jobs could net you a 10 to 20 percent increase in your salary.

Of course, that's not the case for everyone. Still, it's smart to consider—especially if you didn't negotiate your starting salary as well as you wanted—that the only time you have real leverage (outside of when you're being recruited) is when your employer values you and is afraid you might leave. In Stephanie's colleague's case, there wasn't much wiggle room to close the gap in salary between her and her other colleagues since it was a government agency and every pay bump was a set percentage of their salary. But in corporate America, a competing job offer can serve as leverage to ask for a lot more from your employer if you have a good track record there. That's because an employer generally doesn't want to lose you. It costs a lot to replace a valued employee who leaves, especially a mid- to high-level one.

Not only is there a loss of institutional knowledge when an employee leaves, but it can hurt morale and make colleagues feel less engaged with their work. A vacant role can slow down projects and productivity, which can affect revenue. The company must also spend money on advertising, screening, and interviewing, and maybe even pay a recruiting firm, to fill the spot. (Top Echelon, which makes recruiting software, estimates average recruiting fees for using a headhunter are around $20,000.) Overall, the cost of replacing an employee can range from one half to two times the employee's annual salary, according to Gallup.

Plus, the average time it takes to fill any given position is forty-two days, according to the Society for Human Resource Management. Then the new hire still needs to be onboarded and receive additional training to get up to speed, which can result in additional lost time and productivity. A survey of 610 CEOs by Harvard Business School estimates that typical mid-level managers require 6.2 months to reach their break-even point for the time and money invested in bringing them on. Remember *that* the next time you're negotiating a raise.

Of course, if you want to use another job offer as leverage, it requires interviewing with another company. That can take time and effort and distract you from your current job. So I wouldn't recommend doing this unless you're at the point where you're seriously considering leaving.

If you've realized that you're underpaid compared with others at your level in your area or at your company, the first step is to talk to your manager about closing that gap, and make sure to bring evidence of why you deserve to be paid more. That can include market-rate data and specific examples of the ways you've brought value to the company, whether that's additional revenue or cost savings you're responsible for or evidence that demonstrates how your work has improved the business or exceeded expectations. If that doesn't work, though, it can make sense to look around for other opportunities. Interviewing with other potential employers also helps you work that muscle, and it's a good reminder of what your skills and experience are worth in the market. I can attest from experience that the biggest bumps in salary often come from moving from one company to another, or using another job offer to negotiate a better salary with your employer. (I've done both.) And each bump counts.

Think of your wages as the springboard for all your wealth-building efforts. Your earnings play a crucial role in building long-term wealth. The more you earn, the more you can invest. And if you accept a lower salary, there's that multiplier effect, as every raise is typically set as a percentage of your current income. The higher your starting salary, the greater the amount you contribute to your employer-sponsored retirement plan. The greater the base number, the larger your future raises and bonuses. (And if you're already used to living on your current income and you get a raise, you *know* you can afford to put those extra earnings straight into a savings or an investment account and barely miss it!) Consider that you're not just negotiating for yourself, after all; you're negotiating for your future and anyone else you may be supporting now or later.

And research shows that women negotiate harder and with better results when we negotiate on behalf of others, too.

Stephanie, the doctor in Maryland, found that to be true for herself. Until she became the main provider for her family, she says she struggled with asking for more. "I remember in my first job after my fellowship, I actually felt greedy negotiating for more. So I didn't," she told me. "My new boss said, 'We always start people at this much, and then it will go up.' But the fact was, I was better qualified than most of the people coming in. I'd had other job offers. I didn't use any of that. I just worried about seeming greedy."

Claire Wasserman, cofounder of Ladies Get Paid—a platform with resources, tools, and a seventy-thousand-strong community aimed at helping women negotiate for equal pay and power in the workplace—says that's a common concern for women. "Many women have emailed me, saying, 'I feel greedy asking for more.' Or, 'What if they give it to me and I don't live up to it?'" she told me. "There's so much baggage and guilt around money that is gender-based. But it does us a disservice."

Stephanie found that out after she was hired. When he gave her the job offer, the boss who'd hired her had cited median salaries at the hospital to demonstrate that the salary they were offering was fair, so she'd convinced herself that negotiating may not have made much difference. But after she took the offer, Stephanie, who'd moved across the country for the job, discovered that the numbers he used were nearly a decade out-of-date and that colleagues in comparable jobs were earning more than she was. "I didn't make that mistake again," she said.

Years later, when Stephanie was offered the job with the health agency, she did her homework before coming back with a counteroffer. She found out later that she was one of five people with similar backgrounds hired at the same time in comparable positions, but by negotiating, she came in at the second-highest salary. Her three colleagues who were hired with lower salaries did not try to negotiate. But Stephanie had done the research: looking up data on comparable salaries, comparing cost-of-living differences between the two cities (as she'd have to move), and talking candidly with a good friend who worked at another government agency about salary and benefits. She'd learned not only that the cost of living and the salary range for the position she was interviewing for were higher, but also that her medical background counted as creditable years of experience, which could qualify her for more vacation time.

Stephanie ended up asking for nearly 30 percent more than she was making, a number at the high end of the salary-range info she could find for others in similar roles. The final offer came in below that, but close. And she got four weeks of vacation. Had she not asked—as some of her colleagues with similar experience did not—she would have had to start with two weeks of paid vacation and work for years to double that. "Other people had just as much experience as I did, and just because they didn't ask for more, they got two weeks of vacation," she said. "It's important to ask."

While the actual act of asking for more still felt uncomfortable, she said, she felt compelled to do it because she was now the main breadwinner for her family of four. "It can still be very hard for a woman to say, '*I* am worth it.' It was easier to say, 'I am doing this for my family,'" she told me. "By this time, I'd also mentored female trainees on negotiating for higher salaries, so I told myself I was also negotiating for the sisterhood. I didn't want to be another female who was undervaluing herself."

Even then, she remembered, "I still had to call up a friend for support before writing the email for reassurance that I was doing the right thing, because it felt so weird to ask for more. I'm glad I did, though."

Stephanie's one regret, she said, is that she didn't follow the same strategy as the one colleague who was hired at a salary of about $10,000 more than hers. During the interview process, she'd been approached by a headhunter about another job and had turned down the opportunity to interview, since she had already started interviewing with the agency.

Later, she learned that her colleague had been approached about a similar job with the same pharmaceutical company and had opted to go through the interview process. In the end, her colleague was offered that job and turned it down. But she used the offer to negotiate an even higher salary with the agency.

Having the right information in hand to negotiate the best starting salary you can is key, but preparing for and pursuing promotions where you work is also critical. As several studies have found, women tend to hold off on applying for promotions—even when we're more qualified than male applicants. In an analysis of anonymized pay and performance for more than 1.5 million U.S. workers, workforce analytics company Visier found that even though women were more likely than men to be considered "top performers" at work, they were less likely to be promoted into management. Another report estimates that men are *40 percent* more likely than women to be promoted in management roles.

In entry-level jobs, women and men are represented nearly equally. But the gap widens as you advance up each rung of the proverbial career ladder. Only 38 percent of managers are women, according to Lean In and McKinsey and Company's 2020 *Women in the Workplace* report. Just 29 percent of VPs are women, and only one in five C-suite jobs is filled by a woman. In fact, more than one-third of companies had just one female C-level executive or none at all in 2019.

Yes, researchers have found that men are more likely to promote men—and men who are the same ethnicity—which helps perpetuate the lack of diversity at the top. But they have also found that women are less likely to *even ask* for a raise or promotion. One internal survey of female employees at Hewlett-Packard found that women applied for a promotion only when they met *100 percent* of the qualifications. Men applied when they met just 50 percent. So don't hold back!

"I like to tell women, Have the confidence of a mediocre white man," says Ladies Get Paid's Wasserman. "We spend too much energy questioning ourselves."

Getting paid what you deserve is also about finding the right environment and career path that will allow you to thrive and will give you the chance to reach your maximum earnings potential. If you find yourself in a job at a company that will not allow you to grow or to earn what you deserve, it's not worth staying. If you choose a lower-paying career path—or even a lower-paying company—you will miss out on earnings, no matter how effectively you negotiate your salary. And the data show that women still disproportionately choose lower-paying career fields, professional paths, and even employers.

The average man with a bachelor's degree earns *$34,000 more annually* than a similarly educated woman by the time they reach their early fifties, according to an analysis by the Georgetown University Center on Education and the Workforce. That's in part because women are often still paid less even when we're in similar roles. But other factors play into that gap as well.

Even now, as more of us are moving into senior-level jobs and high-paying fields, it's hard to look at the overall data on the college majors and the careers women choose, compared with those men pursue, and not wonder if those choices are based on the assumption that someone else will help take care of us one day. That wouldn't be surprising, given most women are still being raised to believe that they will get married one day and that their partner will be the main provider. In fact, researchers have found that the potential earnings capacities of different career choices are rarely communicated to girls at an early age, as they are to boys. I know it was never a conversation I had with either my parents or my high school or college advisors. I was just urged to pursue a career I was "passionate about."

But this focus on pursuing a passion over a paycheck means that we end up working just as hard as men—often harder—but trailing them in both wages and wealth. Over the course of their careers, a man with a bachelor's degree will see his annual earnings increase by 87 percent, while a woman with a bachelor's degree will see only a 51 percent increase in her annual earnings, on average, the Georgetown University center estimates. And that differential, as Linda Babcock and others have pointed out, equates to hundreds of thousands of dollars of lost earnings for women.

It is possible to feel passionate about what you do *and* earn a lot doing it. (We'll talk more about that in Chapter 10.) But that means considering both your interests and the kind of income you want to have, and choosing a path that allows you to enjoy both. And that is still not happening for most of us.

But wait, you might be wondering: Aren't women better educated than men these days? Wouldn't that increase our earnings potential? Yes, we do outnumber men in college and in graduate school now. But while higher levels of education may lead generally to higher incomes, more education for women does not necessarily lead to the same kind of wage gains as it does for men. In fact, if you take out student loans and you haven't considered the return on investment on that additional education, you can end up in worse shape financially.

The Georgetown University researchers found, for example, that one reason the gender wage gap actually *grows* with a graduate school degree is because women are concentrated in the lowest-paying master's degrees in fields like education and counseling. Even in high-paying fields, women are still far more likely to choose the lowest-paying tracks. About one-third of all students who major in environmental engineering are women, for example—more than in any other engineering field. Yet environmental engineering is one of the lowest-paying engineering fields.

The same dichotomy applies to business and law. Female lawyers make more than twice as much as paralegals and legal assistants, on average, but women make up a much larger share of paralegals and legal assistants—85 percent, compared with just 44 percent of lawyers, according to Georgetown's analysis. And while more women are becoming business majors, the majority still pursue the paths that tend to be the least lucrative, like human resources, where women account for 69 percent of workers. On the other hand, finance is one of the most lucrative business majors, yet only 33 percent of finance majors are women.

That helps explain why disproportionately more women end up in lower-paying support positions in senior management, like head of human resources or public relations—and not in those that are directly connected to revenue and tend to lead to the CEO role, like chief financial officer or chief operations officer. Just 11 percent of CFOs and 16 percent of chief information officers across industries are women. But women account for 32 percent of chief marketing officers and 55 percent of chief human resources officers, according to an analysis by Korn Ferry, an organizational consulting firm. That helps explain why women currently hold just thirty—or 6 percent—of the CEO spots at S&P 500 companies, according to Catalyst, a nonprofit research and strategy organization. And, yes, data show that even women who are in the same C-level or senior management position as men are paid less.

The cross-pollination among traditionally male or female fields isn't as widespread as you might think, either. Economic Policy Institute senior economist Elise Gould and other researchers found that despite women's progress, only about *6 percent* of women are employed in traditionally male occupations. And those male-dominated fields tend to pay higher wages across the board. Architecture, engineering, computer science, statistics, and mathematics are among the majors that lead to the best-paying careers, but less than a quarter of college graduates in these fields are women.

At the same time, only about 5 percent of men are in traditionally female occupations, which pay less. And that matters. Analysts at the National Bureau of Economic Research (NBER) estimate that the choice of occupation and industry could account for nearly half the overall gender wage gap. Even the *employers* women select tend to pay lower salaries. NBER researchers found that women are more concentrated in firms that paid lower wages to *both* men and women across all occupations; and conversely, that more men tend to be employed at firms that pay higher wages overall. WTF?

So, how to address this? It starts with our being more proactive in asking for what we want in the positions we hold; more strategic in the career paths, companies, and even work assignments we choose; and more assertive in going for promotions. We need to do our homework and look at whether the major or career path we choose will provide enough earnings for the life we want. And we cannot count on the fact that our income may be supplemented (or surpassed) by a partner's when we make our career choices.

The persistence of the gender wage gap comes down to three factors—all of which are based on the outdated assumption that our income isn't as important as a potential male partner's income is.

1. **We are paid and promoted less.** That's in part due to gender biases that often result in men being paid more and promoted more quickly. But it's also because we're less likely to advocate for ourselves and ask for more or apply for promotions.

2. **We disproportionately choose lower-paying fields and career paths.** This is true both for those with undergrad and graduate degrees. And even though more women are moving into lucrative fields, we are still more likely to pursue the lowest-paying occupations within that field.

3. **We are much more likely to cut back our hours or take time out of the workforce.** About 42 percent of working mothers have cut their work hours at some point to take care of a child or another family member, versus 28 percent of dads, according to the Pew Research Center. (Moms were far more likely than dads to quit their jobs to care for the kids during the pandemic.) And PayScale finds that women who leave can struggle to reenter the workforce and suffer up to a 7 percent pay penalty upon their return. That can have an exponential effect on our career earnings and the amount of money

we're able to invest along the way (as well as the time it's invested), which helps to explain the gender wealth gap.

If you want to even the playing field and reach your maximum earnings potential, you need to consider all those factors when you plan your career. Of course, not every woman wants to be a CEO, pursue a career in a high-paying field like finance or technology, or take the minimum maternity leave to avoid missing out on money or work opportunities. That's not what this is about. You don't need to compromise on what you're passionate about, or on the time you want to spend caring for a loved one—as long as you plan for it. What's important is that you're making informed choices.

What I heard from the majority of women I interviewed, and experienced myself, is that we often don't factor in money at all when we make choices about our college majors, master's programs, and professions— and even our career paths within those professions. And you can see that reflected in the data.

Thinking like a breadwinner means that if you're investing in a graduate education, you've done the math to make sure it's a smart investment. If you choose to take time away from work at some point, you've planned ahead by saving enough to cover you for several months and strategized about how you'll get back into the workforce and keep your skills up-to-date in the meantime. And if you choose a lower-paying career like teaching, that means you've done the math to be clear on what lifestyle that salary will allow you to have. And if there's a gap between the lifestyle you want and the one you can afford on a teacher's income, you've looked at other ways to boost your earnings—maybe tutoring on weekends and during the summer, teaching an after-school program, or creating online tutorials. My point is, if you want to pursue a profession that does not pay well, be sure you've accounted for that in your calculations. You don't need to give up doing something you love to earn enough for the lifestyle you want. But you will need to be creative, proactive, and strategic about finding other sources of income if your main salary isn't enough to cover it.

Prove Your Worth

Whatever professional path you choose, earning the most you can for the value you bring at all times is key to the breadwinning mindset. That comes down to four steps:

1. **Do your research.** If you're an employee, that starts with checking salary-and-benefits research sites like Salary.com, Glassdoor, Pay-Scale, Indeed, and even the Bureau of Labor Statistics, which has a database showing the annual average earnings for more than eight hundred occupations in four hundred industries by location. It also means looking into the skills and any additional training you may need to be the most effective in your role and to set yourself up for your next promotion.

2. **Track and quantify your successes.** Hold on to emails with praise from bosses, colleagues, or clients. Keep track of your performance and note when you beat metrics or exceed the stated expectations for your job (and make sure you and your boss are clear and in agreement on what those expectations are). As much as you can, quantify the value that you bring in whatever role you have and note awards or training certifications as well, both internally and on your LinkedIn profile. And if you run your own business, track your growth and success stories and ask for testimonials and referrals from good clients.

3. **Talk money with your peers.** One of the most effective ways to get information on how much to ask for—either at your company or from your clients—is to ask other people who are in similar roles or run similar businesses what they earn or charge.

4. **Ask for it.** It may feel uncomfortable. You may feel greedy or underqualified. But the simple fact is, if you don't ask for it, you probably won't get it. Having data to support your case—whether it's showing you're being paid below market rate or demonstrating quantified ways you've contributed to the company—helps you build an objectively strong case for a better starting salary, promotion, or raise. (It's hard to argue with numbers.)

And if you didn't take those steps, remember that you can still course-correct. Stacey, a Philadelphia-based consultant I interviewed, recalls being up for a position at a consulting firm and deciding not to ask for more than the posted salary range because she was sure her prospective boss would give her more.

Instead, he offered her *less*. After some deliberation, she chose to take the position anyway, but she'd learned her lesson. She tracked her performance all year long and compared it with a colleague's who was earning more. After a year, she approached her boss with the data. "I said I had better metrics than the guy he'd hired for more," she remembers. She went through the details of all the additional revenue she had brought to the firm in her role. "Then I asked for a raise."

I'm happy to report that she got it. "I learned you need to know your value," Stacey, who's now a senior partner at a consulting firm, told me. "And you need to be able to articulate that."

Erin Lowry, author of the three-part *Broke Millennial* series, told me she learned her lesson the hard way, too, early in her career. She was up for a content job at a financial technology startup. "They basically said, Name your price," she remembers. "I told them an amount that seemed a lot higher than the salary I'd been making in my job. But when they didn't even counter, I realized I'd probably left a significant amount of money on the table."

After she'd worked at the startup for a year, she remembers her boss swiveled around in his chair, congratulated her on her one-year anniversary, and proposed a small salary bump. She told him she'd prefer a formal review. When he agreed, she did her research, looking at what comparable companies were paying for the job she was doing. She learned that they paid much more for someone in her role, and she was also able to demonstrate that she now had multiple responsibilities that extended beyond the original job description. Erin had also kept what she calls her "success file"—screenshots of praise from clients and colleagues and examples of how she beat her metrics. She compiled her notes and ended up asking for, and getting, a $20,000 pay increase.

Sometimes earning more also requires reframing the way we think about what our work is worth, especially if we're making the leap from a job or an industry that traditionally pays less. Jessica Militare-Walsh, a freelance journalist and former magazine editor, remembers when she landed a contract for a content project recently with a corporate client and learned she'd be paid significantly more than she had ever made for her editorial work.

"The second I found out about it, I went right into limiting-financial-belief mode. Thoughts you naturally go to if you aren't used to making this kind of money. Like, I'm not worthy. What if I can't meet their expectations?" she remembers. "I had existed so long in the mindset of 'I'm never going to earn much,' I had to remind myself that I am creating content for a client and that client is going to make money from the work I do, and think about it like that. This was a breakthrough for me. The fact that I'm going to be making more than I ever did in my life and still have flexibility. It's given me a newfound confidence."

My friend Lisa remembers when she was in her late twenties and was up for a marketing job at a digital publishing company. The research director there advised her to ask for a six-figure salary since she was going to be hired initially on a contract. "Instead of asking for that, though, I just accepted what I was offered—which was thirty thousand dollars less," she told me. When I asked her why, she said she still wasn't entirely sure. "I think it just came down to the fact that I was uncomfortable asking and having that money conversation. I'd never been trained to have it. And the offer they'd made was still more than I had been making in my last job. I justified it by telling myself I also had severance-package money from my last job. But the reality is, the level where you start at a company makes such a difference. It took a while to catch up."

Not long after, her new boss accidentally left a list of the department's salaries out, and she saw that a younger colleague with less experience was making more than she was. She also noted that her boss was making more than triple her salary. "That was the first time I *really* knew that I was being underpaid," she told me. "I didn't make that mistake again."

The Motherhood Penalty

You've probably heard about the motherhood penalty: the notion that women's pay suffers after we have kids, while men's earnings tend to increase when they become dads. An analysis by Michelle Budig, a sociology professor at the University of Massachusetts, found that, on average, men's earnings increased by more than 6 percent when they had children (if they lived with them) while women's decreased by 4 percent for each child they had.

There's no evidence that working moms actually become less productive employees and men suddenly work harder when they become fathers—in fact, studies have indicated mothers are *more* productive than childless colleagues. But some employers assume that will happen. Research shows that we may be passed over for assignments or promotions simply because managers believe that we will prioritize our children over our work. In fact, this bias can begin to affect women's career opportunities before we even have children!

Nadja, a thirty-six-year-old mother of two, remembers when she was pregnant with her first child and working at a legal tech firm in New

York. "People assume you're able to do less when you're pregnant. They think you're not interested in traveling for work anymore, and they're suddenly worried about you 'working too much,'" Nadja told me. And that perception carried over into her return from maternity leave.

"When I came back, my job had changed, and I didn't have as many responsibilities," she remembers. "I know other mothers who said the same thing—the job they came back to wasn't the same job they'd left. Now you've got a reduced role, and that can hold you back from advancement."

Nadja ended up leaving the firm soon after and taking a role with a major technology company. When she got pregnant again, she took steps this time to correct any assumptions her managers might have, making it clear that having another child wouldn't impede her ambitions or performance at work. "After my first experience I decided, okay, I am going to be super explicit about the fact that I can still travel, I will go to meetings and put my hand up, and I'll have serious conversations with my male managers about how I am still the same person and will continue to work hard," she told me. And it worked.

Nadja got months of maternity leave but stayed connected. And when she returned to work, she was able to expand her role and responsibilities significantly. "I thought, *Don't let being a mom impede the way people think of you and your work life*," she said. "That means there is a lot of work to do. But I am very ambitious, and I want to climb here."

Statistically speaking, if you follow convention, you're likely to be underpaid and undervalued, overlooked and overworked. If you don't want to go that route, you've got to approach your career like a breadwinner, tracking your successes and being vigilant about the assignments you take and the salary you make from the get-go—or course-correct as soon as you can. You also want to think about crafting a career path that fits the kind of life you want and can help you hit those goals you set in the earlier chapters.

Negotiating for what you deserve extends outside the workplace, too.

The breadwinner mindset is about looking for ways to negotiate better deals when you spend your money and asking for what you want in every situation. At its core, being a good negotiator is about making sure you're being the best advocate for yourself personally and professionally. So it's worth checking in periodically to ask: Am I undervaluing my skills and talents? Am I compromising on the life I want? Am I advocating as effectively as I can for myself?

Plan strategically and ask for what you want, and you can save yourself a lot of money (and a lot of stress!), boost your lifetime salary by potentially hundreds of thousands of dollars, and ensure that being a breadwinner doesn't have to involve a life of corporate ladder-climbing with no end in sight. The endgame, really, is about building a life you love and can support financially, and having the time to enjoy it.

CHAPTER 9

Do Less, Achieve More

How to Focus on Work That Will Actually Help Your Career

We think, mistakenly, that success is the result of the amount of time we put in at work, instead of the quality of the time we put in.
—Arianna Huffington, cofounder of
the *Huffington Post* and Thrive Global

Somewhere around middle school, I thought I'd figured out the formula for success—or at least for straight As. My approach was straightforward: figure out what my teachers expected of me and then work like mad to exceed their expectations. It was essentially the same strategy I would use when I started working, just swapping in bosses for teachers and extra work for extra-credit assignments. And it paid off, too—at least for a while.

But as I progressed, the expectations became far greater—as did my responsibilities. Constantly trying to manage both became increasingly exhausting, especially as I'd become accustomed to saying yes to any requests from a boss, even if they fell outside the scope of my responsibilities, and trying to handle the lion's share of work myself to prove my value.

For a while I'd considered my capacity for work, and my ability to execute an ever-growing list of responsibilities, as a source of pride. But I eventually got to the point where I simply couldn't take it all on anymore. I was completely overwhelmed. And this happened more than once. In fact, I developed a habit of overworking and overwhelming myself. I'd put in long hours for a particular project and then continue to work those hours even after it was completed because something else would inevitably come up. I'd come home late, irritable, and resentful. I was exhausted, but I had trouble sleeping. Other responsibilities in my life would slip. And then I would find I was off my game at work, too. As a serial overworker, I had trouble recognizing that continually piling more work on my plate wasn't a sustainable strategy.

Maybe I'd been going about this the wrong way. Working harder, I finally realized, only got you so far. At some point, you have to start working smarter. The only problem was that I wasn't sure how to do that. Working harder had become my default setting, and I wasn't entirely sure why.

After interviewing other women, it became clearer. I realized I wasn't alone in feeling that I had to work hard to succeed in every area of my life. From the research and anecdotes I've collected, it seems many of us feel like we have to consistently put in extra effort to prove our value—especially at work.

Sociologists at the University of Virginia and Washington State University analyzed five surveys given in different years to different groups of men and women about work and found that women consistently reported having to work harder than men. And there's good reason for that. "A lot of experimental research has shown that people rate the same performance as better when told it was done by a man. It follows that women have to do *better* than a man in order to get the same evaluation," wrote Elizabeth Gorman, one of the study authors. "This is what women are up against. They have to prove themselves." Constantly.

And this isn't just at the office. Certainly at home, the expectations are higher for women than they are for men. If a man can manage to get his clothes into the hamper (much less actually do a load of laundry!), put his dirty dishes in the dishwasher, and take out the trash, that's often enough. The standards aren't high. After all, we're often dealing with the sons of men who were accustomed to having their dishes cleared and their clothes laundered for them by the women in their lives. Men get praise for grilling on holidays, pitching in with the housework, and picking up occasional grocery items on the way home. Meanwhile, women are expected to have a beautiful home, a full fridge, and dinner on the table every night, even if we don't have time to cook it ourselves.

It's not just the appearance of our homes that must be perfect but our own appearance. Middle-aged men tend to lose their hair and gain a gut—a phenomenon so common it's now cliché—and feel no societal pressure to address either. Women, meanwhile, are pressured to maintain their twentysomething figures (even faces!) well into middle age or fear losing the attention of their spouse—or even hurting their job prospects. In trying to explain the "robust evidence" they found of disproportionate age discrimination against older women in hiring, three male economists from the University of California at Irvine and Tulane University theorized that "older women may in fact experience more discrimination than older men because physical appearance matters more for women and because age detracts more from physical appearance for women than for men." (Ironically, with that last subjective assessment, the male researchers reinforced the very biases they'd cited.)

Women of all ages have been socially conditioned to present ourselves at our best and our homes as an extension of who we are. That doesn't mean we all conform to that. But there is real societal pressure to keep our nails manicured and our lips glossy, to have a flattering, on-trend wardrobe and an HGTV-worthy home. A recent *New York Times* article, headlined "Why Women, but Not Men, Are Judged for a Messy House," cited three separate studies confirming that housework is still considered women's work. And in the workplace, several studies have found that women who are slim and wear makeup are perceived to be more competent than their makeup-free and overweight counterparts. (Although, it's a tricky balance: If you happen to come across as sexy, the effect is reversed, and you risk being perceived as less competent.)

Studies have also found that not only are women judged on their appearance more than men, but that the standards of female beauty are "considerably higher and more inflexible."

All this means that we feel a lot more pressure and exert a lot more effort trying to prove ourselves—and to meet societal expectations that are disproportionately higher for women than for men—in nearly every area of our lives. It's no wonder so many of us end up exhausted. Throw kids into the mix, and the perception that if our titles and salaries grow, so will our workload, and it's easy to understand why so many women intentionally slow down their careers and never move past middle management. While entry-level positions are divided almost equally between genders, the percentage of women falls *by nearly half* at the senior VP level, according to Lean In and McKinsey's 2020 *Women in the Workplace* report, which examined data from 329 organizations. As I mentioned earlier, women represent nearly half the workforce but hold just 38 percent of managerial positions, and the number drops at every subsequent level of seniority.

This multitude of pressures women feel won't subside overnight. But recognizing them for what they are—social constructs devised by men that simply heaped additional responsibilities and expectations on women, rather than recalibrating them, when we started moving into the workforce and into main-earner roles—can help put them in perspective. Ultimately, creating a more equitable workplace and division of labor will require a major shift in how we think about what constitutes men's and women's work and worth.

But meanwhile, it can serve us to better understand where the beliefs and assumptions that drive these pressures come from and whom they benefit, and to look at how we can transform or overcome them so they don't hold us back from the lives and success that we want. Once you start to examine them more closely, it's easy to understand why girls fare so much better than boys in school—yet the *opposite* is true once we graduate and embark on our careers. And why so many women burn out midway through their careers. Here are some of the lessons I've learned from my own experience and from the research I've done.

Lesson #1: Put Your Efforts into Promotable Work

Women not only feel more pressure to prove ourselves, but we're also brought up to be agreeable, accommodating, and helpful—to say yes when asked to assist on projects rather than to push back, guard our time, and focus on the work that makes the most sense for us. This may benefit us early on, as we come across as hungry and hardworking, but it can backfire on us as we move up in our careers. In a 2018 study, Carnegie Mellon's Linda Babcock and fellow researchers Maria P. Recalde and Lise Vesterlund concluded that women actually spend more time than men on "non-promotable" tasks and *less* time on promotable tasks at work. "Across field and laboratory studies, we found that women volunteer for these non-promotable tasks more than men; that women are more frequently asked to take such tasks on; and that when asked, they are more likely to say yes," they wrote. And this was true at all levels.

What's particularly interesting to me is that Babcock says she and her scientific colleagues became interested in investigating this phenomenon in the first place because they'd found it playing out in their *own* work lives. "We actually formed a club amongst ourselves to talk about these issues in our personal lives and how we can make better choices for ourselves," Babcock told the American Economic Association.

The name of the club? I Just Can't Say No. Oh, how I can relate to that! A senior colleague of mine once told me that I would be much more effective if I said "sorry" less and "no" more. At the time, I was in my first managerial role and was a little taken aback. But I realized later that she was right on both accounts. Over-apologizing eroded my authority. And saying yes all the time left me overextended and prevented me from being able to focus on the most critical work. The challenge, though, is that we often feel obliged to say yes—especially if it's our boss doing the asking.

Babcock says that as she and the other members of her club talked about this issue, they looked not only at how it affected their own lives but also at how it might be affecting the lives of those they supervised. What they realized is that they might even be *perpetuating* the problem: "When we wanted someone to do something that was a non-promotable task, we were much more likely to ask women because we knew that they would say yes," she told the American Economic Association.

She and her colleagues weren't alone in their assumptions—and the data back them up. Workplace software company Hive analyzed anonymized data for more than three thousand women and men and found that not only do women complete more work on average, but they are assigned 55 percent of all work, compared with 45 percent assigned to men. "So if women are assigned more tasks and are getting more done overall, why isn't this translating into promotions and more equal career success?" they asked. "One reason could be the type of work women are asked to do."

Yep. This tendency to take on low-profile, non-promotable work ourselves does us no good. We can end up working late or dedicating off-hours to complete these tasks, sacrificing time for ourselves or with our loved ones. Or just not being as effective—or promotable—as we could be in our job.

Lesson #2: Don't Get Swept Up Doing Office Housework

There's a history here. For a long time, most working women *were* in administrative and other roles designed largely to support the work that men were doing. Men were seen as the providers, and women were seen as the supporters, both at home and at the office. While that's changing as more women move into management and the senior roles once held by men, we are still often designated as the default support staff in the corporate world—regardless of our actual titles—charged with buying birthday cards, organizing meetings, and planning events. Joan C. Williams, a law professor and director of the Center for WorkLife Law at the University of California Hastings College of the Law, calls it "office housework." And in her research, she notes that even senior-level women are not exempt from being asked to do it.

I remember clearly when some of my colleagues began referring to me as the "Office Mom" at my New York office—I assume because I was the oldest and most senior woman. While I'm sure they meant the term endearingly, when I heard it, all I could think was that I already had enough responsibilities as an actual mom to two boys and that it undermined my authority as a member of the executive team. (Can you imagine calling the most senior man the "Office Dad"?)

I had a similar feeling of unease when my boss asked me to "run the office" as the team in New York grew. It would have been one thing if most of the team reported to me. But at that point, my team was actually the smallest of four that worked out of our office. The vast majority of people based in the office worked in different departments and reported to different people. I worried that I risked becoming the de facto office manager as well as the "Office Mom," especially after my requests to hire an office manager or support staffer, even part-time, were turned down.

Sure enough, until I wised up and started delegating many of the tasks, I found myself almost solely responsible for dealing with *any* office issues. Those ranged from helping to arrange twice-weekly catered lunches for the full team to getting a broken refrigerator in the pantry fixed, ordering office supplies, and spearheading our volunteer and team-building efforts.

While I didn't mind taking on some of these tasks initially, I quickly realized that if I wasn't careful, I'd end up taking on a new job on top of my regular responsibilities—and one I didn't want!—and taking time and attention away from the work I'd been hired to do. I ended up pulling in two colleagues in management to co-lead the efforts and help delegate office responsibilities. But I remember worrying initially about how to handle the ask, as the additional tasks had little to do with the role I'd been hired for and weren't related to the work for which I was accountable in my performance reviews.

These conflicted feelings aren't unusual. Babcock and other researchers found that "women are more likely to feel pressure to do non-promotable tasks and are more worried than men about the negative repercussions of declining such requests."

And a study led by Madeline Heilman, a New York University psychologist, found that saying no *can* sometimes have negative outcomes for women. In one study, a woman who declined to stay at work late and help a coworker was rated 12 percent lower by colleagues than a male peer who did the same. If a man steps up, researchers found, he is more often praised than a woman is. If a woman does the extra work, it more often goes unnoticed. Yet if she turns down a request, she may be penalized.

This pattern won't change until we start to shine a light on the inequities of these outdated expectations, and leaders work to divide such work equitably among genders or hire someone to do such tasks, rather than assume that a woman will simply take them on. But in the meantime, it helps to be aware of these tendencies so that you don't get caught up in them.

In the end, I told my boss that it made sense for me to share these responsibilities with the leads of the two largest teams in the office, a man and a woman, and he agreed. We met regularly and partnered to come up with solutions to office issues that arose, plan informal events like a weekly breakfast, and eventually to find a new office space. We also created a group with members from all four teams to plan upcoming morale-building events. And after reaching out, I was able to tap the office manager at our headquarters to help with office support and meal planning. This still required some time and effort, but a lot less than if I'd just taken it all on myself, so I was able to focus more on my job responsibilities again.

In addition to specific requests, there are all the small daily tasks that it's assumed women will instinctively do. Heilman found that women's assistance often happens in small, unseen ways, like cleaning up after an office party or setting up a conference room for a meeting; whereas when men help out, it tends to be in more visible and high-profile ways. This may be deliberate. Men are more likely than women to seek recognition for the extra work they do—ensuring their name is listed on a presentation they helped create even if they don't present it, for example. And they're more likely to select out-of-scope assignments that can provide them with more visibility and connections, even if they aren't technically promotable. Because they're thinking strategically. We should be, too.

"My observations are that women get points detracted from their gravitas the more office housework they do. Doing office housework, no matter how seemingly important it could be, doesn't get you to be viewed as a leader," the executive coach Kameka Dempsey, who consults with senior-level management teams, told me. "It's a dance for women, because you don't want to come across as arrogant, but you need to exert some level of authority among peers. That type of behavior, where you think, 'Oh, I can just take care of it myself,' can have negative consequences you don't even realize."

Of course, when you're starting out in your career, you will be doing some tasks that seem more like chores—that comes with the territory. And no matter your role, not every task you volunteer for has to benefit you. Sometimes you're just pitching in to help. And that's okay. But it is worth considering the time and effort required, along with the risks and benefits of saying yes, before you volunteer for or agree to something that's not inherently part of your job.

Obviously, telling a boss "that's not in my job description" is probably not the right response. But you can explain how taking on outside tasks could negatively affect projects that are a core part of your responsibilities (by delaying delivery dates, for example) or prevent you from being able to do your job effectively. Or you can demure by pointing out that you are tied up with _____ (fill in the blank with a high-priority project). Or ask to share the responsibility with a male colleague. The point is to be mindful of the work you accept and to ensure that you're not setting yourself up to succeed at non-promotable office housework at the expense of the work you were specifically hired to do.

Lesson #3: Value Your Time as Much as a Man's (Maybe More!)

If I asked if your time is as valuable as a man's, I'm sure that you'd say yes. (I hope so anyway!) But our actions don't always reflect that. The inherently sexist message that women's time is less valuable than men's is insidious—it's found its way deep into our subconscious. And it's systemic. It starts in the home and extends into the workplace and just about everywhere else. Men may have perpetuated this belief, but women have been conditioned to adhere to it. We may not be wholly conscious of it, but the data show that we often behave as if our time is less valuable than that of our male peers at work and partners at home—willingly picking up the necessary but often unrecognized grunt work at home and at the office, while protecting men's time from it. So it's important to be mindful of that in every aspect of your life to ensure that your values and goals, not your cultural conditioning, are guiding your choices.

Jennifer Crews, an executive consultant and mom of two who lives near New York City, remembers working with a colleague who was a few years older than she was. Over the years they worked together, she noticed that in every meeting he would turn to whatever woman was seated closest to him and ask her to take and distribute the notes—even if there were men in the room. And the women would acquiesce. It came to a head when Jennifer was running a meeting on a separate project she was spearheading and invited him to it. "He asked me if I would take notes," she remembers, laughing. "I said, 'No, but you are welcome to.'"

He was taken aback, she says—it was likely the first time he'd gotten such a response. But he agreed.

In her essay in the *Washington Post*, Joan Williams, who coauthored the book *What Works for Women at Work*, notes that even successful women in high-status positions—like lawyers, academics, and even executives—told her that they've been expected to bring cupcakes for a colleague's birthday, for example, or order sandwiches for office lunches or volunteer for committees. The implication being, of course, that their male colleagues' time is too valuable to waste on tasks like these. Her suggestion for when someone asks you to take on work that's time-consuming, undervalued, and non-promotable is to practice what she calls the art of gender judo: Say no, but in a way that gently reminds them that there are junior (and male) workers perfectly capable of doing it as well. For example: "I'd love to serve on the paper clips committee. But that's the perfect stretch assignment for David, our new junior hire, down the hall."

Or as one California lawyer recounted to Williams about being asked to make coffee, smile sweetly and say, "I'm not sure you want someone with my hourly rate making coffee."

Of course, we can't all get away with a snarky response like that, and most of us are not making an attorney's hourly rate. But we can practice our own form of gender judo. I wasn't much of a note taker or coffee maker myself, but I realized I had been guilty of volunteering or agreeing to do office tasks throughout my career that took time away from more important work and maybe undermined my authority as well. It was work that needed to be done, sure, but it didn't need to be done by me. And that is a key distinction. The challenge of doing work that other people can do—especially more junior people—is that it takes you away from the work that *only you* can do. That's not a good use of your time. (Can you imagine if Jennifer had actually tried to run the meeting and also take notes?)

Time is like money. How we spend it determines how we'll spend the rest of our lives. Our minutes, like our dollars, can be used to bring us closer to the future we want—by investing them in work that's meaningful, courses that improve our skills, and relationships that enrich our lives—or they can be sucked up by others' demands and meaningless tasks. I'm not saying that binge-watching *The Great British Baking Show* or scrolling through Instagram is a waste of time, especially if that's how you relax; we need to give our brains a break at times. I'm talking about being mindful of where our time, as well as our money, is going so that we don't look back later wondering where it all went and wishing we'd made better choices.

Lesson #4: Take Control of Your Calendar

When we talk about the work that's most important, it's not limited to what you're doing at the office. Many of us have activities that light us up outside our jobs. It could be working on a passion project that we hope could turn into a full-blown business one day. It could be journaling with the idea that those entries could eventually become a series of articles or a book—or just journaling as a creative outlet. It may be reassessing our career path and exploring potential new directions. Or taking time to write out and research a business idea we have.

But if our calendars are packed with meetings, tasks, and household to-do lists, the risk is that this work ends up being deprioritized. We're not getting paid for doing it (yet anyway). There's no one asking us to do it. There's no immediate sense of urgency. And there may not be any immediate recognition—or results. But that doesn't mean this kind of work isn't important. In fact, it may be the most impactful work of all in the long run.

Kate Brodock, CEO of Women 2.0, a global platform for female and underrepresented founders and women in tech, calls it "white space." It's space we get to fill in however we want. This is the time we allow ourselves to dream of what could be, and to create. Or just to unwind and clear our minds, creating the space for new ideas. It's work that only we can do, or solo self-care activities we need to do. And it's not something we typically schedule on a calendar. But we should. Otherwise it's easy to get distracted by the endless stream of emails and tasks that can feel urgent but ultimately aren't that significant.

"It's about creating the space for the important but not urgent priorities," she said. "You have to be able to recharge and to carve out time to think more long-term. Those periods of time are so important to productivity at the end of the day."

Brodock now schedules blocks of white space every week on her calendar. But she says guarding this unscripted time required a shift in mindset. "I have understood that a lot of what was driving my tendency to work so many hours is that I felt guilty not being 'productive' all the time," she told me. "I realized I had to be okay with the fact that I didn't need to work so much. It actually wasn't getting me further. I was just doing more stuff."

A colleague of mine with three young kids who works remotely and often works in the evening, as she is an hour ahead of our headquarters, began blocking out an hour from the late afternoon to early evening so that she could be assured that she'd have time to sit down for dinner with her family before she had to jump on work calls again. There were times when meetings conflicted, but for the most part, it allowed her to protect that time. Several of my male colleagues block out an hour for lunch daily and several hours a week for "focus time." Since you can set calendar settings to "private," other colleagues don't have to know that you've blocked time for a meal with your family or white space.

Essentially, though, you're giving it equal weight with the work meetings that get scheduled. And that's important.

The breadwinner mindset is about being less reactive to others' demands for our time and more protective of the time we need to do our best work and to be our best selves. Take control of your calendar and you take control of your life. Your time is a finite and precious commodity. Before you give any away, make sure that you've already reserved enough of it for the things that are most important to you.

Lesson #5: Don't Mistake Being Busy for Being Productive

It's easy to confuse busyness with productivity. And to feel guilty when we claim unscripted time for ourselves, especially when there are other things that need to get done. (And aren't there always other things that need to get done?) But by being mindful of our time, and allowing ourselves the space to recharge or to brainstorm or to strategize about our future or our business, we're using time in a way that actually allows us to be more productive in the long run.

Part of the reason I realized I often felt overwhelmed was that I was not only taking on additional work indiscriminately, but I was trying to excel at everything I was doing in my life at once—or at least to not let anything slip—rather than prioritizing what was most important and delegating or pushing off the rest.

Even as I was writing the proposal for this book—work that I believed was important and that, ultimately, only I could do—I'd notice the pile of dirty clothes in the hamper or the dishes in the sink or a work email that cried out for a response (even on the weekend). Or I'd realize I still hadn't gotten through a Friday to-do list. And I would postpone writing and prioritize those tasks instead. I'd get back to my book later, I told myself. The reality, though, was that many of those tasks could be handled by other people or pushed off. The result of continually prioritizing them was that it took me months to finish the proposal, and I began to get resentful in the meantime that this never-ending to-do list was keeping me from finishing something I really cared about.

It's tempting to blame others for taking our time. But often the reality is that *we* aren't prioritizing it. Maybe it felt easier in the short run for me to just get through the finite tasks on my list so that I could feel an immediate sense of accomplishment. Maybe it was a sense of guilt at devoting hours to a project that might never pay off monetarily. Maybe it was the pull of a very real list of tasks that had to get done by someone, and vestiges of the Supermom syndrome that constantly had me thinking I *should* do them. But the fact was that I was the only one who could prioritize the work that I believed in—and that I was the only one who could do it. And if I didn't act as if it was important, why would anyone else?

The same holds true for you. And what I realized was when I did start treating the work as important, other people did, too. They helped protect the time for me to focus on it.

I began to carve out specific hours to write, and my family honored them. The feelings of guilt didn't completely go away, but the relief I felt when I looked at the hours I'd cleared was palpable. I finally started making real progress. I know that not everyone has flexibility like this, and sometimes loved ones aren't as supportive as you'd like. But what I'm really getting at is the importance of prioritizing your time and delegating work that's less important so that you can focus your energy and time on the work and the people you love.

Lesson #6: Do Less to Do More

Delegating, as several studies have confirmed, is something that does not come naturally for most women. A series of five studies from

Columbia Business School found that women "have more negative associations with delegating and feel greater guilt about delegating than men." The result, researchers found, is that they were actually *less* productive while simultaneously keeping subordinates from being able to develop their skills. Oof.

"There is a paradox in delegating. You might at first think that doing more tasks—more and more paper, more and more computer entry, more responsibilities—is always more productive," writes economics advisor and author Jeffrey A. Tucker for the American Institute for Economic Research. "What you discover over time is different. Once you master a task, the best use of your time might be to train an understudy so that you can move on and take on another task or innovate in another direction . . . *This* is how you grow to become ever more valuable." It's a difficult mind shift, especially for women, he acknowledges. But it's crucial. "Instead of looking for more things to pile on your plate, you should try to do the opposite. Get things off your plate so that you can take on new challenges and innovate."

Looking back, I could definitely see a tendency to take on (and hold on to) tasks outside the scope of my job responsibilities and a reluctance to hand off tasks to the people who reported to me. Eventually though, I realized that I had to get more comfortable delegating rather than giving in to my innate urge to take on the work myself to prove my value. I also had to shift my own mindset to understand that doing more tasks didn't equate with being more productive.

The more you're able to delegate tasks, the more you're able to focus on the high-level work that could have the greatest effect. Technically, you may be "doing" less, but you'll be having a greater impact.

Jennifer Crews says she learned early on the dangers of trying to do it all. "I noticed so many women in roles that were very tactical where they focused on productivity, while men occupied most of the leadership roles that were more strategic and got to set the direction. I wanted to be in a strategic role," she told me. "I learned not to conflate urgency with importance and to have laser focus on those things that have a real impact on the business."

Protecting your time and energy often starts with setting boundaries and expectations at work, both during and after regular office hours. Otherwise, precious off-hours can easily be eaten up responding to work emails or picking up unfinished tasks if we let it happen. (I've certainly been guilty of both.) But here's the thing: No research indicates that those extra hours give us any advantage. In fact, working longer hours may actually be counterproductive.

Lesson #7: Working Harder Than You Have to Is a Waste of Time

For months I was mystified by how chill my good friend's husband, Clinton, was about his job. He came home consistently at the same time. When he wasn't at work, he wasn't talking or even thinking about it—or didn't seem to be, anyway. In fact, he was building a completely separate business as a speaker on the side. And he often spent his downtime writing, practicing, and giving talks, or taking workshops to hone those skills. Yet he was in a senior management role at work and the primary breadwinner in their marriage. How was he able to disconnect and still be effective in his job? I felt like I was thinking about work almost all the time, and often doing some on weekends.

When I asked him about it, he told me that as long as he was hitting his targets (and he was) and his boss and his team were happy, he didn't *need* to put in any extra effort. Putting in additional effort—especially when he had outside interests that he wanted to have enough headspace and energy to pursue—would have been a waste of his time.

It seems so logical, but this was a mind-blowing revelation to me. The more I thought about it, the more I realized this is the major mindset shift many of us need. In fact, working harder and longer hours can often be *counterproductive*. Devoting valuable time and energy to a job during our off-hours keeps us from being fully present with family and friends. It can undermine the kinds of outside pursuits that can pay off more in the long run. It's not serving us. And frankly, it may not be serving our employers either.

Despite our country's glorification of overwork—surveys have found that one-third of Americans work on the weekend and a quarter do work between 10:00 p.m. and 6:00 a.m. during the week—the data show that working more doesn't necessarily produce better results. In fact, it doesn't take long to reach a point of diminishing returns. Stanford researchers estimate that after about forty-eight hours a week, or an average of nine and a half hours a day, a worker's output drops sharply. And, if Clinton's example weren't compelling enough, a group of economics researchers released a study in April 2019 that found working longer hours than someone else in the same job doesn't even earn you more money! It can actually lead to a 1 percent *decrease* in wages.

Yet women in particular have been conditioned to draw a correlation between the amount of time and effort we exert and the results we produce. It's not just about proving our value. At school, we learned that if we worked harder, we'd be rewarded. Putting in extra time—doing extra-credit work—resulted in better grades and commendations. But the same doesn't hold true in the workplace.

Lisa Damour, a psychologist who wrote a book about stress and anxiety in teenage girls, noticed in her own practice that boys often seemed to skate by at school, putting in extra effort only if their grades started to slip. Meanwhile, girls "relentlessly grind, determined to leave no room for error"—convinced they must put in the maximum effort at all times. The result, she found, is that the boys gained a good sense of their abilities and calibrated their efforts accordingly, while girls defaulted to putting in extra effort on *all* their work, regardless of their level of competency.

"What if those same habits that propel girls to the top of their class— their hyper-conscientiousness about schoolwork—also hold them back in the workforce? What if school is a confidence factory for our sons, but only a competence factory for our daughters?" Damour asks in a *New York Times* essay. "For boys, school serves as a test track, where they build their belief in their abilities and grow increasingly at ease relying on them. Our daughters, on the other hand, may miss the chance to gain confidence in their abilities if they always count on intellectual elbow grease alone."

In fact, while girls often built up an incredible capacity for work, they still felt a lack of confidence in their abilities. And that can carry over into their careers. In their book *The Confidence Code*, Katty Kay and Claire Shipman found that a lack of competence is less likely to be an obstacle to advancement at work than a lack of confidence. "Underqualified and underprepared men don't think twice about leaning in," they wrote. "Overqualified and overprepared, too many women still hold back. Women feel confident only when they are perfect."

It's not just the belief that we must meet 100 percent of the qualifications to apply for a job or to be successful in a role that holds us back. It's also the idea that if we don't exert maximum effort all the time, we've somehow fallen short.

A Shift in Mindset

If we want to be successful without being stressed out, to do work that is intellectually and emotionally and financially rewarding—and to have a high-level role as well as a life outside work—we need to shift our thinking around this.

The breadwinner mindset is about allocating your time so that you can be most productive. That doesn't mean working more hours. That means channeling your time and energy into the most critical work, where you can see the biggest return on your investment of time and effort. It also means identifying those areas of work that require less time and effort on your part, either because you're so competent that you can complete it with minimum effort or because it's work you can delegate to, or share with, someone else.

Economy of time is an important concept. We are often overly generous with our time and reluctant to ask for or arrange support, to our own detriment. How we manage our time inside and out of our careers is key to being able to build wealth effectively, and being able to have time to enjoy it. But learning this for myself involved thinking that was counter to everything I'd believed when I first embarked on my career.

The fact is, your time is finite. And so is your energy. And you need time to recharge. So it follows that you should allocate the time you have to the work and the people most important to you. This may be challenging when you first start your career, but it becomes increasingly important as you advance and the demands on your time increase. Delegate anything that doesn't have to be done by you so that you have more time to focus on the work that can *only* be done by you. Ask for help. Enroll other people in helping you focus on the work you do best. Protect your time fiercely. If you don't value it, no one else will either.

The mental hurdle for many women—one that may keep us from going after higher-level opportunities—is the belief that in order to pursue a career path with high earnings potential, we have to continue to take on an increasingly larger load and deprioritize everything outside our careers. While the unjust paradigm may still exist that says women must work harder than men to prove our value, there's another way to approach it so that we don't have to keep working harder and longer. We work smarter.

Once I grasped that I was valued most for my skills and experience—not for the hours I put in at the office—I began to channel my efforts accordingly. I signed up for workshops to hone and expand my skills and took on projects at work that could raise my profile and range of experience. I began to delegate more work to junior colleagues and to narrow my focus on work that could be done only by me in the organization.

The more strategic I was with my time and effort, the more effective I became. And being able to get the work done more efficiently allowed me more flexibility and time for other projects that were important to me (like this book). As you progress in your career, the most value you bring to a job—or to your own business, if you have one—isn't your capacity to work, but the skills, expertise, perspective, and experience that are unique to you. To be able to apply them most effectively, you need to allocate your time accordingly.

Ultimately, it isn't working harder that will allow us to succeed—it's working smarter.

CHAPTER 10

Beyond Passion

How to Do What You Love
and Get Paid (Well) for It

Everyone's got some greatness in them . . . But in order to really mine it,
you have to own it. You have to grab hold of it. You have to believe it.
—SHONDA RHIMES

WHEN I WAS young, I used to ask *a lot* of questions. So many that my mom, exasperated, finally said to me one day: "You should become a reporter. Then you can get paid for asking questions."

I was only in middle school at that point, but I was intrigued. And when my parents gave me a copy of *Newsweek* a few years later, I read it cover to cover, imagining how incredible it would be to get paid to do what the people who wrote those articles must get to do each day: ask interesting people questions about interesting topics in interesting places. At the age of thirteen, I declared that I was going to be a journalist when I grew up, and that I would work at *Newsweek*.

To their credit, my parents didn't try to discourage me—even though we lived in Dallas at the time, 1,500 miles away from *Newsweek* headquarters, and I was just starting high school and had never taken a journalism class. I'd go on to join my high school newspaper. And when I went off to study journalism in college, I felt lucky to already be so certain about the profession I wanted to pursue. I felt especially fortunate when, in my late twenties—after years of sending emails and months of interviews, calls, and waiting—I got a job as a junior-level reporter at *Newsweek*.

I loved the work I did so much that it hardly felt like work most days. It felt meaningful. It allowed me to spend time with fascinating and often inspiring people. And I was writing every day, something I'd enjoyed doing since I was a kid. I remember several times as a reporter, both at *Newsweek* and at the newspapers where I'd worked beforehand, saying to myself, "I can't believe I'm getting paid to do this!"

Ultimately, that's what we want, right? A job that doesn't feel like one. Work that is so enjoyable and fulfilling that it often doesn't even seem like work. The only problem was that I wasn't getting paid very much to do it. (I'd made so little in my first job that I'd qualified for food stamps and had to get an extra part-time job just to cover expenses.) In all the career conversations I'd had with my parents, my professors, and my college advisor, the subject of salaries had strangely never come up. The message had simply been to pursue what I was passionate about and the money would follow.

Aligning Passion with Pay

Eventually, my salary did grow. But by the time I had that midnight wake-up call in my early thirties, I realized that the income I was making was not going to be enough to support the life I wanted—or even the short-term goals we had to expand our family and find a home big enough to accommodate a second child. So in order to earn more, I decided to shift course and move into management.

While I have no regrets—I've earned and learned a lot as I've moved up in management—I realize now, looking back, that maybe I went about it the wrong way. What if I'd been paying attention to the salary from the start and thinking like a breadwinner? Would I have made different choices? Probably. I'm pretty certain I still would have pursued journalism. But maybe I would have picked up an extra part-time job sooner so that I could be sure to cover my bills and still save some money. Maybe I would have moved earlier onto the editor track, which paid more. Maybe I would have sought out higher-paying publications rather than taking the first journalism job I got. Maybe I would have advocated more for myself early on and actually negotiated my salaries.

I also began to wonder if maybe I'd asked the wrong question when I started thinking about how to increase my income. Rather than asking how I could get paid more to do what I loved and did well, I'd asked, What else can I do to earn more?

The underlying assumption, of course, is that you can do what you love *or* you can get paid well. But unless you are lucky and talented enough to become a pro tennis player, say, or a pop star—or you happen to love and be adept at business, financial analysis, or performing surgery—you typically can't have both. More commonly, our passions and interests don't align in obvious ways with high-paying occupations. So we feel we have to either pursue a job we love that doesn't pay us what we need or take a job that pays well and try to indulge our passions on the side.

The problem with the advice we often get to just pursue our passions is that it leaves out a critical part of the equation: the pay! I can't tell you the number of people who told me how incredibly lucky I was when I mentioned how much I loved my reporting job—as if I'd won the lottery!—without even considering the fact that I was getting paid so little that I could barely cover my bills. (This advice also assumes that we all know what our passions are, and many of us don't. We often discover them along the way.) Maybe when the end goal was to get married, and making a little money on the side was sufficient, the idea of dabbling in work we enjoyed without worrying about how much we were paid for it was okay. But not anymore.

Carrie's Story

Carrie, a leadership consultant with a dark bob and a commanding presence, knew she wanted a career—but she was less certain about what it would be. She started as a singer and then worked for a few years in acoustics. "My family was really supportive of my non-traditional route," she remembers. "So when I got my master's degree in voice, I thought, 'Oh, it'll be fine. I'm smart. I'll figure out how to make enough money.'"

That "it will be fine" attitude carried on, she says, until she woke up in her thirties, after switching careers a couple times, single and stressed out about her money and her future. "And I thought, 'Oh wait! I actually don't know how I am going to make any money.'"

She can laugh about it now. After going back to get an MBA, she launched her own successful consulting group and is now living in Michigan with her boyfriend and their newborn baby. But she still shakes her head when she thinks about how being able to actually provide for herself (or anyone else) was never a part of the conversation when it came to career choices.

When Carrie was young, her mom quit her job as an architect to stay home with Carrie and her siblings. "I got the sense, even then, that she was not happy—that this derailed what could have been a very successful career in architecture. And it became a big thorn in her side," Carrie remembers. "I saw that growing up and I thought: 'I am not going to do that. I am going to pursue a career above all else.' And I just assumed the money would follow! It wasn't until my late twenties that I realized it doesn't. We're encouraged to pursue our passion, but we don't talk about money."

The fact is, if you focus only on going after your passion, the pay often *doesn't* follow. I say that from experience. But we can do work we love—work that we feel so compelled to do, and so enjoy doing, that it often doesn't feel like work—and also make a good living. We just have to consciously seek that out, rather than assume the money will naturally follow.

"You want to be doing something that you love, or something that is logically going to lead to something you love, in order to do your best work. That desire will make you more creative and more resourceful, and will help you get further faster. And it will help you persist," write the coauthors of *Just Start: Take Action, Embrace Uncertainty, Create the Future* in a 2012 *Harvard Business Review* article. "But, let's be real. None of this guarantees wealth, or even financial success."

Maybe, instead of trying to identify our passion and thinking about how we can indulge it, we can look at what we naturally enjoy doing and are good at—basically, what we have to contribute to the world. And then look at what needs we can fill with those gifts that will also allow us to earn enough to support the life we want.

Ikagai: Get Paid to Do What You Love

If you want to spend most of your time doing purposeful work you love *and* get paid well for it, you have to figure out how to match what you do well with what employers or clients need and then factor in what they're willing to pay for it. That's not often the way we approach our careers though. Certainly not the way I did at first.

But in spring 2019, I went to an all-day workshop that transformed the way I looked at work. It was taught by a successful entrepreneur who'd founded a digital company, sold it for big bucks, and now devoted himself to helping other entrepreneurs level up and scale their businesses. I wasn't an entrepreneur then, but he emphasized that even employees must think entrepreneurially, especially now, as well-established industries are being disrupted by upstarts and few people can count on staying with one employer for long. We're all, in a sense, building our own brands and value.

He talked passionately about a concept called *ikagai*, a Japanese word that translates roughly to "reason for being." I was skeptical at first, tired of the old tropes like "Chase your bliss." If you do what you love but make so little money you can barely cover rent, how blissful is that? I'd been there, and I didn't want to go back. But I also didn't want to spend my days doing work I didn't love just to make money, something I was worried was beginning to happen. The *ikagai* model seemed to address both. And it resonated.

As he spoke, I took out a piece of paper and drew a line down the middle. On one side I wrote the things I'd done that week that I really enjoyed—work that felt effortless or fired me up and gave me energy. On the other side I listed the tasks that felt like effort and left me drained. When I was done, I had a lot more on the "lot of effort" side. And I realized that many of the actions on the effortless side were being squeezed in among the others. Uh-oh.

Next he asked us to make two lists:

- What we love to do
- What we're good at

Then he asked us to review those lists to see where there was overlap between them and where they had these additional criteria:

- What the world needs
- What others will pay us for

As I looked over my lists, a pattern slowly began to emerge. I realized with a start that as my job description evolved, I'd started spending a lot more of my time doing work that I didn't enjoy and that didn't leverage what I was best at—what some call our "genius." The creative aspects of the job that had attracted me to it in the first place had been shrinking, and I found myself spending more and more time on process-oriented tasks, project and people management, and meetings. And as I reviewed the lists of what I loved and knew I was good at, I realized that a lot of that was being channeled outside my job.

This is the kind of assessment we are rarely taught to do. We may do strengths training and generally identify what we're good at, but we often don't audit our day-to-day to-do lists with an eye toward identifying where we're most effective and what tasks drain our energy and play against our strengths. Nor do we consider whether our natural strengths and interests are being leveraged as they could be.

Are You Doing the Right Work?

Men have gotten accustomed to dumping the work they don't want to do on the women around them. We have not had that luxury, historically. So we often pile on responsibilities and plow through them without giving much thought to what we're best at, what comes naturally, and what might be better handled by someone else. That's especially true early in our careers, as we're trying to figure all that out—and sometimes just trying to pay the bills. Yet even as we progress in our careers, we often don't think to ask if the work we're spending much of our time on actually suits us, and allows us to hone our strengths and work most effectively. How often are we doing work that only we can do?

It's not just that we tend to take on extra work (including, yes, a lot of that office housework and other non-promotable work) but that we often end up taking on roles or responsibilities that don't necessarily align with our interests, talents, or true desires. We may be good at doing them, but that doesn't mean they serve us or allow us to have the impact we want. That's a lesson I had to learn myself. When I started to feel exhausted after work, I initially thought it was a result of taking on too much—and there was definitely some of that. But as I dug deeper, I realized some of it was also a result of the *kind* of work I was taking on.

I'm not just talking about avoiding that non-promotable grunt work. It's also possible to find yourself in a job spending a majority of your time doing higher-level responsibilities and tasks that . . . you just don't enjoy and that don't play to your strengths. Part of our work as breadwinners is getting to a deeper understanding of how and where we can add the most value—to a company or business, and also to the world—and then figuring out how best to support that work. Maybe that's consciously building a team of people with complementary skills and preferences, adjusting our role so that we are able to spend more time on the work we find most meaningful. Or maybe it's finding or creating a new role for ourselves.

As I sat in that all-day workshop, I wondered: Was it possible to get to a point where I was spending more of my days doing the kind of work that I *did* love? Work that came naturally to me and that gave me energy and joy but also supplied the income I wanted? And would that mean finding a new job, or just redefining the one I had? After a few hours of jotting down ideas and connecting the dots between my various interests and talents, I began to get an idea of what that might look like. It wasn't a specific job, but it was a sort of job description that could be applied in different ways.

A few months later, I got a call about a role that lined up surprisingly well with the description. While I ultimately chose not to take the job, it was validation that there is something very powerful about getting clear on what you're seeking. I don't know if the universe organizes itself to send it your way—though some people believe that—but I *do* know that if you aren't clear on what you're looking for, you won't recognize it when it does show up. So it's beneficial to spend some time writing out what an ideal job description or an ideal workday would look like, even if you don't know exactly where it would be or what the actual job title would be.

That doesn't mean that we'll *always* do everything we want. "I don't know one person who says that every single day at work is pure bliss.

That just seems inauthentic," Lisa Johnson, who is the VP of marketing at a patient-driven telehealth company in New York, told me. "What I look for is a company and a role that aligns with my set of values. I think that's more important. I love what I do, but I don't need to be living my bliss every minute."

We can work toward a place, though, where we are spending more and more of our time doing work that brings us joy and plays to our unique strengths. We can look at each position we take as an opportunity to identify the kind of work we most enjoy and excel at and then consider how we can do more of it in a way that allows us to have the most income and impact. And we can look for companies that embody our values and offer opportunities that play to our strengths.

Along the way, we may also need to take some jobs that just pay well or that will allow us to hone our skills in service of the work we eventually want to do—or the life we want to be able to afford. But I can say from experience, and from interviewing dozens of women who are passionate about the work they do and *also* passionate about getting paid well for it, that it is possible to design a career that supports the life you want, allows you to do meaningful work you enjoy, and compensates you well for it.

It's Not Just About the Paycheck

Directing the majority of our focus and energy into what we're already naturally good at is nearly the opposite of what we're taught to do in school (outside of the arts and athletics). As students, we were encouraged to put extra effort into areas where we were *not* performing as well in order to bring those grades up, so that we could get good marks across the board. That makes sense if you're building a basic foundation of skills. But it doesn't serve us as well once we become adults.

Yet we often make that mistake in our careers: We expend a lot of energy trying to improve our competency levels at tasks and roles that we are not that great at or don't enjoy. Instead, we should be leaning into what we are naturally good at and enjoy doing in order to hone those skills even further, then seeking to surround ourselves with people who have complementary skills. Otherwise, the risk is that we become competent at a wide range of tasks but not exceptional at any. Not only can that make us more easily dispensable, but it means we may not get the opportunity to deepen the skills and work we are innately good at and have the kind of impact we want to have. We may end up in a role that we don't excel at or in one that we're competent at (and maybe even well-compensated for) but don't enjoy.

That's what happened to Mayumi Young. At twenty-seven, she *seemed* to have an enviable life. She had been hired a couple of years earlier by a global telecom company and had been promoted twice since. She was serving as international finance director, traveling the globe, and earning a sizable salary. Based in Southern California, where she lived in an upscale town home, she frequently traveled to the company's offices in Europe, Australia, and New Zealand.

But she told me that she'd pursued a career in accounting simply because she'd gotten an A in her accounting 101 class in college, learned it was a lucrative profession, and had a lot of student debt to pay off. In the end, that foundation would enable her to create a business she's passionate about. Initially, though, after graduation, she got hired by a major accounting firm to do audits, and then recruited by the telecom company—an offer she took mainly because it offered her a higher salary, a better title, and the chance to travel. But the hours were long, the work could be tedious, and, while she was good at it, it didn't excite her. While she did love traveling, doing so much of it also began to take a toll.

On one of her many business trips, she remembers waiting in an airport when a woman with a young girl struck up a conversation, asking her what she did for a living. "I gave her my usual answer and made it sound really good," she told me. The mother turned to her daughter, who was about eleven, and said, 'Wouldn't you like to be her one day, too?'"

"That girl looked right at me, and I suddenly realized I wanted to take it all back. I wanted to say, Scrap that. I'm actually miserable. I'm exhausted, and I'm unfulfilled," Mayumi remembers. "I wanted to tell her instead: Figure out what you really want to do, what lights you up, and go after that. It was a radical wake-up call for me. I decided, in that moment, I was done."

Within a few weeks, she submitted a letter of resignation. "I definitely *do not* recommend this as a strategy," she told me, laughing. "But I was desperate. I didn't know exactly what I wanted to do, but I knew it wasn't this."

After she left her job, she took some time to try to figure out what it was she really wanted to do. "How do you create a career and a life that is in alignment with who you are? I'd never asked myself that before," she told me. "It started there, setting an intent. I realized I wanted to serve other people using my gifts and talents, and that whatever I did had to *both* make money and have purpose."

On reflection, she realized that her interests fell into three spheres: entrepreneurship, education, and finance. She had a strong finance background and accounting degree and knew that she had a natural talent for communicating tough concepts in ways that were easy to understand, and she'd always been entrepreneurial-minded. So she then began looking at how to combine those interests and skills in ways that would allow her to make a difference and also make money. She started by creating a high school financial-literacy curriculum that was picked up and piloted in a local charter school, where she was then hired to become the development director. Then she launched a financial education program for adults called Club Freedom. Over time, her vision and ambition continued to evolve.

Eventually, Mayumi found a way to combine all three of her interests. A CPA, she decided to launch her own company, CPA MOMS®, which pairs CPAs who have kids with small businesses and startups that need accounting help, allowing those moms to create their own book of clients—and their own schedules—so that they have more time for their families and themselves. She developed end-to-end software to support them, and educational content to help them build their businesses, and in 2020 began franchising her company nationwide. At the same time, she began building a community of similarly minded socially conscious entrepreneurs in San Diego, where she lives with her husband, with the intent of looking at how they could collaborate to have a significant impact.

"Ultimately, I believe that our job is to discover what our unique talents and gifts are and then to offer them to the world. That is the journey of life," she told me. (But you want to get paid well for them, too!)

Getting the Work and Income We Want

Figuring out how to combine our passion with the paycheck we want can take time. Often we may find ourselves veering one way or another— either earning a lot but feeling unfulfilled, as Mayumi did initially; or doing work that fills us up but leaves us scrambling financially, as I did—before settling on a path that allows us to both do work we love and make enough money to support the life we want.

"You can't just make money out of passion. But you have to discover who you are, what brings you joy, and what you're great at. And I've learned the only way to figure that out is by trying different things and seeing what you like and don't," Mayumi told me. "And in the beginning, it's usually a whole lot about discovering what you *don't* want to do."

The trick, I realized, is in creating a path that allows us to do increasingly more of what we love and that comes naturally—and to find or allow others who are better suited to do what doesn't. That realization was eye-opening for me; it helped me understand why I had found more success and contentment in some roles than others. It also had an almost immediate effect on the way I operated at work. I began to hand off more responsibilities that didn't support my strengths—not just non-promotable work but also work that didn't align with what I knew I was innately good at—so that I could focus on those responsibilities that would allow me to leverage my skills. I also spoke candidly with my boss about how I might apply my skills more effectively and about the work I wanted to be more (and less) involved in. Ultimately, I ended up transforming my role entirely.

Stop Searching for Your Passion (It'll Come)

Outside of ignoring the question of pay, the other problem with the "Pursue your passion!" advice is that it assumes we all know what our passion is, or that we have just one. But as I've learned, as have most of the women I interviewed, we often don't realize what kind of work we really enjoy doing until we try it. (I knew I had an interest in journalism, but I didn't discover my passion for it until I started doing it.) And we need not limit ourselves to one career path or profession, even if it's one we love. It's possible to find work that's fulfilling and that plays to our strengths in ways we might not have imagined initially.

Take Terri Trespicio. By her midthirties, she had built a successful career in media, advancing to become a senior editor at a national women's health magazine—"my first big job that aligned with what I *thought* I wanted to be." But after a few years in the role, she says she looked at the women in the top two roles of executive editor and editor in chief, both of whom she liked and respected. "And I saw two women who were totally stressed out and exhausted," she told me. "My executive editor was already there when I got to work in the morning, and she was still there when I left. She was just muscling her way through pile after pile of tasks. And I noted with dread that I didn't want to be her."

Terri enjoyed being an editor and host of the magazine's daily call-in show—"being that person with the cool job to talk about at parties." But she also realized that she needed a path that would allow her to earn more but not demand so much of her time and energy that she had little left for anything or anyone else.

When a new editor in chief arrived, layoffs soon followed. And Terri was among those who got a severance package. It was just what she needed to chart a new course. Anticipating that she might leave, she'd already been making connections with women she admired. She wasn't sure exactly what to do next though. "So I asked myself, What am I good at? I thought, 'I can write and listen and take ideas and turn them into something people will listen to and read. I can do any kind of content.' Then it was time to look at what people needed."

She reached out to a woman who was the editor of another magazine, explained she'd been laid off, and asked if there was anything her magazine needed. "She said, 'Our sales department needs some content we can sell.' I said, 'I can do that,'" Terri told me. Then she got a second client, the former publisher of the magazine where she'd worked, who was now leading a small startup.

She wasn't chasing a passion. She was looking pragmatically at where her talents met the market's needs. And that's key. It's less about pursuing your *passion* per se than it is about leaning into work you enjoy and are good at—and figuring out how best to apply it so that you can earn what you want. Within one month of being let go, Terri had two clients who were paying her more than she'd ever been paid. Within two months, she was earning more than double her old salary. She still hadn't figured out *exactly* what she wanted to do. But when an opportunity came along for her to media train authors and experts, it started to click into place: what she was good at, what she enjoyed doing, what people would pay for, and what the world (or a good number of clients, anyway) needed.

After interviewing dozens of people over her career as an editor, Terri had firsthand experience in watching people struggle to convey what they meant. She found she had a natural talent for helping them crystallize what they were trying to say, and she enjoyed it. "I realized I was good at that, and it was fun," she told me.

So she delved into it, thinking about the different ways that process could be applied. "I realized I was retrofitting a brand message," she said. "And then I realized, *this* is what people need."

Over time, she built a successful branding business, expanding her services to include helping others do everything from generate branded content to TED talks. (Her own TEDx Talk, "Stop Searching for Your Passion," has gotten more than 6 million views.) She started to add paid courses and online offerings, and then later, live events and retreats. But all of it came back to the core talent she'd identified years earlier. In fact, her LinkedIn profile reads: "I do one thing exceptionally well: I identify, distill, and articulate critical brand messaging—and I do it for a range of individuals and companies across a range of industries, from financial services to fashion, and from seasoned pros to budding entrepreneurs."

By discovering and focusing on what only she could do—and continuing to hone her skills in that space—Terri found that she could spend more and more of her time doing work she enjoyed, and that the work she did became increasingly valuable. "Over time with the business, you get a better sense of what you're really good at, what people need, and what you enjoy," she said. "The goal is, how do I get so close to the bone of what I am good at that I only have to do that one thing?"

She also got better at understanding the kinds of clients and projects that best suited her. She learned she preferred short, finite projects versus long-term retainers, so she focused on clients with specific problems to solve and restructured her business and pricing to support this. "You can absolutely shape your business for how you work best," she told me. "I do start-to-finish projects. They've gotten shorter and shorter, but more expensive."

Over time, she's also arranged her daily schedule so that it fits her natural rhythms. "I know I can do my best work in the morning, so I take a break in the afternoon, take a nap, and then work again in the evenings," she said. "I judge everything around my idiosyncratic style of work and my energy levels. A lot of running your own business is curating your time."

Nearly a decade later, Terri is not only making the money she wants, but she's also at a point where she can pick and choose clients and create a schedule that supports the kind of life she wants. "This idea that you need to know exactly what you should do from the start—you don't. You just need to pitch a few tents, and you'll learn," she told me.

This journey of discovery, she stresses, is not the same as simply pursuing your passion. "If you are sitting around waiting for your passion to show up, you could be waiting a long time," she said in her 2015 TEDx Talk. "So don't wait. Instead, spend your time and attention solving your favorite problems."

Over time, she said, she's come to view passion through a different lens—as something that arises naturally as you move in the direction of work you enjoy and that meets people's needs and makes a positive difference in their lives. Ultimately, she said, "Passion lives in realizing what you have to contribute."

Terri's story resonated with me. As I thought about what I might want to do next, it became clear that it wasn't about focusing so much on a particular role or title, but rather on the impact and the life I wanted to have. And that would inform whatever work I did.

Ultimately, we all want to feel like we're making a contribution—that the work we're doing matters. That it is purpose-driven and makes a difference in people's lives. And that we can make enough doing it to support our own lives.

One of the joys of getting to a place in your life where you're not in financial-survival mode anymore is that you have the opportunity to reflect more on how you *want* to spend your days and the kind of work you want to do. You can allow yourself to make choices guided by where you can create the most value and impact and get well-compensated for it (and have fun doing it!)—and feel less bound to a particular job title or career path. It's a different way of looking at success, one that we get to define ourselves.

PART IV

The Breadwinning Life

*How to build relationships—and
a life—that you love.*

CHAPTER 11

Now What?

What Happens When We Earn More

Biological sex should not determine what we are capable of, what we aspire to, and what we do in our life.
—ANNE-MARIE SLAUGHTER, AUTHOR,
LAWYER, AND POLITICAL SCIENTIST

IF I ASKED whether you want to earn a lot of money, the answer would probably be, Heck yeah! But if I asked whether you want to earn more than your partner, the answer might be different. One of the things I noticed as I spoke with other women about making money is that even if we plan to earn a lot, we still tend to assume our current or future partners will, too. Even ambitious, breadwinner-minded women don't generally set off to be the main earners for their households.

But millions of us end up there—whether we planned for it or not. And just as it takes time to get comfortable asking for more and investing our own money, fully inhabiting a role we hadn't anticipated having can take some adjusting, too.

If you're single, you know who's responsible for managing the finances and household (you!). If you're in a relationship and you each earn about the same amount of money, dividing the bills and household tasks can also be pretty straightforward. That's where my husband and I started.

But if your income and job demands start to exceed your partner's, it can get trickier. That's especially true if either of you had different expectations of how those responsibilities would break down. That's the time to start talking about what feels fair, both in terms of housework and covering expenses. (We'll talk more about that in the coming pages.) An income gap—regardless of who earns more—can also create an uneven power dynamic in a couple. But that can be mitigated by ensuring both of you are involved in the money-making decisions, management of finances and future planning, and that each partner's opinion is treated as equally important.

Throw kids into the mix, too, and things can get even more complicated—as I discovered. Then we're talking not just about bills and household tasks but about who's taking care of the little ones. And it's not a simple matter of splitting childcare fifty-fifty, because, unlike household chores, we actually *want* to spend time with our kids. Each partner also generally comes with preconceived notions of what being a good parent means and of who is supposed to take the caregiving lead, which may be based on memories of parental roles that look different from the ones we find ourselves in.

You may not have or want kids, so may be tempted to skip ahead (and that's fine!). But I found that this perceived conundrum in balancing our responsibilities at home and at work lies at the heart of many women's apprehensions about wholly embracing a breadwinner mindset and achieving their full earning potential. Whether or not you're married or plan to have kids, understanding where these concerns come from can be enlightening. In the coming pages, we'll take a deeper look at the cultural conditioning many of us have gotten around our responsibilities at home, and look at the impact that has—not just on working moms but on working women generally.

I'll also share my experience as the primary breadwinner for my family of four for the past dozen years. Yes, I am living proof that it's possible to be committed to your family and to your professional ambitions. (And you'll hear from others as well.) I'm deeply involved and connected with our sons, and I have the added joy of knowing I am helping to provide a wonderful life for my family and setting an example for our boys. I'm in a position now to support our sons with all the resources they need to thrive, to help cover their college costs, and to set them up for financial success as adults. That's an incredible feeling.

But getting to this point was a journey, and it required me to confront many of the ideas I'd absorbed growing up about money, marriage, and motherhood. As I've learned from personal experience—and you've probably figured out by now—in order to fully embrace a breadwinner mindset and enjoy all the benefits that come with it, we must first confront the beliefs that stand in the way.

Confronting Conventional Norms

When what had seemed like a temporary financial arrangement became our new normal, both my husband and I struggled initially in the face of cultural expectations. Victor was ashamed at first to admit to his father, a former commercial airline pilot who'd been the sole breadwinner for much of Victor's childhood, that I earned more than he did. I was ashamed to admit that I sometimes preferred the comforting rituals of work to the unpredictable periods at home with my young kids, especially during their temper-tantrum years.

I felt guilty about prioritizing work over family at times. Victor felt guilty about not contributing more financially. I felt shamed by my stepmother, who still cooks complicated dinners nearly every night for herself and my dad, when she made offhand comments about my kids subsisting on take-out, chicken nuggets, and pasta. And I felt guilty when I worked late and missed dinner altogether.

Upending the conventional breadwinner model meant upending our own ideas of what our marriage would look like and how our household would operate. It wasn't just a matter of who earned or contributed more, or how we divided our financial obligations. This new dynamic forced us to face all the underlying, unspoken emotions and assumptions we had about our roles.

Many of those feelings came from expectations we'd carried with us, those we realized we'd had for ourselves and those others had for us that we had internalized over the years or heard about regularly. It's not just news headlines that warn against upending the conventional breadwinning model—the one that values women most for their looks, homemaking, and parenting abilities and men for their moneymaking abilities and professional status. Our own, sometimes well-intentioned, family and friends can do the same.

"Almost all of the women around me in my family—even my aunts and older cousins—were homemakers. No one was telling me it's important to be a breadwinner," remembers Michelle, a thirty-eight-year-old Brooklyn mom who runs a consulting firm. "But I had one really badass grandma. She always worked, and when her husband passed away, she continued working and supporting herself—and she truly loved it. I think she was the only example I had growing up of a woman who worked both to support herself and really enjoyed it."

"Even now with friends and family, honestly, sometimes you really have to spell it out for them: Our household *depends* on me working," said Michelle, who earns more than double what her husband does. "Still, when there's a family event and my brother says he can't go because of work, it's okay and no one says anything. But I don't get the same reaction when I say I can't go because I have to work."

Mothers-in-law who stayed home themselves to raise their sons, in particular, can struggle to understand how their son's wives could value their careers as much as their sons do (maybe even more!).

"My mother-in-law actually called my mom and said, 'You need to tell her to stop working. It's inappropriate for her to be working,'" remembers Alyson, who runs a New York–based PR and marketing firm and lives in New Jersey with her three kids. "I couldn't believe it. But she hadn't worked, and my sister-in-law stopped working when she had kids and didn't go back even after the kids were in school. So I'm sure that was part of it."

Jennifer, a mom of two in New York who works in the pharmaceutical industry, remembers when she first got married in 2006, "My husband made more than me and was very comfortable in that role, and he felt very secure."

Then she went back to school to get her master's degree and, after she leveraged it to get a major promotion at work, began outearning her husband. She vividly recalls a visit to her in-laws shortly after. "His mother sat down with me and said, 'I don't understand why you have to work and why you can't let him be the breadwinner,'" she remembers. "No woman in his family works. They just didn't understand it."

Christine, a colleague of Jennifer's, met her husband when they were both graduate students. After they got married, he became a pharmacist, and she went to work for the pharmaceutical company. Within a few years, her income exceeded her husband's. "But he couldn't admit to his family that I made more," she said.

After she gave birth to their son, her in-laws began pressuring her to stop working. "My mother-in-law had been a physician, but she gave up her practice when she had kids," Christine told me. "I remember she said to me, 'Don't you know that kids with mothers who stay home do much better than kids who don't?' I looked her in the eye and said, 'My mom worked the entire time I was growing up, and I think I turned out fine. So, no.'"

Still, Christine said she felt initially like she had to do "all the traditional mom things" on top of her job. She dropped off and picked up their son from daycare every day. She took him to doctor's appointments and playdates and stayed home whenever he was sick. "My husband said he was worried he would get fired if he took too many days off for his kid," she remembers. "His boss had told him, 'That's what you have a wife for.'"

Breadwinning Versus Caregiving:
It Doesn't Have to Be a Choice

As Christine found, all these societal expectations about breadwinning are heightened when kids enter the mix. It's something I experienced firsthand, as my breadwinning potential came smack up against my cultural conditioning as a daughter, a wife, and—crucially—a mother. When I was growing up, my dad was the sole breadwinner for many years for our family and then the primary one. I had no reason to think the model would be much different when I became a parent.

My mom stopped working when I was born and didn't go back to work until I was in middle school. She was the one who taught me how to read, took me to dance class, and came to all my recitals. I can still picture her, leaning over the edge of the ice rink when I competed in figure-skating competitions, pumping her fist in the air and cheering me on. And I remember her looking me in the eye and reassuring me that I was beautiful when a high school boyfriend broke up with me and insisting that I deserved better than him anyway.

I don't have as many memories like that of my dad. I mostly remember him being distracted at the dinner table and heading off to his home office as soon as my sister and I cleared the table. Once, I remember him bringing me to the university where he worked and letting me try the coffee in the faculty lounge (which I mixed with four heaping spoonfuls of sugar and promptly spit up). But the only times I remember really bonding with him were Sunday mornings after church when the whole family would go for long drives around Dallas, checking out new neighborhoods and restaurants. I cherished those hours because it seemed like the only predictable period of time I had with him.

When I was thirteen, my parents split up and offered my sister and me the choice of which parent to live with. We didn't seriously consider moving in with my dad, much to his surprise and disappointment. For my sister and me, that seemed inconceivable. We were with our mom every day. We mostly spent time with him on Sundays.

I wanted to have a successful career when I grew up and to get married and have a family. I didn't plan to stop working altogether when I had kids. But I'd assumed I would slow down, maybe even go part-time for a while to spend more time with them. I didn't want to be a Sunday mom.

What I hadn't factored in was the possibility that I might be the main provider when we had kids. And how exactly that would work.

While I enjoyed the newfound confidence I felt about my earning power and financial status and the comfort of being able to provide for myself and my family, I hadn't anticipated how my breadwinning ambitions would run headlong into the expectations I had for myself as a mom and a wife. I didn't want to follow my dad's model and devote myself entirely to breadwinning, nor did I want to follow my mom's lead and give up my career for years to be a full-time caregiver to our kids. But I had no model for how to blend both roles.

Because it has been framed as a binary choice—you're either the breadwinner or the caregiver—we often grow up believing the two are incompatible. And breadwinning has been associated for decades with men, while we are still brought up to believe that caregiving is primarily a woman's responsibility. So it can be difficult to imagine how to merge the two successfully. But we can, as I've learned. It just requires us to redefine our roles based on our reality—and not on our expectations or childhood experiences.

I remember calling my dad late one night, after a particularly grueling day at work. When he asked how things were going, I broke down. Between sobs, I told him the financial pressure of being the primary earner was intense. I loved my job and relished making a good living. Yet I'd been working late so often, it seemed like I never got to spend time with my family. At home, I was often tired and distracted, responding to work emails on weekends and sometimes working after the kids went to bed during the week. There was a moment of silence, and then he said softly, "Now you know how I felt."

As I listened to him describe for the first time the pressure he felt as the sole provider for much of my childhood, I sympathized with him and had a new appreciation for the sacrifices he'd made. But after I got off the phone, I began to realize it was my experience with my dad growing up that had led me to equate being the main breadwinner with thinking about work and money all the time. And to believe that taking care of my family financially meant not having the time or bandwidth to take care of them emotionally. That being the main breadwinner meant giving up time with loved ones in order to work to provide a better future, hoping that one day they would understand and appreciate your sacrifice.

But did it have to be that way?

Did being the primary breadwinner have to come at the expense of my being as involved as a mother and wife as I wanted to be? How much of the pressure that I felt was based on actual work demands, and how much was driven by my own beliefs about how the main earner was sup-posed to behave? Were my workaholic tendencies driven by my boss's expectations, or were they an outcome of what I'd witnessed myself growing up? How much of the pressure I felt was emotional, the result of cultural expectations I carried about the level of responsibility a mom *should* have for her home and family as well as for her job?

After that call with my dad, I began to look more closely at where the beliefs I'd adopted about breadwinning and the roles a husband and wife "should" have came from. And I wondered what might change if we began to redefine those roles for ourselves.

A Quick History Lesson

The male breadwinner model rose to prominence in the 1950s when one income was enough to support a family and a middle-class lifestyle.

And in the nearly seventy years since, corporate policies and cultural expectations, even public school schedules, have continued to support it. Despite the gains of the women's liberation movement in the 1970s, the prevailing assumption was that men would continue to be the ones to have a full career, and women—even if we did work—would hold secondary, supportive roles. We'd still be expected to manage the household and swap our paid work for parenting or caring for loved ones as the need arose.

It was as if husbands and wives had an unwritten social contract—at least, those in middle-class and upper-middle-class enclaves. (Breadwinner moms were historically more common in low-income areas, where moms were also more likely to be single.) The unspoken assumption was that the husband would take care of the income, and the wife would take care of the household. Staying home with the kids was often seen as a choice and a privilege, a luxury that only women with successful husbands could afford. "Opting out" was a status symbol, and the implication was that women could simply opt back in whenever they wanted. For much of the twentieth century, the typical assumption was that if a mom worked, it was because she had to—not because she wanted to.

But that's changing. More women have been moving into the workforce because they want to, and their income has become increasingly important as the costs to raise a family continue to climb. Two-income households are the norm today among married couples, and two paychecks are often necessary in order for many families just to maintain a middle-class lifestyle. By 2013, nearly half of all households with kids—or 16.4 million households—had a mother bringing in at least 40 percent of the total household income.

Even in those families in which the husbands earn a lot more, many wives have discovered that "opting out" of the workforce after kids and then back in again years later is not easy, especially given the speed at which technology has disrupted nearly every industry. In 2003, a group of highly educated, accomplished working mothers with high-earning spouses made the cover of the *New York Times Magazine*, under the headline "The Opt-Out Revolution," for choosing to drop out of the workforce just as they were hitting their stride professionally in order to stay home with their kids.

A decade later, the *New York Times* ran a follow-up article that included many of the same women, called "The Opt-Out Generation Wants Back In." While those with elite college degrees and the most well-connected social networks had found it relatively easy to return to the workforce, Judith Warner reported, the jobs they found usually paid less than their previous positions and were less prestigious. And the women she spoke to who lacked high-powered networks and prestigious degrees, or those who had since divorced, she wrote, "often struggled greatly" professionally and financially.

The decision to stop working also shifted the dynamic at home for these women in unexpected and unwanted ways, "transforming them from being their husbands' intellectual equals into the one member of their partnership uniquely endowed with gifts for laundry or cooking and cleaning; a junior member of the household, who sometimes had to 'negotiate' with her husband to get money for child care," Warner wrote.

The economist Sylvia Ann Hewlett, founder of the Center for Talent Innovation in New York, surveyed thousands of women in 2004 and again five years later and found that roughly a third of what she described as "highly qualified women" had left the workforce in the interim to spend time at home. As with the "Opt-Out" wives portrayed in the *New York Times*, most discovered it was much harder to return to work than they had hoped. Eighty-nine percent of those who'd left said they wanted to go back to work, but only 73 percent of them succeeded in getting back in—and notably, only 40 percent got full-time jobs. And those who went back to full-time work took jobs that paid, on average, 16 percent less than those they'd had before. About a quarter of the women surveyed took jobs with fewer management responsibilities or said they had to accept a lower job title than the one they'd had when they left.

I remember one of my mom friends, a talented photographer and former magazine photo editor with an Ivy League degree, telling me at the playground how she had quit her job when her son was born. A few years later, when her son was still a toddler, her husband divorced her. But in the time she'd been out of the workforce, the magazine industry had transformed from print to digital. She had no digital experience and struggled to find work in her field. When we spoke that afternoon, she was planning to apply for loans to cover a master's degree program to bring herself up to speed so that she could get hired back into the field she'd left. "I never would have quit my job if I'd realized I was committing career suicide," she told me.

Men generally haven't had to deal with these dilemmas. The assumption has been that they will continue to ascend in their careers post-kids—it's not even a question that comes up—because there'll be someone else caring for the family and doing most of the work at home. So they can focus on making money and doing the fun stuff with the kids. While mom is washing dishes, making meals, cleaning, and looking after the kids on a daily basis, dad gets to take the kids to ball games, or on fishing or camping trips, or just sit on the couch with them watching TV. At least that's been the traditional arrangement.

But when the mom has a demanding full-time job, especially if it accounts for a significant portion of the family's income, that arrangement no longer works, as I learned myself.

Trying to Do It All

When I first became the main breadwinner for my family, I'll admit I felt angry. Angry at being thrust into a role I hadn't prepared for. Angry that I didn't have the "luxury" of staying home longer with our newborn. Angry that I was suddenly the one carrying most of the financial responsibility, not just for my future but for my family's, too—a possibility I'd never planned for and still felt ill prepared to handle.

And when I wasn't angry, I was often steeped in sadness or guilt. It wasn't that unusual for me to burst into tears in the shower. Or in the bathroom at work. Or, once, in front of my boss. Eventually, I got a therapist. And I spent entire sessions talking about how overwhelmed, exhausted, and confused I was by the sudden surge in responsibilities I felt I had to manage.

At home, all I could see was the dust on the bookshelves. The dishes stacking up by the sink. The water stain on the ceiling from the leaky pipe that needed to be fixed. The dirty shower curtain that needed to be replaced. The sag in the middle of our mattress. The toddler bed our oldest was already outgrowing. The stains on the shades I'd bought for the living room. The half-dozen prints still leaning against the walls, waiting to be mounted. Everywhere I looked, there was something to do. Our baby crying to be fed. Our toddler tugging at my leg. The dirty clothes piling up in the hamper. The formula needing to be mixed and warmed. The work emails waiting to be answered.

When I looked in the mirror, I noticed prematurely gray roots peeked out weeks after I got my hair colored. Were the bags under my eyes just the temporary effect of my constantly interrupted nights or the new normal? My high-heeled shoes made me wince when I walked—all of them tight, now that my feet had grown a half size with my second pregnancy. My work wardrobe needed an update. All my dresses were tight around my chest, which had swollen from nursing, and around my stomach, which had yet to return to its flattened pre-pregnancy state despite daily sit-ups.

It seemed like I was spending an increasing amount of effort and money just to keep up my appearance—new under-eye concealer, Spanx, stretch-mark cream . . . Even when I wasn't spending on myself, I felt like I was hemorrhaging money: on daycare and clothes, shoes and books for the boys. Groceries, toiletries, diapers, wipes, and baby bottles. And later, on baseball and soccer, and the clothes and equipment that came with them. Birthday gifts, field trips, trips to see the grandparents. Although my husband was covering some of the bills, I started to fear that I was less a parent than a human ATM. That I was spending more money than time on my boys. It seemed like every event I planned with them turned into a shopping trip.

I'd always excelled in school and at work. I was accustomed to pleasing my teachers and my bosses. Now, suddenly, I was struggling to stay on top of my life. It wasn't a matter of excelling anymore, but of just getting everything done. And the stakes had never seemed higher. I was now in management, responsible for a team, a budget, and aggressive metrics—the most demanding role I'd had yet. I couldn't afford to lose this job, or even miss a paycheck, with the expenses we had. I was trying to adjust to my first management role while also adjusting to being a parent of two—and the main provider for our family. I had never had so many competing priorities or operated on so little sleep. This constant feeling of falling short all the time, no matter how much I scrambled, left me with a crushing sense of sadness and self-doubt.

The result was a never-ending to-do list. I woke up an hour before my family and stayed up late, working after the kids were in bed. I was juggling housework, playdates, and work meetings, afraid to let anything go for fear it would all unravel. I was continually shifting my schedule around to make it all work. Very often it didn't. In my attempt to squeeze everything in, there was very little margin for error. I was constantly texting or emailing with apologies for being late or absent. I felt like I was in a perpetual state of scrambling.

My husband and I alternated dropping off and picking up the kids from daycare and preschool, and he began picking up more household tasks. But for nearly a year after our youngest was born, I was still pumping milk for him and getting up most nights to nurse. Even after I stopped, I continued to insist on managing most of the family logistics—formula feedings, birthday parties, playdates, mommy-and-me yoga—so that I could feel connected to the kids and their daily lives, since I worried I was less present for them day to day.

Wait—isn't this supposed to be a book *promoting* breadwinning for women? I promise this story has a happy ending. Read on.

Separating Needs from "Shoulds"

Looking back later, I wondered why I didn't ask my husband for more help when the kids were young. Why didn't I hire a house cleaner or a part-time sitter to relieve some strain, even if it cut into my earnings? Why did I feel such pressure to take almost all of it on myself?

It seems obvious now that as my work hours, demands, and salary grew, I would need more help at home and with the kids in order to manage it and continue to provide the essential income for our family. But I couldn't see that initially through the blur of busyness that clouded my days. What I eventually realized was that being the main breadwinner itself wasn't the burden. It was the weight of the cultural expectations—and the bulk of the household work—that I was carrying. Sure, there are pressures that come with being the main provider in a marriage or family, but what's really hard is trying to do that *and* everything else.

At first, the thought of Victor taking on more caregiving duties actually seemed more of a threat to my identity as a mother than a relief. And during particularly stressful times, the idea of him taking care of us financially seemed like a welcome alternative (*If only Victor earned more*, I would tell myself). Only later did I realize that could have been the most dangerous choice of all: to give up my income. And to give up the parts of me that lived outside my children and my home. That initial instinct to cut back on my career, I came to understand, sprang not from an actual desire to stop working or to lower my professional ambitions, but from deep-rooted beliefs I'd inherited about what being a good mom required and the fear that I would fall short if I were also the main provider.

So creating a new dynamic that worked with my husband required being honest about what was most important to each of us—what pieces of parenting mattered most, and how we could stitch those together so that we each felt ownership of some parts and were able to share the others. Then we figured out how to split up or outsource the critical household tasks so that they didn't take us away from what mattered most: spending quality time together.

I had to examine what I was doing because I felt like I *should* be doing it rather than because I wanted to do it. What was I doing out of guilt? And what was I doing out of genuine desire? When my career and earnings took off, the reality was that I couldn't continue to take on as much at home as I had, so some things had to go. I began by looking at what I didn't want to let go of: taking the kids to school, spending time with my family in the evenings, and finding activities we could do together, even if it meant just getting a treat from the local bakery together on a Saturday morning or having a weekly family-movie night.

Did I really want to make the house my domain? Did I want to cook and clean and schlep my kids to all their playdates and activities? Or did I believe that I *should* want those things? Honestly, I wasn't sure how much would change at home if our salaries were similar. While I loved spending time with our kids, I didn't need to make dinner for them every night or be at every single one of their sporting events, as long as one of us was there, for them to know I cared about them. And I knew I didn't want to give up the career I loved (or the income!) to stay home with them, no matter how much my husband was earning. I'm ambitious. It felt good to succeed and to earn enough to help provide a nice life for my family. That wouldn't change even if my husband got a better-paying job.

A New Path Forward

The assumption that women should be the ones to curtail their careers to handle the management of the household—or simply try to do it all!—is unrealistic these days. It also devalues the work that women do, both outside and inside the home. It treats a woman's career as a precursor to marriage and potentially parenthood, not as a decades-long opportunity to build experience, relationships, confidence, capabilities, fulfillment—and wealth. It presumes women will be perfectly willing to cede our independent income to fulfill our duties as wife and mom: a job with endless hours replete with menial tasks but with no vacation days, no time off, and—oh, right—no pay. Or that we will simply pick up a second shift of (unpaid) work if we insist on retaining our jobs. When you think about it like that, it seems almost inconceivable.

And yet . . . Women *are* still the ones most likely to put their careers on hold—even when they're high earners. (Moms cut hours and quit working in much higher numbers than dads in the pandemic to care for kids at home.) And even if we work full-time, we're still taking on most of the household and caregiving duties. Fewer than a third of different-sex couples in a 2016 study had reached approximate equality in sharing housework. According to a 2020 report by the Institute for Women's Policy Research and Oxfam, women still spend two hours more *each day* cleaning, cooking, and running household errands. University of Texas researcher Joanna R. Pepin and her colleagues found recently that married mothers actually spend *more* time on housework than single mothers.

I knew plenty of women who worked full-time and also carried most of the load at home. One friend, Stacy, worked in sales in a New York City suburb. She and her husband both worked full-time—in fact, she earned more than he did—but he still expected her to have dinner on the table when he got home each night, as his own stay-at-home mom had done for him and his family growing up. Stacy was also the one who did all the grocery shopping and often shepherded their two kids around from school to sports practice to social activities. At one point, her family obligations became so great that she had to cut out of work early to squeeze in school pickups or grocery runs and was penalized by her company for not logging enough hours, nearly costing Stacy her job (and the family its main source of income).

And Stacy's situation isn't unusual. The Institute for Women's Policy Research–Oxfam report, which looked at data from the Bureau of Labor Statistics' American Time Use Survey, found that women across the country who work full-time spend 22 percent more time on unpaid household work than men who *work exactly the same number of hours* outside the home do, on average. Other research has found that women who earn more than their husbands actually take on even *more* of the household responsibilities, too.

The question is why.

CHAPTER 12

Letting Go

How to Free Yourself from Expectations That Hold You Back at Home

The chores of the day kill the dreams of a lifetime.

—MELINDA GATES

YOU MAY NOT be married, and you may not have kids, but you probably still have some notions about who should be responsible for what household tasks in a relationship.

Growing up, we often adopt ideas about gender roles from watching our parents or seeing how other couples are portrayed in popular culture. And those ideas can then inform the way we approach the division of labor if we do get into a relationship and the childcare responsibilities if we also have kids. The challenge these days is that many women—and men—have been conditioned to believe that women *should* pick up most of the household chores and childcare duties. And that can be an overwhelming and self-defeating goal if we also have or want a flourishing career (and create resentment if we also bring home most of the income). Getting to a more equitable division of responsibilities at home requires that both partners take a closer look at the assumptions they brought into the relationship and be willing to adapt to the realities of their unique situation, rather than be bound by expectations or cultural beliefs.

From a purely practical perspective, if we have a capable partner, we won't have to voluntarily pick up most of the responsibilities for taking care of the home (and kids, if we have any). Unless, of course, we've been led to believe those are inherently our responsibilities.

In dozens of discussions I've had with wives and mothers in their twenties, thirties, forties, and fifties, it became clear that was still the case for many of us. So that means it's not *just* about getting our partners to step up at home and do a fair share of the work and childcare. It's also about being willing to let go of some of those responsibilities ourselves. And given women's cultural conditioning, that can be just as difficult. Why?

Some clues emerged in the conversations I had with working wives and mothers in comments like:

- It's just easier to do it myself.
- If I don't do it, it won't get done. (Or it won't get done *right*.)
- I can handle it all—and aren't women better at multitasking anyway?
- I feel guilty not spending more time with my kids.
- I feel selfish taking any *me* time.
- If I don't _____ (fill in the blank), I feel like I'm being a bad mom.

I know I've had all these thoughts at one time or another. They can affect any working woman with a partner or family, but can be particularly stressful—and resentment breeding—for those who are the main providers for a household. In this chapter, we'll examine where some of these common beliefs come from and how to transform them so we can pursue our ambitions and full earning potential without guilt.

Let's take a look at some of the biggest offenders.

Belief #1: If I Don't Do It, It Won't Get Done

There is some truth to this one. Research shows that while men's attitudes about women working have evolved, their willingness to pick up more household tasks has been slower to catch up. Recent surveys find that men between eighteen and thirty-four years old in opposite-sex relationships are no more likely to divide household labor equitably than older couples are. "I think a big reason is simply that men are happy for their partner to bring home another paycheck, but aren't as happy to do more chores," *New York Times* gender and families correspondent Claire Cain Miller said in a recent article.

The sneaking suspicion that we're taking on a disproportionate amount of responsibilities at home often arises long before kids arrive (if kids arrive at all). Many women complained to me that their husbands were "helpless" around the house—or acted that way, anyway—assuming their wives would pick up tasks like laundry and cooking that their mothers had once done for them.

One friend, Suzanne, the founder of a literary arts organization, remembers getting home from facilitating a six-day professional training to find the house a mess and her husband sitting on the couch. This became a common occurrence, one that made her increasingly anxious as she began working longer hours to build her business and support their lifestyle. She had the choice of ignoring the mess, asking her husband to step up, or just doing it herself. "Asking him often meant an uncomfortable conversation," she told me. "It was usually easier just to do it myself." (That was a common refrain among many women I interviewed.)

But there are signs that things are changing. In marriages formed before 1992, researchers found that both husbands *and* wives seemed satisfied to have the wife do most of the housework and childcare. But later studies that looked at marriage data from 2006 found that the most content—and even the most sexually satisfied—couples were those who divided housework and childcare the most equitably.

Men *have* doubled the overall time they spend on housework since 1965. But a gap remains: Women still do about two hours more household work per day. And working women are more than three times as likely as their male counterparts to run the household, nine times more likely to manage their kids' schedules, and nearly eight times more likely to require time off to care for a sick child.

Conventional gender norms are hard to break—especially when they go all the way back to childhood. Even today, data show boys are assigned fewer chores than girls are and get paid more for them! When those boys get older, they also tend to pick up the kind of household work that pays more, like fixing the car, landscaping the yard, and doing repairs around the home. Men still gravitate toward tasks that involve feats of brute strength or technical skills like carpentry, which are deemed more "masculine." Meanwhile, women pick up the lowest-paying work, like laundry, cooking, cleaning, and childcare—tasks that our own moms were most likely to do. Of course, that's also the work that must be done on a daily basis, while yardwork and DIY projects can be done on weekends or whenever there's time. So this conventional division of labor means women end up working at home every day and for more hours.

Linda, a mom of two in Arizona, remembers that even as her work hours and her earnings as a financial planner surpassed her husband's, he refused to take on additional housework that he considered women's work. "So I was making most of the money. I was paying all the bills. But I was also arranging childcare, child activities, making sure the kids got where they needed to be, getting them off in the morning. It all fell on me. I was also the one who had to try and manage all the spending. I did all grocery shopping and cleaning," she remembers.

When I asked what her husband did, she replied: "He took care of the lawn."

Let's be real here. Childhood chore assignments aside, neither gender is inherently better qualified to fold laundry or pull weeds or do many other necessary household tasks. What it usually comes down to is what we each enjoy most (or hate least) or feel most comfortable doing. Some chores get picked up naturally—one person likes to cook, another prefers to do the grocery shopping. But there will inevitably be those tasks that no one wants to do—at least not every single day. And they need to be either split or outsourced.

Not everyone can afford a housekeeper, of course, and dust and dishes pile up daily, which means you either need to talk about who's doing what and when or risk having it grow into a much larger problem. "When women tell me about how much they're doing at home, I always ask them: What does your husband do? They tell me he doesn't *care* as much. It seems like so many women are just assuming the lead at home," Heather, the thirty-four-year-old New York City sales director, told me. "That's why talking about it is important. I've been absolutely upfront with my husband that we need to split the labor fairly."

Belief #2: If I Don't Do It, It Won't Get Done Right

Even though we know what a Sisyphean task it is to maintain a tidy home, especially with kids, there's still a social equating of a perfect home with a perfect home life, an illusion perpetuated by Instagram influencers, glossy magazine spreads, and popular HGTV shows. It's easy to fear being socially shamed for falling short of expectations that we've internalized about what our home *should* look like: dust-free shelves, home-cooked meals, well-appointed furniture, and a well-dressed woman at the helm with a ready smile and (if she has a family) her adorable kids by her side.

I pretended that I didn't care whether our home was perfectly put together, but I soon realized I actually had some pretty deep-seated expectations about what our home and home life should look like based on my own suburban upbringing and the TV-show depictions of home life I'd grown up with. I felt responsible for almost all things kid- and home-related. And true confession: Deep down I believed that I was innately better at maintaining a well-furnished, well-kept home and making sure the kids ate a healthy diet, dressed well, and got good grades. After all, my mom had been the one in charge of home decorating, plus meal prep, clothes shopping, and homework help when I was growing up.

It wasn't a conscious bias, but it began to manifest itself in offhand comments I made about the way Victor did things. When I learned he'd served the kids chicken nuggets and applesauce for the third time in a row one week, I was overcome with a dizzying swirl of shame (what if the other parents find out?), anger (how hard is it to make a box of pasta?), superiority (I could surely do better!), and guilt (so why didn't I?).

I complained about the potato chips and doughnuts Victor regularly brought home. (Fig Newtons were the closest things to cookies I'd had as a kid, and soda was banned entirely.) I complained about the way he did laundry, throwing my delicates in with the boys' socks and under-wear in hot water. And the way he cleaned, passing over the eco-friendly, softly scented cleaners I'd bought in favor of scrubs with concentrations of bleach so high that even in the middle of winter I had to open the windows after he cleaned. I complained when he rearranged the living room furniture after vacuuming, and about the cheap bath mats and hand towels he bought. No matter what I said, what I really meant was, *That's not how I would have done it.*

"I can't do anything right," he sighed one night, after I exploded in frustration when I couldn't find the boys' pj's he'd put away. "I'm just trying to help out here."

I finally realized that in order to support the life we wanted finan-cially and be able to enjoy it, I needed to let Victor take on more tasks and appreciate that he might have a different (possibly better) approach, even if it didn't meet my specifications. I needed to release some of the preconceived ideas *I'd* been holding on to around the division of house-hold labor and the way things should be done. And I needed to be clearer about what was important for me to own.

That required taking a more probing look at my assumptions and what actually mattered to me. Beneath many of the arguments we had,

I realized, was a nagging fear that my husband and I may not share the same values. When I brought home organic applesauce and yogurt for the boys and then he gave them potato chips, I worried that I cared more about us all eating healthy than he did and was even more determined to take on that task. When he let them eat on the couch in front of the TV, instead of having dinner at the table together, I feared the kids would miss out on a favorite family tradition that I had growing up and thought was important.

The problem was, outside of agreeing that we wanted to raise kids in New York City and send them to a good public school, my husband and I had never talked explicitly about our values and how we wanted to raise our kids. I had just assumed that I would be the one making the decisions about what we ate, how we furnished the home, what the kids wore, and when they went to bed—as my mom had. I hadn't factored in the possibility that I might be working so much, and so late, that I'd be the one missing dinner some nights, falling asleep on the couch before the kids went to bed, or responding to work emails while my husband and the boys played cards or watched Netflix together.

My husband had quietly started picking up the slack as my earnings, responsibilities, and hours at work grew. And I had let him. But we had never talked about what was important to us in terms of raising the kids and running the household. So, belatedly, we did. I realized that, as long as we both committed to ensuring the kids eat healthy food most of the time, I didn't really care whether it was my husband or I who picked up take-out or made dinner at home. Nor did I care that much if my kids ate the same meal three nights in a row as long as it was relatively nutritious and included fruits or vegetables. And I didn't mind if the kids ate on the couch occasionally, as long as we both agreed to have some meals together each week as a family.

Once I was able to assure myself that my husband and I did share the same basic values (even if he was more lax about letting them eat junk food), I recognized that a lot of the feelings bubbling up were related to my guilt at not being more involved—not real concerns about the kids' well-being. Being honest with myself allowed me to loosen my grasp a little. I started to let go of some responsibilities, and of my singular vision of how they should be carried out, and to prioritize those things that mattered most, rather than feeling like I had to be involved in every aspect of our household. In my case, it was ultimately less about dividing tasks straight down the middle and more about figuring out what worked for us at a certain point in time—if I had to work late three nights a week, for example, it made sense for him to take care of dinner those nights—and determining what was most important to me and what I could let go.

Mandi, the thirty-two-year-old mom who lives outside New York City, says she became accustomed to picking up most of the childcare responsibilities and household tasks when she was on maternity leave from her digital content job. "I gained confidence in caring for our baby because I had to—I wasn't special. But then I got so focused on the baby, I didn't leave a lot of room for my husband to help," she told me. "I've had to recognize that I can self-sabotage by setting up the baby to need me."

She remembers when she was working remotely during the pandemic, asking her husband to feed their baby while she took a conference call. "And then I hear the way he's eating, and I barged in there to show him how to hold the spoon the 'right' way. And the next thing you know, I'm feeding him and my husband is off doing another project," she recalls. "Now when he sees me doing something with the baby and he says, 'Oh, I could never do that as well,' I realize it's important for me to say 'yes, you can.'"

Belief #3: I Need to Give
100 Percent to My Family and to My Job

Even when women say their spouses willingly pick up more of the housework, adding kids to the mix ratchets up the pressure on working moms. Pediatrician Alison Escalante blames it on the "should storm." The moment that parenthood approaches, she says, women get caught between two incompatible beliefs. "Mothers should fully devote themselves to their children. And workers, whether parents or not, should fully commit themselves to their work," she writes in *Psychology Today*.

These competing beliefs can set us up to fail from the start. Then we often end up internalizing our inability to do both simultaneously, deeming ourselves at fault for our failure to measure up to—let's be honest—impossible standards. So why do we continue to subscribe to these self-defeating ideals?

While women have been raised to be the primary caregivers and optional breadwinners, men are still raised to be the primary breadwinners and optional caregivers. That continues to inform the way many of us approach our careers, our marriages, and our share of the household responsibilities—whether or not we have kids. The difference is, women often don't feel like the caregiving role is optional, even if we have the more demanding, high-paying career.

After several therapy sessions, it became clear that it wasn't postpartum depression I was suffering from after my second son was born (the initial diagnosis). I was suffering from Supermom complex—this belief that I could be the primary breadwinner but had to be the primary caregiver, too, or else I was somehow shirking my duties as a mom, and my family would suffer the consequences. *I* would suffer the consequences.

This may seem illogical. And yet, consider this: Working mothers spend as much time doing activities with their children today as *stay-at-home* moms did in the 1970s.

The rise of "intensive mothering" over the past three decades coincided with the rise in moms working outside the home, creating an untenable situation for women who either didn't want to or couldn't afford to put their careers on hold. "The moment I started in pediatric practice 10 years ago, I knew there was a problem," Escalante writes in another *Psychology Today* article. "The stress mothers feel is not because they aren't working hard enough, aren't mindful enough, aren't organized and efficient enough . . . [It's that] the cultural ideal of motherhood is an all-absorbing devotion to her children."

And it runs deep. Belgian researchers Loes Meeussen and Colette van Laar, who tracked the rise and impact of intensive parenting, found that moms bore the burden across Western cultures—still expected to be fully devoted to the task of caring for their kids, even putting their kids' needs before their own. This pervasive social identity had spread beyond affluent moms to middle-class and even working-class moms, they found, and was deeply entwined in a woman's sense of self. In other words, if we failed to devote ourselves fully to the cultivation and nurturing of our kids, we'd fail to fulfill a basic part of our identity. No pressure there!

In fact, this pressure to be the perfect (read: super-involved) mom, they found, led women to actually take over household and childcare tasks from their partner and, not surprisingly, to experience parental burnout at far greater rates. It also made it much more difficult to balance a career, ultimately leading many women to curtail their career ambitions.

"The way it was traditionally set up is that the man is the breadwinner, and the woman does *everything* else," says Michelle, the thirty-eight-year-old Brooklyn mom who runs a consulting business and makes more than double what her husband does as a writer. "So there was a little bit of friction when we were first together, and we realized I made a lot more. That had a lot to do with confronting these roles he assumed we'd fill. But then he adjusted to it."

Still, she admits that *she* had the tougher time adjusting to their shifting roles after they had their daughter. Because she runs her own business, she found it difficult to take any time off after the birth. Her husband took paid leave and ended up staying home with the baby for more than four months. Michelle says she tried to work from home. "I was on the laptop answering emails with my baby asleep on my chest three days after giving birth," she remembers. "But my husband basically became the primary caregiver. And I was really uncomfortable about that. It didn't feel natural, and I had terrible postpartum anxiety . . . It was like this feeling that *I am supposed to be with her.* I really had to examine that."

I remember thanking my husband every time he "watched the kids" when they were young, as if this were not a required duty as their dad. (In his defense, he didn't make a big deal about it—I did.) My expectations were so low for him initially that I would thank him profusely every time he cooked a meal for the family and washed up afterward, or when he washed and folded the laundry or took the kids to a weekend music class. Not only would I thank him, but I would *apologize* when I wasn't able to take them, or when I had to work late and wasn't able to get them from daycare. I didn't even realize how often I was doing it until a friend of mine pointed it out and reminded me that my husband was as much their parent as I was.

Yet I continued to insist on doing most of the childcare, refusing to cede the caregiving role to my husband in my mind even after he quit his full-time job, began freelancing from home, and started to pick up more responsibilities around the house. This actually started to create tension between us, since he felt like I wasn't recognizing the unpaid work *he* was doing. (Sound familiar?)

It culminated one night in a shouting match in our kitchen. I'd come home after work for dinner before heading out to a friend's book party. My husband and I were standing at the kitchen counter, arguing over who would go to the boys' parent-teacher conferences the next evening. Both of us wanted to go, but only one of us could, as the other would need to stay home and watch the boys, who were then both in elementary school. As I argued that their schooling was *my* purview, the fight escalated. "Why?" he asked. "Why not me? I do everything else."

I felt my face flush with rage. At that point, I was working in a new job at a news organization headquartered in New Jersey. In order to make the morning news meeting, I had to leave for the office around 7:00 a.m. I'd wake the boys, kiss them good morning, and then rush off to catch a shuttle to the office, which wasn't located near any public transportation. At night, the commute home could take anywhere from sixty to ninety minutes. I'd often arrive home just as they were finishing dinner and end up eating alone. I felt like I was grasping for anything I could hold on to that would keep me tethered to my family and allow me to feel like I was still essential to its functioning.

I still spent time with the boys on weekends and went over their homework many evenings. And I arranged to drop them off at school on days when I could come into the office a little later. But without my realizing—or acknowledging it, anyway—my husband, who was now working about thirty hours a week from home as a contract editor, had begun to pick up most of the household slack. "Honey, face it. You are the primary breadwinner," he said as we faced off in the kitchen. "And I am the primary caregiver."

"No, you're not!" I insisted adamantly. "We share caregiving duties."

"Well, I get the boys ready and take them to school most days. I pick them up. I take them to their doctor's appointments," he said, and listed off a host of other responsibilities he'd picked up recently.

I refused to listen, stomping out the door to meet my friend. The idea of ceding the caregiving role seemed inconceivable. Later that night, when I recounted the argument, my friend listened patiently, then asked: "Jenn, what exactly would he have to do for you to think of him as the primary caregiver? I mean, look at you—you're out tonight and he's home, putting them to bed."

She was right, of course. And so was he. But that only made me feel worse. It turns out that even when our partners willingly take over more of the parenting duties, we still have to deal with the residual guilt of not doing them ourselves. Whether it's culturally driven or not, the feeling is real.

I wondered what the perfect solution would be. Would it be a fifty-fifty split, with each of us bringing in near-equal earnings and dividing up the work at home and caregiving responsibilities evenly? That was what many of the women I'd interviewed said they wanted. But that was unrealistic. The chances of both halves of a couple consistently earning the same amount are slim. It's also not easy to split the responsibilities at home straight down the middle when kids' activities overlap, and the lines between work and personal time continue to blur. Plus, evenly dividing up our tasks wouldn't have solved one of the biggest issues. What I wanted most was more quality time with my kids and my husband, and the chance to connect with my boys in a meaningful way—not another dozen household tasks added to my to-do list.

Belief #4: I Can Handle It All—And Aren't Women Better at Multitasking Anyway?

No. Actually, the data show women are no better at it than men. In fact, a growing body of research shows *no one* is good at it. Researchers have found human brains actually cannot manage multiple activities simultaneously—particularly when two tasks are similar and compete to use the same part of the brain. Not that that's kept us from trying!

Leah Ruppanner, an associate professor of sociology and co-director of the Policy Lab at the University of Melbourne, found that while mothers are more apt to take on more and try to multitask, the result is *not* that we're more efficient, just that we're more stressed out. While both parents report feeling more rushed or pressed for time after they have a baby, she found the effect was twice as high for mothers as for fathers.

"If I could do it all over again, I would have hired more help," said Beth, a mom of three who runs a digital media company in New York. She and her husband were earning about the same salary when they had their first child, but she liked her job better, and it had benefits, so he quit to stay home and started doing projects on a freelance basis. They left New York City for the suburbs when their kids were four and two and she was pregnant with their third. Her husband picked up some of the household work and pitched in with school pickups and other responsibilities, but she says she ended up managing all the activities and logistics after he struggled to stay on top of them.

"The kids' academic schedules, extracurricular activities, medical appointments, teacher conferences, tutors, religious education requirements, school volunteer obligations, social schedules—oh, the birthday parties!—summer camp registrations . . . planning family vacations. All of that fell to me," she remembers. "When you have three kids and a full-time career, it's just an ungodly amount of stuff to handle. And I was a pretty low-key mom compared to my friends."

The pressure of being the main earner, and also trying to do a significant amount of household tasks, started to get to her. Ultimately she transferred to her company's Midwest office, a move that significantly reduced their cost of living and her commute time and improved their quality of life. Still, she acknowledges that reaching out for, or hiring, more help earlier on would have saved a significant amount of stress. "I just barreled through my checklists feeling stressed out and resentful," Beth said. "In retrospect, it would have been better to regularly set aside time to communicate everything that needed to be done to keep our family life on track. That would have allowed us to consciously divide the work in a more equitable way."

Sometimes shifting that balance and easing that strain is as simple as asking a partner to step up.

Nadja, the thirty-six-year-old marketing manager, was pregnant with the first of their two kids when she took the senior management role at the legal tech firm in New York. "For a while, I was just trying to do it all," she recalls. When she wasn't working, she was cooking meals, taking prenatal yoga classes, reading reviews of baby gear, building their registry, and helping to prepare their nursery. She and her husband hadn't talked about it—she'd just instinctively started handling all those responsibilities, on top of her full-time job, even though her husband could work from home and had a more flexible schedule. "There came a point at which it was just overwhelming," she told me.

In fact, she remembers the exact point. It happened one weekend morning during her second trimester. "The garbage needed to be taken out, and I was tying it up, and the smell was making me queasy. And I remember thinking, 'It's the weekend, and I'm stuck doing all these household chores.' I was so exhausted, and I just broke down and started crying, which was very unusual for me. And I said, 'I can't do this anymore.' My husband got really worried."

So they sat down together and talked about what had to get done, and he committed to taking on more of the household chores like making dinner—and, yes, taking out the trash. "I realized I had been doing everything and *hoping* he would help, but I hadn't actually asked him," she told me. "Making it more visible to him was really helpful. He did step up, and he took several things off my plate, and that also lessened the mental load for me."

"Unpaid work is really invisible, undervalued work that takes hours and hours of time," Eve Rodsky, author of the bestseller *Fair Play*, told me. "How can we value women's time if we don't recognize the work it takes to keep a household running smoothly? We need to invite men to the table and make the invisible, visible."

When the pandemic forced many parents to work from home with kids who were attending school remotely, a lot of those "invisible" everyday tasks women typically picked up became much more visible to everyone in the household—and the sheer amount of competing priorities made multitasking impossible, prompting many women to reevaluate how the unpaid work was being divided.

Kristy Wallace, CEO of Ellevate Network, a global professional women's network, and mother of three kids ages five, seven, and ten, says that when her family began to quarantine, she initially tried to put to-gether schedules for her kids and prep food ahead of time for snacks and meals so that she could work effectively from home. But by day three, with the five of them together in their New York home, she says, "It just fell apart. I was completely overwhelmed."

So she wrote out a list of everything that had to get done during the day—from making beds to making breakfast to putting dirty clothes in the hamper. "I realized I had the capacity to do about twenty percent of the list, but I was carrying one hundred percent of it. It was all in my brain," she told me. So she called a family meeting. "And I told them, I can effectively do about twenty percent of this. We need to figure out who is going to do the rest."

After she went through the list, tasks were divided not just between her and her husband but among all family members. "It forced us to look at what every single person has to do to support our ecosystem," says Wallace.

Belief #5: I Feel Guilty Not Spending More Time with the Kids

This is a biggie for working moms. Parental guilt is real, no doubt. But is there any research-backed reason to worry about taking time for your-self, or time at work, at the expense of spending more time with your family?

It's been more than a decade since the first meta-analysis—which looked at sixty-nine studies over fifty years—established that kids whose moms worked when they were young suffered *no* negative conse-quences. Since then, a slew of studies have gone further, showing that outcomes among kids of working moms are often *better* than among kids whose moms stay at home. They've found that kids with working moms are more successful in school and have lower levels of depression and anxiety. Daughters of working moms grow up to be more successful in their careers, and sons grow up to take on a more equitable share of household responsibilities. "Kids of working moms grow into happy adults," concluded a 2018 Harvard study.

"Women are socialized to believe mothers should stay home with their children, so when you separate from your kids every day for work, it can be painful," acknowledged Harvard Business School professor Kathleen McGinn, who led the study, which ultimately analyzed surveys of more than one hundred thousand men and women. "As we gradually understand that our children aren't suffering, I hope the guilt will go away."

The same holds true for taking time for ourselves. In fact, if we don't make time for self-care, it becomes much harder to take care of everything and everyone else in our lives. "Generally, you're working at a deficit unless you find a way to fuel yourself," Stephanie Kramer, a New York marketing executive and mother who's writing a book about pregnancy and work, reminded me. "It shouldn't feel like guilt—it should feel like the right thing to do, knowing all of the responsibility you are carrying."

In fact, taking time to care for yourself and your needs may actually help you be more present, engaged, and energetic when you *are* with your kids so they can get the most out of that time.

In a study published a few years ago, Amy Hsin, from Queens College–City University of New York, and Christina Felfe, of the University of St. Gallen in Switzerland, found that mothers who work full-time often trade quantity for quality when it comes to time with their kids. They tend to spend less time doing unstructured activities, like watching TV together or sitting beside their kids as they play video games, but more time on activities that "positively influenced children's development." Activities like reading or doing arts-and-crafts projects together. As a result, Hsin and Felfe said, kids with working mothers actually tend to have improved cognitive development, compared with those with stay-at-home moms.

In other words, how we spend the time we have with our kids can be more important for their development and well-being than how much time we spend with them.

Allowing dads the chance to spend more time with the kids also has positive effects for both. This seems intuitive, but there's actual research behind it, too, showing that the more engaged dads are in a positive way, the better the social, behavioral, and psychological outcomes for kids. But while we may know that rationally, it can be difficult emotionally to give up that time.

"When I went back to work after having our son, it gave me comfort to know my son would be at home with Dad," remembers Adrienne, a thirty-three-year-old chief operating officer of a marketing analytics firm in Los Angeles, who became the sole breadwinner after she and her husband had their son three years ago. "Still, I stressed about the guilt of being away from our son. It hurt me to my core."

Adrienne's husband is supportive and helped to reinforce the fact that it's about the quality, not quantity, of time—and that her financial contributions to the family are equally important. "He reminds me, 'The way you are there for him is that you're providing for him,'" she says. "Sometimes I actually sit down with our son and say, 'Do you like these things? Do you like living here? I love buying you toys and having this house, and part of the reason I can do that is because I go to work and I take these phone calls for work.'"

"Sometimes I think, what if things were different and I could spend most of my time with our son?" Adrienne told me. "But I also realize I am probably a better mom because I am out of the house working, doing something I love, and when I am home, all I have is love for him."

There is something to this. A study published by the American Psychological Association found that moms with jobs, whether part- or full-time, tend to be healthier and happier than moms who stay at home during their children's infancy and preschool years. And when researchers from the University of Maryland started examining how working parents have been spending their time at home, they discovered something interesting. "By increasingly incorporating their children in their own leisure activities, parents deepened their time to circumvent the simple zero-sum trade-off between work and other areas of their lives," they found. In other words: We may actually be figuring out how to schedule our downtime activities more efficiently so that we get more time to connect with our kids, pawning off some of the housework to our partners (or outsourcing it) and incorporating our kids into activities we might have once done alone, like exercising.

That held true in our home, where we often brought our kids with us to walk around the park or to go to the neighborhood store to pick up a few groceries, just to get some extra time with them.

While those of us who are working moms may carry residual guilt for not having more time with our families, the research is pretty clear that our kids are doing just fine: The quality of time we spend with them is more important than the quantity of time. And allowing men to pick up more caregiving duties can be beneficial for everyone.

Not only is it insulting to both genders to assume that women are somehow inherently better suited to stay home with the kids and run the household while men are better suited to bring home the income, but there's also no evidence to support this model as ideal for a family. Especially today. In fact, both parents may end up paying the price if they're constricted to one domain. My dad regrets that he didn't have the chance to forge deeper connections and experiences with my sister and me growing up—it still makes him sad that we never considered living with him. Meanwhile, my mom gave up a decade of her career (and earnings) to stay home with us and had to start her career all over again in her forties, going back to school to get an MBA in the midst of her divorce.

It's worth noting, too, that researchers have found women have no special disposition or genetic advantage that makes us naturally better parents than men. One Israeli study, which compared hormone levels and brain scans of primary caregivers in both heterosexual and same-sex male couples, found that *all* of them—whether female or male—showed activation in what scientists call the "parenting network" of the brain as well as increased levels of oxytocin. In other words, engaging in hands-on parenting can prime a parent's brain for caregiving in the same way pregnancy and childbirth do. "What we thought of as a purely maternal circuit can also be turned on just by being a parent," neuroscientist Kevin Pelphrey, a professor of neurology at the University of Virginia, told *Science* magazine. "It's clear that we're all born with the circuitry to help us be sensitive caregivers."

Nor are men genetically predisposed to be better breadwinners. In fact, when Christin Munsch, the University of Connecticut assistant professor of sociology, analyzed fifteen years of data on married couples from the National Longitudinal Survey of Youth, she found that being the primary breadwinner actually has a detrimental effect on men's health, especially if they're the sole provider. As men earned a greater share of the household income, she found, they experienced greater declines in both their psychological well-being and overall health. (Interestingly, being the breadwinner seems to have the opposite effect on women. As we earn more, Munsch found, our psychological well-being and level of happiness actually rise.)

Finding a Better Balance

The fact is, our society has placed expectations on both women and men that have little to do with our innate talents or what we may individually value or enjoy.

Let's face it. Not every woman likes cooking and home decorating. Not every man wants to devote himself to his job. We may be assigning roles to each other without any consideration of what we are actually good at and what we enjoy doing. And in assigning breadwinning to men—and letting them off the hook when it comes to most caregiving and household responsibilities—we do a real disservice to women. The reality today is that a woman's income is often essential to the household, and that income is in jeopardy if she's also expected to pick up the bulk of the household duties. (Assigning the lead caregiving role to women can similarly do a disservice to men, who have less of an opportunity then to deepen the bonds with their kids and be more involved in their lives.)

Ultimately, everyone should have the opportunity to make the contributions they want inside and outside the home. Both men *and* women should have the chance to pursue their professional dreams and their full earning potential and to engage in activities that are personally fulfilling, too. That's possible only when there's an equitable division of labor at home. And that's not a static arrangement. It can mean shifting most of the household responsibilities from one partner to the other so that each gets the chance to focus more fully on building a career or a business at different times.

It became clear that in order for me to be an effective (and happy) provider, my husband and I would need to recalibrate the roles and responsibilities we assumed we'd have once we started a family. And we'd have to let go of the cultural expectations we'd been hanging on to that didn't serve us—along with any guilt or shame that came with not meeting them.

What if, instead of feeling bound to a seventy-year-old division of household and paid work that no longer works for many of us, we created a new model that allows us to honor our ambitions, whatever they are? One that allows us to differentiate between what we truly want versus what our culture tells us we *should* want? One that gives us the chance to leverage our skills and indulge in more of what brings us joy, rather than feeling like we must take on certain tasks or risk being branded a bad spouse or parent? One that allows each partner to feel that she or he is contributing an equitable amount to the overall functioning of the household—whatever form that takes?

That doesn't mean splitting the work fifty-fifty, an impossibility for most. It means dividing up responsibilities in a way that respects each other's time and abilities and allows both of you to have quality time with each other—and with your kids, if you have them—and also have time to devote to the passions or pursuits that fill you up and bring you joy.

CHAPTER 13

Beyond "Having It All"

What Do Working Women Really Need to Succeed?

We have to understand that we can have it all, if we're not trying to do it all at once.
—MADELEINE ALBRIGHT, FORMER SECRETARY OF STATE

IT'S HARD TO write a book about breadwinning without addressing the question that's plagued working women for nearly forty years now: *Can we have it all?* A lot of digital ink has been spilled debating the question, and I bet you're probably sick of hearing it. Yet it persists. Even when I spoke with women who were just starting their careers, they told me they'd wondered about it. And they weren't sure of the answer.

Does anyone really have it *all?* Who knows? And who cares? The idea of having it all, like that Supermom ideal, mostly just leaves working moms feeling like we've failed for not living up to some superhuman standard. It's not unlike the notion of "work-life balance." That's another fallacy that (1) men never seem to worry about and (2) is about as realistic as having a perfectly fifty-fifty household in which both partners earn precisely the same amount and do exactly the same amount of housework. That's not how life works! And holding any of these concepts up as ideals to aspire to is not just unrealistic; it's disempowering. It undermines our own sense of agency, happiness, and satisfaction.

The question to ask is this: *Are you setting yourself up for the life that you want? That* is the breadwinning mindset. And it is one that allows us to determine for ourselves what we want in our lives and to define for ourselves what success is.

Consider that men are already brought up to think, *What do I want for my life? And how am I going to get it?* Once women start thinking like that, it begins to inform all of our choices so that they support the life we want. *Having it all* is a meaningless ideal. Breadwinning is real. It is a means to an end. It gives us the tools to create our own happy ending. And it enables us to decide what that is.

When you think like a breadwinner, you have the chance to think about what you really want and how to make it happen. That's what breadwinning allows you to do. You take the steps to build your credit. You invest money to start growing wealth. You save so that you don't get stuck. You spend with intent so that you get the value you want. You know where your dollars go—in fact, you tell your dollars where to go. And you create opportunities for yourself. You stop trying to measure up to some external ideal, and you start asking yourself what *you* need in your life to feel fulfilled and happy.

But it's worth looking at why this question of having it all has persisted for so long: Why are women still being made to feel like we must choose between a career and kids? Why do systemic barriers and biases still exist that keep us from reaching our full potential professionally—whether we have kids or not? Why have our congressional lawmakers, and most of our companies, failed to adopt the sorts of policies that would make it easier for all of us to ascend as far as we want to go professionally without feeling as if we must sacrifice our personal lives to get there? In this chapter, we'll look at those questions and how we can take charge of our happiness and define our "all"—on our own terms.

Where Did the Notion of "Having It All" Come From, Anyway?

What's interesting, and a little ironic, is that the woman who's credited with popularizing the term expressed no interest in having kids herself. What she did want was a career and a partner—and a lot of great sex. But we'll get to that.

I actually met her briefly when I was general manager of some of the women's magazine sites at Hearst, including *Cosmopolitan*. Helen Gurley Brown still had an office there well into her eighties, though she'd long since given up editing the magazine. Yes, the woman who helped make "having it all" an aspiration for working women everywhere was the same woman who'd once decreed that there be no mentions of motherhood in the magazine she edited for nearly three decades. Brown, in fact, became a household name after her bestseller *Sex and the Single Girl* was published in 1962, and didn't get married herself until she was in her late thirties. Reportedly, she even argued against the title of the other bestseller she'd write two decades later, which would end up having a more enduring legacy than the book itself: *Having It All*. It's also worth noting that the book cover specifically referred to love, success, sex, and money. There was no mention of marriage or family.

Brown—who turned *Cosmopolitan* into one of the most popular magazines in the world with a mix of sex and beauty tips and career advice—was actually not the first to publish a book with that title. In 1980, two years before Brown's book, Joyce Gabriel and Bettye Baldwin published *Having It All: A Practical Guide to Managing a Home and a Career*. True to its title, the pair offered "practical" tips for working moms trying to manage their households, such as "strive to do two things at once, like letting your nail polish set while you blow-dry your hair." (Of course, multitasking is second nature for working moms now. And it looks a lot more like checking work email on your phone while blow-drying your hair, or packing the kids' lunches while practicing the pitch you have to give later that morning.) It was Brown's bestseller, though, that propelled the term into the mainstream lexicon, where it took on a life of its own.

Years later, Brown herself said, "I never, so to speak, had it all. But I had *my* all, which is what I wanted: work and love."

And that is key. What Brown was actually advocating in her book was a breadwinner mindset. She encouraged women to pursue their own career success, make their own money, and seek out a partner who could appreciate that. Brown did so herself, and created the life that she wanted with both a lucrative career and a partner she loved. You can bet she wasn't asking herself if she had it all. Because by her definition, she did.

When "Having It All" Became "Doing It All"

Somehow, over the years, "having it all" became shorthand for women with flourishing families and successful careers. When commentators asked "Can women have it all?" what they often meant was, Can a woman actually manage a career on top of all the caregiving and other work she does at home?

That's been the message for several years now from the men in power. Sure, women can have a career—as long as we are *also* willing to continue to manage the household and handle, or arrange for, childcare. This is where the conundrum of "having it all" started. Even if women were spending eight hours or more a day at work, nothing was expected to change at home. We were supposed to, I guess, just compress all the unpaid work we usually did neatly into our weekends and weekday evenings and sort out the remaining logistics: childcare, school drop-offs and pick-ups, playdates, and extracurricular activities. As if handling all these other responsibilities weren't also a full-time job.

When it comes down to it, what "having it all" really seems to mean is working two full-time jobs, only one of which pays. No wonder it feels like an impossible standard.

Dictating to women what we *should* aspire to rather than letting us decide what *we* want for our lives does not serve us. It's set up to leave us feeling "less than" if we choose not to get married or not to have a family or not to pursue every promotion at work. Or if we cannot seamlessly juggle all the responsibilities of being a wife, mother, and breadwinning career woman. So who *does* it serve? Mostly the men who don't want things to change at home. By asking only if *women* can have it all, the question implies that (1) men already do, and (2) it is women who must figure out whether they can continue to fulfill their duties as a wife and a mother and a household manager while *also* pursuing a successful career. (And if not, which will they choose?)

At its heart, "having it all" is not an ideal to aspire to but a perpetrator of not being or doing enough. It conveniently lets men off the hook by setting this up as an aspiration for women, while simultaneously putting the onus on us to accomplish it—and then treating it as a failure when we fall short. But in reality, it is the policies, biases, and assumptions perpetuated by men in power that have prevented so many of us from being able to realize our potential without burning ourselves out in the process. If we choose a different path, or we don't have it *all*, as defined by our culture, we have somehow failed. When in truth it is often the system that has failed us.

So, What If You Do Want Kids and a High-Powered Career?

So where does that leave those who do want to raise a family and rise to a senior-level role? In the coming pages, we'll examine the structural barriers and biases that can leave women wondering if we can do both effectively—where they come from and what it will take to upend them.

We'll also look at how to navigate around them in the meantime to set yourself up for success, and explore the types of policies that could better support working moms *and* dads (and anyone caring for a loved one) in the future.

If you're in your twenties or thirties and worry that you may one day have to choose between having a family and an ambitious career, rest assured it is possible to have both. But there can be a tension between the two. And that's not the result of any shortcoming on your part, but of a country that has fallen short in supporting working parents. (And of course, going back to caregiving, there's also the matter of partners picking up their fair share of household responsibilities.)

The family–work quandary is often framed as a uniquely female problem. But it's not, really. Dads want time with their kids, too, and with their partner (and for themselves!). They're just discouraged from asking for it. Corporate America has largely designated Dad as the primary provider and Mom as the main caregiver, and its policies and practices tend to reinforce that—even if most companies would never admit it. Adhering to those assumptions provides a convenient pretext for a company to overwork its male employees and to relegate its female employees to lower-profile, lower-paying roles that make it harder for us to reach the top.

Corporate policies and workplace cultures were designed to support the professional ascension of male breadwinners with stay-at-home wives, after all, and many have simply not evolved to match the realities of today's economy or households. This hurts both moms *and* dads, but only moms are made to feel guilty about it.

The Overwork Problem: A Case Study

A few years ago, Robin J. Ely, a business professor at Harvard University, and Irene Padavic, a sociology professor at Florida State University, were asked to advise a prominent consulting firm that wondered why just a few of its female hires progressed to the partner level. When the pair surveyed more than one hundred of the firm's male and female consultants about the disparity, most pointed to what the professors called the typical work-life narrative: "High-level jobs require extremely long hours, women's devotion to family makes it impossible for them to put in those hours, and their careers suffer as a result." (In a 2012 survey of more than 6,500 Harvard Business School alumni across various industries, they noted, 73 percent of men and 85 percent of women also invoked it to explain women's stalled advancement.)

"Believing this explanation doesn't mean it's true, however," the professors said.

Sure enough, as the two wrote in the *Harvard Business Review* in 2020, they found women weren't held back because of trouble balancing the competing demands of work and family—men, too, suffered from those and nevertheless advanced, they noted. "Women were held back because, unlike men, they were encouraged to take accommodations, such as going part-time and shifting to internally facing roles, which derailed their careers."

The core culprit, they found, was actually a culture of overwork. Most workers reported feeling emotionally conflicted by the firm's demand for 24-7 availability, with men and women alike describing "in heart-wrenching detail their interactions with disappointed children." But working moms paid the higher professional costs, they said, because of an institutional bias that moms should be the only ones to slow down.

When the researchers presented their findings, they were surprised to find that the firm's leaders nonetheless "continued to maintain that women were failing to advance because *they* had difficulty balancing work and family."

What the researchers realized was that framing it solely as a working moms' issue—that *women* feel uniquely conflicted because we have an innately stronger devotion to family that keeps us from focusing on our career progression—allowed male employees to justify their devotion to work at the expense of time with their families *and* let the firm avoid taking responsibility for the very real costs of promoting an always-on culture of overwork.

Like other businesses, the firm adhered to the narrative in corporate America that pushing employees to work longer hours gives a firm a competitive advantage (even if it means workers face wrenching choices at home, the erosion of personal time, and eventual burnout). But that's not necessarily true. In fact, there's growing evidence, as I mentioned earlier, that valorizing long work hours and an on-demand culture doesn't translate to better productivity and results. What it does do, though, is make it seem nearly impossible for anyone to advance to the highest echelons without fully committing to work at the expense of family and personal time. (Side note: It also leads to more employee health problems and turnover.)

The Harvard and Florida State researchers said they hoped that as more data show the business advantage of reasonable hours, this firm and others will shift in that direction, too. "If and when those forces gain traction, neither women nor men will feel the need to sacrifice the home or the work domain," they wrote. "Demand for change will swell, and women may begin to achieve workplace equality with men."

Clearly, most companies are not there yet. Workplace cultures and attitudes still need to evolve to better support us and our ambitions and to fully recognize our contributions at home and at work. And until government and corporate policies change, there will continue to be tension for any woman *or* man who has a family and big professional ambitions. We are still living in a corporate system that was designed to promote men's careers, often at the expense of family time, with women playing supporting roles.

Ultimately, asking whether women can "have it all" is just another distraction from the real question: What needs to change in order to allow us all the chance to be successful at home and at work? Let's work toward *that*.

What Do Working Moms Need to Succeed?

Really, it's the same as what working dads need: support. Because we can't possibly do it all. A breadwinning mindset is important. But raising a family while simultaneously managing a successful career or business also requires recognition from our partners, our employers, and our government of the value of both.

It requires that our culture recognize that each partner must pick up a fair share of the responsibilities at home. It requires that companies recognize that reasonable work hours, paid leave, and flexibility aren't just perks but critical for many working parents (and anyone caring for loved ones) in order for them to do their best work and ensure that they can sustain their employment. It requires that we recognize *as a country* that without childcare, and school schedules that more closely mirror work schedules, many parents—especially those who cannot afford childcare to fill in all the gaps between school and work schedules and school vacations—will continue to drop out of the workforce, placing additional financial strain on their families, and risk not having the chance to reach their professional potential. (We saw the effects when the pandemic suspended in-person schooling.) And as a society, we will be worse off for that. It requires a recognition that if we want more women in management and senior levels, we need to stop framing it as a choice between being an involved parent or having a high-powered career. This is beginning to happen, but creating lasting change will require a concerted and sustained effort from both genders.

It helps when we stop treating this as just a working *moms'* problem. Policies that benefit working moms benefit working dads, too. It's worth pointing out that while no one is going to regret not having done more household chores, most working dads say they wish they had more time to spend with their kids, too. In fact, surveys have found that many are experiencing the flipside of the "having it all" coin: They're still feeling pressure to be the main earner while also trying to be more involved as a dad. One study found that nearly six in ten male breadwinners with children would prefer to work fewer hours and have more time with their families, even if it meant taking a pay cut. One benefit of moving to a model where parents can share childcare and breadwinning responsibilities more equitably is that they both have the chance to spend time with their kids and form stronger bonds early on.

The broader solutions are pretty straightforward, and I'm certainly not the first to propose them. But actually implementing them on a large scale requires a major shift in thinking for those who still hold most of the power in this country. That requires an awareness and acknowledgment that we cannot continue to base our corporate policies, our school schedules, and our household division of labor on the assumption that women will simply stop working or scale back their careers when we have children. That's not just unfair, but also unrealistic for most families. (And it puts women in a precarious financial position.) It's hard to maintain a middle-class lifestyle on one parent's paycheck anymore. And what about single parents? Why are we perpetuating a system that's so archaic and rigid that it forces *anyone* to feel they must choose between having a child or having a paycheck?

The good news is that many companies and a growing number of politicians are starting to recognize this and to take steps to change it.

Better Benefits and Symmetric School Schedules

It is not unreasonable for companies to offer access to backup childcare (or even host their own on-site) and to provide several weeks of paid leave for new parents and those caring for ailing loved ones. It's not difficult for businesses that don't need workers to be on-site to allow employees to work remotely—as we learned in the pandemic—or to allow some flexibility with work schedules. In fact, these kinds of benefits can actually *save* companies money over time, helping to reduce missed workdays and office-space costs, improve employee productivity, and increase retention. Researchers have noted additional benefits, too. Let's take a closer look at each.

1. Subsidized Childcare

Ironically, Congress *did* pass legislation to provide working parents with subsidized childcare—half a century ago. The 1971 Comprehensive Child Development Act would have set up a network of nationally funded childcare centers to provide education, nutrition, and medical services on a sliding payment scale. It was vetoed by President Richard Nixon, who claimed it had "family-weakening implications." In the years since, no legislation has made it out of Congress, but childcare costs have skyrocketed. The average cost for daycare (not including extended hours) is more than $12,000 a year—more than a quarter of the median annual income for women *before* taxes are taken out. And the average annual costs for a nanny can be $30,000 or more.

A full 85 percent of employees in a Care.com survey said they wish their employer offered benefits like backup childcare access or discounted childcare. Unfortunately, the percent of companies that actually offer them now is significantly lower. (And that was before the pandemic.)

By early 2020, almost eight in ten parents with kids under the age of three—or about 11 million Americans—are working. Finding adequate and affordable care for their kids can be a challenge, and it's one that disproportionately affects women. In a 2018 survey conducted by the Center for American Progress, moms were 40 percent more likely than dads to report that they'd personally felt the negative impact of child-care issues on their careers. (And we know they cut hours or quit work more than dads did during the pandemic.)

Challenges in finding enough childcare coverage can force parents to cut hours or change jobs—or put careers on hold altogether. Even in normal times, when childcare arrangements fall short, it can mean missed workdays and lost productivity. That can also cost companies. A recent analysis by the national nonprofit Council for a Strong America, which represents a coalition of business executives, pastors, and military, sports, and law enforcement leaders, found that U.S. companies lose an estimated $12.7 billion annually when employees' childcare arrangements fall through.

That happens more often than you might think. A survey by the nonprofit research group Child Care Aware found that in a given six-month period (pre-pandemic), *45 percent* of working parents experienced childcare issues that led to more than four days of missed work. In fact, employers that provide access to childcare report that childcare services have decreased employee absences by 20 to 30 percent and reduced employee turnover by as much as 60 percent.

Patagonia was one of the first companies to offer subsidized on-site childcare, opening a childcare center at its headquarters in 1983. It has since opened one at its four-hundred-employee distribution center in Reno, Nevada, as well. The outdoor clothing company reported recently that 100 percent of its new moms had returned to work over the previous five years and estimates that it earns back 90 to 125 percent of its paid subsidy for the company's on-site childcare programs.

Providing on-site childcare isn't cheap, though, which may explain why only 4 percent of U.S. companies were offering free on-site childcare, with another 4 percent offering subsidized on-site care before the pandemic, according to the Society for Human Resource Management's 2019 Employee Benefits Survey. But the list—which includes big names like Boeing, Clif Bar, Cisco, Disney, Home Depot, and Procter & Gamble—was growing. And employers who've provided paid or subsidized care often say they can earn much of it back between tax credits and improved workplace productivity and retention.

The Families and Work Institute's *2016 National Study of Employers*, which includes a nationally representative group of employers, found that another 5 percent of employers overall and 9 percent of larger employers—including Google, Amazon, Facebook, Apple, and Prudential—contracted with a childcare provider to offer backup or emergency childcare services in case an employee's childcare arrangement falls through. That number was slowly growing before the pandemic. Starbucks captured headlines when it announced in late 2018 that it would offer subsidized backup childcare to all its employees for $1 an hour for in-home care and $5 per day for center-based care. Bright Horizons, the largest operator of employer-sponsored childcare centers, said in 2019 that it had seen a 70 percent increase in companies offering backup-care benefits over the previous five years.

ReadyNation, which represents more than two thousand senior business leaders, has also called on lawmakers "to protect and expand programs that enhance the affordability and availability of quality child care," which could incentivize more employers to provide access to it as they reopen offices post-pandemic.

2. Remote Work Options

A 2020 analysis by University of Chicago economics professors Jonathan Dingel and Brent Neiman found that nearly 40 percent of U.S. jobs—ranging from engineering to legal, business, and administrative roles—can be done entirely from home. Yet before the pandemic, only around 8 percent of all employees worked from home at least one day a week, according to the U.S. Bureau of Labor Statistics.

Of course, that changed with the pandemic, when many businesses were forced to allow employees to work remotely. And many said they wanted to maintain that flexibility even after it was safe to return to the office. Gallup reported that 60 percent of U.S. employees who had been working from home during the pandemic preferred to work remotely "as much as possible" in the future. That doesn't necessarily mean full-time but having the option to work remotely for at least part of the week. A separate survey by Morning Consult found that nearly half of those working remotely during the pandemic said their ideal arrangement would be to continue working from home one to four days a week. The shift was enough to prompt the *New York Times*'s questioning headline last year: "Is the Five-Day Office Week Over?"

For millions of workers, it may be. When the coronavirus pandemic forced many companies to move to a remote-work model, both workers and their employers found that productivity often improved. (That builds on research like a well-known study from 2014 led by Stanford University professor Nicholas Bloom, which tracked remote workers at a Chinese travel agency and found they were 13 percent more efficient than their office-based peers.) In a survey by the National Bureau of Economic Research, more than one-third of firms with employees who switched to remote work expected remote-work arrangements would remain more common at their companies even after the COVID-19 crisis ended. Employers overall predicted that 27 percent of their full-time employees would continue working from home after the pandemic, according to a survey released by the Federal Reserve Bank of Atlanta. And the number was even higher in some sectors—43 percent of employees in business services were expected to continue working remotely at least a few days a week.

Employers who do offer flexible work options say they've found employee morale and loyalty improved. According to Global Workplace Analytics, 72 percent of employers say remote work has had a high impact on employee retention. That's not surprising, because it takes a huge amount of stress off parents. Allowing them to work from home when necessary means that if a child needs to be picked up from school, or if a nanny calls in sick or has to leave early, a parent can still get work done and avoid taking a full day off—or falling behind at work. Not having to commute can also allow time to squeeze in a doctor's visit, a parent-teacher conference, or some errands without disrupting work.

3. Family Paid Leave

The United States remains the *only* developed country in the world that doesn't offer mandated paid maternity leave, much less paternity leave.

During the pandemic, though, the government offered tax credits to incentivize companies to begin offering paid sick leave and time off. Under the Families First Coronavirus Response Act, employers with fewer than five hundred full-time or part-time employees could get refundable payroll tax credits designed to reimburse them for the cost of providing leave to employees affected by COVID-19. The act also provided emergency paid family leave for parents unable to work if their children's schools or childcare services were closed because of the pandemic.

Alight Solutions, a provider of benefits administration and other services, reported in spring 2020 that nearly half of the 246 employers it surveyed had implemented or started to implement an extended sick-leave and paid-time-off policy, and another 11 percent were considering it—even those too large to qualify for the payroll tax credits.

How long such benefits will remain in place is unclear. (The Families First Act was set to expire at year's end.) But as with providing the opportunity to work remotely, companies are facing increased pressure to continue offering paid sick-leave benefits and to expand parental-leave policies.

While paid parental leave is still not required of companies, Congress did pass the Federal Employee Paid Leave Act in 2019, granting federal employees up to twelve weeks of paid time off for the birth, adoption, or foster of a new child. And more than half a dozen states have passed legislation mandating paid-leave policies.

California was the first to implement a paid family-leave program in 2004. It extended the duration of paid family-leave benefits from six to eight weeks starting in July 2020.

New Jersey's Family Leave Insurance Program was next, taking effect in 2009. Paid family leave is (as of this writing) now mandated for at least some employers in Massachusetts, New York, Rhode Island, Washington State, and Washington, D.C., too, with bills pending in other states, the Society for Human Resource Management reported. Connecticut employees are funding that state's new paid-leave program by contributing 0.5 percent of their income via a mandatory payroll tax as of January 2021. And on January 1, 2023, a paid-leave law will take effect in Oregon, providing twelve weeks of paid time off for family or medical leave to employees across the state. (It will be funded by a new payroll tax paid by both workers and employers with twenty-five or more employees.)

These paid-leave policies can make a critical difference in the number of new moms who return to work. On average, nearly 30 percent of working women nationwide now leave the labor force when they have a child. But when researchers looked at the New Jersey and California companies who gave paid leave to women who had adopted or given birth, they found that *20 percent fewer* left their jobs in that first year, and there was up to a 50 percent reduction after five years, compared with rates before the policies went into effect. Over the long term, they discovered that having paid time off nearly closed the gap in workforce participation between mothers with young children and women without kids.

That can pay off for companies as well. In a survey by the Center for Economic and Policy Research taken seven years after California implemented its paid-leave legislation, the vast majority of California businesses reported positive or neutral effects on productivity, profitability, and turnover. Notably, a majority of businesses in California (87 percent) said they had *no* increased costs as a result of the program, and 9 percent indicated that the program had actually generated cost *savings* for their businesses by reducing employee turnover or reducing their own benefit costs.

It's not just paid maternity leave that we need though—paid leave for fathers is equally important. Studies published by the U.S. Department of Labor and the National Bureau of Economic Research found that paternity leave can improve outcomes for children, reduce the risk of mothers' experiencing postpartum health complications, and increase gender equity at home and in the workplace. Ensuring that fathers can meet work demands and responsibilities at home, Labor Department researchers concluded, "can significantly increase the personal and economic well-being of their families."

Despite findings like these, more than 80 percent of U.S. employees still don't have access to *any* paid parental leave through their employers, according to the Society for Human Resource Management. But it's becoming easier to find companies that do offer it.

In fact, several major companies have announced expanded policies in recent years. About a dozen big ones, including Adobe Systems, Etsy, Netflix, and Spotify, offer at least six *months* of paid leave. Nearly two hundred well-known companies now offer at least sixteen weeks of paid maternity leave. And many offer paid paternity leave as well. As of 2019, the independent nonprofit Just Capital identified more than a dozen major companies that offered sixteen weeks or more of paid leave to *both* mothers and fathers. They include Alphabet, American Express, Citigroup, DocuSign, Estée Lauder, Facebook, Juniper Networks, Netflix, Prudential, Square, TD Ameritrade, Twitter, VMware, and ZenDesk.

The bottom line: Where you work matters. While the country doesn't mandate paid family leave, a growing number of states and companies are recognizing the value and benefits of offering it. If you want to have a family, look for employers with policies and benefits that will support you and your ability to cover expenses and spend time with any future kids. Having leave that's paid can make a significant difference in your finances and ability to build wealth when you're taking on the added costs and responsibilities of raising a child.

Why work for and support companies whose policies don't work for or support us? Dozens of companies do. Seek them out. Support companies that support women with your dollars. Work for a company that will support you in achieving your unlimited potential *and* having a family if you choose.

4. Universal Pre-K and After-School Programs

The vast majority of parents—70 percent—work full-time until 5:00 p.m. or later, but the average closing time for public schools is *2:30 p.m.* On top of that, schools are closed 80 percent longer than the paid holidays and vacation time a typical worker gets, or about thirteen more days off each year than most working parents have, according to the Center for American Progress. It doesn't take a math whiz to see how big the childcare gap was for parents to fill even before the pandemic.

The United States has one of the shortest school years in the world. Most U.S. schools operate on a nine-and-a-half- to ten-month calendar and offer a six- to seven-hour school day (including lunch). The schedules were established when America was still primarily an agrarian country, and they haven't been updated much since. While there have been calls to switch to a year-round calendar with regular but shorter breaks and to extend school days, neither has gained much momentum in the United States. Public schools say extended days would encroach on teacher prep and grading time, and cost more than their budgets allow. And there's no consensus among parents or educators on shortening the summer break or moving to a year-round schedule like some countries have, including Japan, South Korea, and Australia.

After-school programs fill the gap at some schools, but they are not required. At my son's elementary school, the parent-teacher association helped create and support the after-school program—and participating families pay about $500 per month. The program at my older son's middle school is funded and run through a nonprofit organization. It didn't cost us anything, but we also weren't assured a place. We had to enter a lottery each year for him to participate. (Fortunately, he got in, but the uncertainty created a lot of anxiety.) Not surprisingly, there's widespread support among working parents for these programs. A reported 90 percent of adults surveyed say after-school programs are important to their community, but the Afterschool Alliance, a nonprofit public awareness and advocacy organization, estimates that only one of every three students who could benefit has access to these programs.

Starting kids in school earlier has gained more traction. As of 2017, all but six states—Idaho, Montana, New Hampshire, North Dakota, South Dakota, and Wyoming—were contributing to provide pre-K programs to at least some students, and about 1.5 million kids participated nationwide, according to the Education Commission of the States. Only two states, Vermont and Florida, offer truly universal free pre-K, meaning they're not capped in any way, so every child can enroll in the pre-K programs (and most do). But several cities have also taken initiatives to establish universal pre-K programs, including Boston, Charlotte, Detroit, Houston, Nashville, Los Angeles, and New York City. These sorts of programs can save parents literally thousands of dollars. (Even the part-time preschool in our neighborhood charges nearly $5,000 per semester.)

A lot of research also shows the longer-term benefits of providing pre-K schooling to all kids. One study by a University of Chicago economics professor looked at outcomes including health, crime, income, and IQ—and the increase in a mother's income after returning to work, thanks to childcare—and calculated that the return on investment for high-quality pre-K programs can be as high as 13 percent. And a Center for American Progress analysis estimated that the United States would see a net benefit of $83.3 billion for each annual cohort of four-year-olds enrolled in high-quality pre-K programs.

If the rest of the country offered universal pre-K to children, that would cut childcare costs for millions of Americans and allow parents to go back to work earlier. If the government provided resources for after-school programs that extended school days to match workdays—instead of putting the onus on individual schools, PTAs, and parents to come up with the money—parents wouldn't have to scramble to find childcare or be forced to cut back work hours or drop out of the workforce entirely in order to ensure their kids were supervised in the afternoons.

These are straightforward solutions. But they require a commitment from our government to invest in working parents. In the meantime, if you want kids, make sure you factor those into your calculations when you look at where to start a family and what schools your future kids might attend.

So What Do Working Moms Do in the Meantime?

The truth is, having kids and a career competing for your time and attention can be emotionally and physically taxing. But having *any* two competing priorities is tough. Getting clear on your values and what needs your attention most at any given time can help—as can asking a partner to pick up more of the unpaid responsibilities. And if you're in the financial position to do so, you can hire someone to do some of that household work.

But it's also important to remember that prioritizing your career over time with your loved ones on a given day doesn't mean they're any less important to you overall. And as any working mom can tell you, there will be many instances—sometimes several in a day, as we've learned during the pandemic—when you have to choose where to direct your time and attention. But you can be committed to your family and to your career, and both can be thriving. It's just a matter of figuring out where you're willing to compromise or delegate and what is nonnegotiable.

For nearly fifteen years, work was the main focus for Latrise. Single and ambitious, she worked her way up to senior management at a major consulting firm. Then she got married—to a man with three kids. And a couple of years later, they had a daughter. "Suddenly I now had the responsibilities of being a wife and a mother, and people depending on me, and I still had all my responsibilities at work," she told me. "I was exhausted. And I was in this role, competing with men for promotions who didn't have the same responsibilities I did. Every day, I was thinking, 'This is not sustainable.'"

She lives in New Jersey, and until shifting to remote work during the pandemic, her commute to the office in New York City could take more than three hours round-trip. She'd wake their daughter up in the morning, make breakfast, and get her ready for school, then rush to the train to get to the office. She'd try to be back in time for dinner and to get her daughter ready for bed, and often was so tired that she went to bed soon after herself. On weekends, she had her stepkids (who lived with their mom during the week). "I was so tired," she remembers.

Latrise said she was almost ready to quit. But she confided in her mentor, who suggested that she talk with a new female executive who'd recently been hired. She introduced the two, and Latrise, to her surprise, was able to shift to an entirely new role under the new hire—still at a senior level but internally facing, which allowed her more flexibility and the ability to work remotely. The shift made it much easier for her to be there for their young daughter in the mornings and evenings, which was important to her, and also be able to focus fully on work in between. "I feel like I finally found the right kind of balance."

Latrise may seem like one of the lucky ones—and in some ways she is. She had an opportunity to make a lateral internal move to another senior-level role, retain a high salary, and find the flexibility she needed. But she was also strategic. She had gotten clear on what she needed in order to make it work—and she articulated that and reached out to a mentor to look for a solution. In the end, her employer benefited as well, by not losing a longtime and well-regarded employee, and the institutional knowledge she'd accumulated, and allowing her to apply her skills in a new role.

At some point, almost every working mother with big career ambitions will reach what feels like a crossroads. If she continues to advance professionally, taking on larger roles with more responsibilities, she wonders, will she need to sacrifice more time and attention for her family? And if so, will the paycheck and prestige be worth it? Is the work she's doing meaningful enough to justify the time and energy she is devoting to it? If the answer is unclear, then she may feel like she's in a quandary. We often worry that we must either hold ourselves back in our careers and suffer the financial and professional consequences, or miss out on time with our family and fear that our kids will suffer the consequences.

The good news is that doesn't need to be the case. For one, when you're in a more senior role, you often have *more* control over your schedule, not less, since you're doing more strategic work and have a team to handle much of the execution. And more companies are also recognizing that in order to retain the best talent—especially women—and to get the best out of their employees, they need to allow for some flexibility.

There *are* companies that offer flexibility, reasonable hours, and generous family-leave policies. There are roles that allow us to make a difference and a good income without feeling like we need to be "on" all the time. And it's possible to find childcare coverage that more closely matches our work hours. But these are not (yet) the norm, so it's still largely on us to seek them out.

I think of Jessica, who decided to have a baby on her own in her late thirties. Before she went to the sperm bank, she switched from journalism to a job in PR at a healthcare organization that offered better pay, nine-to-five hours, some flexibility, and paid leave. That way, she was able to stay home with her son a little longer to find a good childcare arrangement before she returned to work. She could work from home if he got sick. And she was able to count on regular hours so that she could be home by six o'clock every night, in time for dinner.

This all requires some strategic planning, of course. And even with the best planning, things can still go awry. But planning ahead can help ease some of the tension and provide you with more choices.

I can remember times in my career when even with a helpful partner, I thought, *This isn't working.* When I got the job that required me to commute more than three hours a day round-trip, for example, it meant I woke the boys at seven in the morning and then headed out the door to catch a shuttle that would take me to the office. I often didn't return home until seven or eight at night. So I essentially had an hour or two, at most, with my family before putting the boys to bed. I missed dinner most nights. I missed taking the kids to school. And I was exhausted. I had almost no time to myself. Because I took a shuttle with other work colleagues, my commute often felt like an extension of work—in fact, we often did work en route to or from the office. But I still needed to physically be in the office nearly nine hours a day.

Although I enjoyed the job and it paid well, even a few weeks in I realized that the schedule wasn't sustainable. We didn't want to move at that point, with both boys in school and strong roots in our neighborhood, and working from home or a satellite office that was closer to us wasn't an option.

That experience crystallized my nonnegotiables for me. I realized I needed to find a job that allowed me to work in an office that was close enough that I could leave for work after dropping the kids at school and be back in time to eat dinner together at least a few nights a week. I needed to be able to carve out some time for myself and for exercise. And I needed an employer that would allow me at least some flexibility, so if I needed to work remotely some days—or leave work for a school event or kids' doctor's appointment—I could do so without feeling like I was sneaking around. And with my next role, I did.

Sometimes you may also end up choosing to stay in a role you've mastered a little longer so that you have more stability, and more time and mental energy for your family. That can mean that your career progression slows during certain periods, but that doesn't mean it has to stall out or can't accelerate again. My friend Heidi calls it "slow-rolling" career advancement.

Last year Heidi, who's the vice president and general manager at a large land-development company in Colorado and mom to a thirteen-year-old boy, was offered a promotion to a significant senior role. But it would have required her to move her family across the country. "I absolutely wanted to pack my bags and go. It was such an opportunity. But my family didn't want to move, and there was no question my son would suffer if I took this role," she told me. "I have a senior leadership role now with responsibility for a large business, but I am senior and experienced enough to handle that and not sacrifice time with my son. I knew if I took that next step now, it would throw my life out of balance."

Ultimately, she turned down the promotion. "It was tough, but I'm happy with my role now because I have a teenage child at home. I am at the place where I want to be right now," Heidi told me. "But I am still driven to have a C-suite role."

The Power of Planning Ahead

You can start to set yourself up *before* you start a family, if you plan to have one, by considering commute times and nearby pre-K, childcare, and after-school programs when you're thinking about where to live. And consider remote work, paid leave, and childcare policies when you're thinking about where to grow your career. If you've built up enough contacts and expertise, it may even mean striking out on your own so that you have more flexibility in your days and work and aren't bound to one company and its policies. And of course you want to consider whether the person you're with will be a true partner and step up at home so that you can both be successful at work. Or if you want to go it alone, consider what kind of childcare and support system you'll need.

What I realized, belatedly, is that I hadn't factored much of that into my career planning. I assumed I could just manage it all. I hadn't chosen to work at *Newsweek* because it offered extended maternity leave (though, notably, without pay for most of it). I learned about that when a colleague got pregnant. I hadn't even checked the maternity-leave policy at my next employer until I learned I was pregnant with our younger son, Sebastian. I didn't consider just how taxing that shuttle commute would be. Looking back, I realize that had I been more strategic, seeking out employers with more generous leave policies, flexible work arrangements, and closer offices, I may have saved myself both money and stress. In the end, I found a career path that worked. But it took some time, and some stressful trial and error, to realize what I needed in order to feel like my life was in balance.

The good news is that it's getting easier to find employers with policies that better serve working parents. Sites like Fairygodboss, Glassdoor, Working Mother, and PL+US (Paid Leave for the United States) list companies with the best paid-leave policies and other benefits to support working parents. The number of companies that offer extended paid leave, access to childcare, and the ability to work remotely—or the flexibility to adjust work schedules when we need to—is growing. These benefits are no longer seen as fringe offerings but as critical to ensuring companies can attract and retain the best talent. We've also seen more women start their own ventures, putting into place the kinds of policies they wish they'd had at other companies.

There's a growing understanding, too, that being a good mom (if we choose to have kids) doesn't require us to be available 24/7. Sometimes we spend extra time at home with our partner or family. Other times working late or traveling for business takes precedence. And that doesn't mean we love our loved ones or our work any less.

"There's a limited amount of time in the day, so there's always a push and pull between work, family, and personal time," my sister, who practices medicine and is married with two kids, told me. "When I feel like I'm really excelling at work, I often feel like I'm not putting enough focus on my family, because if I'm excelling, work is usually absorbing most of my focus. That being said, I do think it's possible to have a rewarding career, a close family, and engaging outside interests."

To do that, she said, will involve some compromises. "I will never be PTA president, but my kids love me, and have said they are glad I am their mom, which is good enough for me," she said. "Likewise, I will probably never be at the absolute top at my field, but I am still really good at my job, and that's enough. So, philosophically, maybe having it all is finding a balance that works and being satisfied that the components are enough."

If that's the way it's defined, she told me, "I have often had it all."

Defining Our Own "All"
(It Doesn't Need to Include Kids)

We are daughters and sisters, mothers and wives, friends, activists, and leaders. We are not just our ambitions. We are more than our jobs. We are multifaceted human beings with limitless love and potential but limited time. How each of us defines "having it all" should reflect what's most important to us at that time and what we need in our lives to feel fulfilled. That's it. Not someone else's definition of what we should be, do, or have in our short time on this spinning planet. But ours.

You don't need to have kids, you don't need to be married, and you don't need to have a high-powered, demanding career to have it all. The reality is, you *can* have everything you want in your life. You just can't *do* it all at once. And that's okay.

Simran, the widowed mom of one who recently launched a skincare startup in San Francisco, told me that she defines having it all as achieving her top three priorities at any given time in her life. "And as long as I feel good about those three things, I feel like I have it all," she said.

Simran's son is grown now, but when he was younger and she was raising him on her own, she said it was all about having a fulfilling career, having time with her son after school and on weekends, and ensuring that she got Friday and Saturday night to herself. (She hired a sitter those nights.) "As long as I got all those three, I really felt like I had it all," she told me. "Having a relationship took a back seat, so some might think I didn't have it all. But for me, it was not in my top three. So that was a conscious choice."

"Our culture has given us a very narrow standard for what 'all' is—being able to be a successful career woman and be a mother and be feminine and put together," Suzanne, a writer and founder of a Connecticut-based literary institute, told me. "Defining your *own* 'all' early on and letting the definition continue to be both central to your work and elastic seems to be crucial to the process of moving into our own version of success."

How has Suzanne defined it for herself? "Work that has staying and growing power, empowers me, meets my financial goals, and allows me time to grow personally, stay healthy, learn about the world around me, and have a blast doing it!"

"We have always based 'having it all' on someone else's determination, when in reality it has to come from inside," Susan McPherson, the owner of a socially minded consulting firm in Brooklyn, told me. She has a simple definition. "The true moments I've felt like I have it all are when my alarm goes off and I am feeling optimistic and looking forward to the day."

"For me, it's really more about thinking how I want my life to look. How do I want to express myself, and how do I want to be in the world? And then creating from there," consultant Jennifer Crews told me. "I decided that I wanted to do challenging work that mattered and had a positive impact *and* I wanted to be a present wife and mother *and* I wanted to have space to take care of myself physically and emotionally. I created my work life so that I could check all those boxes. Even though some days it feels like I'm not giving each part of my life one hundred percent, I've decided that's fine. On any given day I can't be one hundred percent of everything."

What's important is to ask ourselves what *we* want. To ask what success means *to us*. And to stop allowing others to define that for us. That's what the breadwinner mindset is all about: taking control of our future and writing our own stories.

Those critical distinctions shifted the way I approached my work and the questions I began asking. What kind of work could I do that would allow me to have more time and headspace for my family but still provide a sizable income? What would it look like if I paid more attention to the impact I could have in a role than the title? Were there companies that offered opportunities for advancement but also offered more flexibility and the ability to work remotely sometimes? (Yes, there are a growing number of them, including Acorns.) And what investments could I make now that would provide income to supplement my paychecks and eventually decrease my dependence on them?

Ultimately that process would change the choices I made, too, and allow me to keep moving closer to the kind of life I wanted—one that included fulfilling, well-compensated work and quality time with myself, my family, and my friends.

My husband's income and mine may flip-flop in the future, but my mindset and my commitment to building enough wealth to support the life I want for myself and my family will remain the same. Now, with more than a decade of hindsight, I can see clearly just how much shifting my approach to money, and acting accordingly, has improved our quality of life and my sense of self and purpose.

Early last year, as I was walking one of my kids to school and laughing at something he said, I felt a wave of happiness roll over me, and I was struck by an unexpected thought: This *is what it means to have it all.* Or, at least, all that truly matters. Having a life you love, a life that you helped create—it doesn't have to look like anything but what makes you content.

These days my husband and I sit on the back balcony, sipping tea and looking out over the garden our downstairs neighbor has planted, in a home we love that's in a neighborhood that brings me joy. I run in the 526-acre park that's three blocks away. I eat and shop at the restaurants and boutiques that run along the avenue at the end of our block. My kids can walk to great schools within a six-block radius of our home. In other words, I'm actually living out the vision I conjured up that morning, over a decade ago. Thanks in part to a series of choices I began to put into place then, we've been able to raise our kids in the city we love and to travel (in normal times), visiting far-flung friends and family across the country and taking our kids on vacations to destinations that will help them expand their horizons and their minds. But that doesn't mean I've stopped visualizing what our future could look like.

What's most empowering is that I feel confident I can live out my dreams instead of leaving them to chance. Whether a partner earns more or less than we do, whether we end up with a partner (or family) or not, whether we're moving up the ranks or are just starting a career, we can feel secure about our ability to create the life we want. Embracing a breadwinner mindset allows us to take control of our finances *and* our futures.

And the possibilities are endless. When we reach one goal, we can set another—pushing ourselves beyond previous thresholds of possibility while appreciating how far we've already come and what we've already been able to create.

Because here's the thing: You don't ever really have it *all*. There will always be dreams that pull you forward: a bigger home, a business of your own, new skills you want to learn, a long list of destinations you want to visit, opportunities to have a greater impact. But that's what goals are for—and you know you'll reach them eventually because you are choosing to take the steps you need to get there. Having the freedom to choose the life you want is the joy of breadwinning.

You get to decide how your story is written. You get to write your own unique happy ending. You can choose what having it all looks like—and enjoy every minute of that life. That's living like a breadwinner. And if you've read this far, you're on your way.

CHAPTER 14

Find Your Allies

How to Cultivate a Network of Wealth-Building Women

The success of every woman should be the inspiration to another. We should raise each other up.
—SERENA WILLIAMS

IN FALL 2015, not long after I'd been hired as a VP at a financial startup, I flew out to its headquarters in Southern California to meet the rest of the then eighty-person team. I was working out of a tiny WeWork space in New York at the time and hadn't been to the main California office yet. I dressed up for the occasion in a bright blue dress and high-heeled sandals, curling my hair and slipping on a silver cuff bracelet and small hoop earrings. At the all-hands team meeting, I stood before the entire company as the president strolled in wearing a T-shirt, jeans, and flip-flops. He introduced me, then gave me a few minutes to talk about myself and lay out some of the goals for the financial wellness site we were building. As I spoke, I remember scanning the crowd and having two thoughts: *Wow, I haven't seen this many hoodies in one place since college.* And, *Where are the women?*

Much of the team was made up of guys in their twenties and early thirties in T-shirts and various stages of facial-hair growth. I spotted just a handful of young female faces sprinkled in. For a moment, I imagined I was there on assignment as the journalist I had been, thinking about how I would write a description of this scene. A futuristic office that seemed designed for a band of young gamers with ergonomic chairs, massive monitors, and shared scooters for darting around the office. An informal dress code that seemed lifted from a college dorm. A selection of snacks that could've been snatched from a grade-schooler's lunch box: fruit gummies, animal crackers, Cheez-Its. Cold brew on tap and six-packs of double IPA in the fridge.

I later learned that women represented less than a quarter of our company at that point, and there was only one in management besides me, who'd been hired the same day. (The vast majority of women were in customer support or administrative roles.) The ratio would change significantly over the following years: By 2020, the company would grow to more than 350 employees, and women would make up nearly half the senior management team. But on that day, I remember feeling acutely aware of my gender.

True, I was now working at a fintech startup, a mash-up of two industries—financial services and technology—notorious for being heavily populated with bros. But you don't have to be in a mostly male industry to be the "only" in the room. Because regardless of industry, the higher you rise, the smaller the number of women. Since 2015, when LeanIn.org and McKinsey and Company first launched the annual *Women in the Workplace* report, which surveys close to three hundred companies with nearly 13 million employees, researchers have noted: "Corporate America has made almost no progress in improving women's representation. Women are underrepresented at every level, and women of color are the most underrepresented group of all, lagging behind white men, men of color, and white women."

Although women earn more bachelor's and advanced degrees than men do, the 2019 report found that women are less likely than men to be hired or promoted at almost every level. But the disparity is particularly acute in management. "Women are less likely to be hired into manager-level jobs, and they are far less likely to be promoted into them," the researchers noted, citing a "broken rung" at the step up to becoming a manager, which they identified as perhaps the biggest obstacle women face on the path to leadership. As a result, women account for just 38 percent of managerial positions. And the number continues to shrink as you ascend through the levels of management, to 29 percent at the VP level and 28 percent at the senior VP level in 2020. In the C-suite, men outnumber women by nearly four to one. Initially, that was almost exactly the ratio at the startup where I worked. (Fortunately, our CEO was committed to diversifying our company, particularly at the senior management level.)

"Is It Just Me?"

If you're the only woman at your level, it can be lonely and isolating and that much harder to keep up your momentum—and that may help explain why a lot of women do start to drop off as they approach senior management, or not go for promotions in the first place, keeping them from reaching their full earnings and wealth-building potential. That's one reason why it's so important to find and connect with other women who can relate to you and your situation, even if it means looking outside your company (and it often does).

Is it just me? I'd asked myself so often, internalizing the micro-aggressions and subtle sexism I'd experienced repeatedly in my career. For years I'd interpreted so much of what I'd heard as something *I* needed to adjust or fix. My voice. My wardrobe. My stance. My ambition. Was I too assertive or not assertive enough? Was I talking too much or too little? Was I speaking loudly enough, or was I too loud? Was my dress too tight or not flattering enough? I was expending a tremendous amount of effort and energy every day trying to figure out how I needed to show up in order to succeed. It was not only draining, but it also started to erode both my confidence and my identity.

It's hard to focus on the substance of what you want to say at a meeting if you're worried about whether you'll even be able to get a word in—if you'll have to cut in or talk over someone to be heard and risk being admonished for being too brash. If you're concentrating on modulating your tone and emotions when you talk with the male manager who told you that you were "too defensive," you're not able to pay as much attention to what you're actually saying or hearing. If your male boss tells you that you're "too ambitious," it's hard not to feel like throwing in the towel. And if you feel like your peers can't relate because they're men, it can be pretty lonely at work. Sometimes it feels as if loneliness is the price you pay for promotions as a woman.

So it's key to remember as we ascend in our careers that even if they're not standing next to us, there *are* other women in management and senior-level roles standing with us—if not yet as many as we hope for. And many of them are having similar experiences. Finding and connecting with women who are in comparable roles, even if they're in different divisions, industries, or cities, can provide you with valuable perspective and support.

Someone You Can Trust

"The work will get hard for different reasons in your career," Latrise, the New Jersey–based executive at the consulting company, told me. "To know you can make a phone call at any moment and know you have someone you trust to talk through it with is so important for women, especially when there are still so few of us in management. I've realized I can't be successful without the network and relationships both."

Still, Latrise said it took her a while to recognize the importance of having female networks and mentors. "I spent much of my career being a lone soldier—I didn't even seek mentors out," she told me. "But I've since realized I would not be here if I didn't have them."

After she had her daughter and was struggling to balance her work and her family—especially with the long commute into New York

City—she credits her mentor with helping her move into the new internal-facing role that had more flexibility and allowed her to work remotely. "When I was really feeling stuck, I was suffering in silence for a while," she remembers. "And then, when I finally did reach out to my mentor and said the words to her, new opportunities opened up that I hadn't even thought of."

Latrise, who has been with the same consulting company for almost all her career, says she was also fortunate to be assigned a sponsor early on as she advanced up the ranks. She remembers learning that her sponsor organized regular trips for senior-level women from across the company to allow them informal time to connect with each other. "You had to pay for it, but if you were invited, you definitely felt you should go," she told me. When she moved into a senior role and got an invite, she says, "It was the best investment I ever made."

Latrise went on three separate trips with more than a dozen senior-level women, who flew in from around the country. In between, she says, they would get together for dinner or drinks when one was in town. "It was because of that experience that I started to build other types of relationships with these women," she told me. "We'd find ourselves in smaller groups having really honest conversations. It really helped to strengthen those relationships."

A New Level of Networking

It's not just about networking but about being around women who can mirror the experiences you've had and remind you that you're *not* alone—women who can inspire and uplift and support you, and who know better than almost anyone else what you're going through. One of the most affirming and mind-blowing aspects of spending time with other ambitious women was the sheer number of shared experiences, the continuous string of confirmations that what I was witnessing in the workplace wasn't unique to me or something that I had to fix in myself, necessarily, but more often something that needed to be fixed within a system that was built by and for men with wives at home. Having peers who were going through similar experiences helped me keep perspective and get advice that was directly relevant to my situation (and hard to find anywhere else).

"It's hard to function effectively professionally if you feel isolated. Being around people who have multiple shared experiences is so important," says Kate Brodock, the CEO of Women 2.0, a fifteen-year-old company focused on gender, diversity, and inclusion in the tech and startup space. "There's a level of comfort when you are around people who've had shared experiences that allows you to feel comfortable asking questions and allows you to seek solutions and grow together."

Brodock told me that the importance of community really hit home years ago when she led a global, sixty-plus chapter organization that focused on women in technology and entrepreneurship before joining Women 2.0. "I remember when we opened a chapter in Milan, Italy, and all of a sudden these women were coming out of the woodwork and saying, 'I didn't even know there *were* other women in tech,'" she said. "The mobilization of these communities—whether by location or WhatsApp or whatever—I heard time and time again, was a game changer."

Early in my management career, my idea of networking was checking LinkedIn a few times a week and having the occasional coffee or drink with a former boss or colleague. Then a few years after I moved into management, I joined my first female networking group called TheLi.st. My female boss at the time was already a member. She had encouraged me to join and covered the annual fee. Initially I was skeptical. If anything, it seemed like a time-suck when I already felt stretched thin. And the other members all seemed to be way more accomplished than I was—they were publishing best-selling books, running companies, winning big awards, doing TED Talks. It was an intimidating crowd. I lurked for several months without posting a thing to the Google group.

And then one day, as I was starting to do interviews for what would become this book, I posted a callout for anyone who was the breadwinner—either the main earner in a relationship or supporting herself if she was single—to be interviewed. I got a flood of responses. Women I'd never met in real life, women who I knew were busier than I was, were offering up thirty to sixty minutes of their time for interviews I wasn't sure would ever see the light of day.

The first woman to volunteer, the Brooklyn-based entrepreneur Susan who runs a socially minded consulting company, spent more than an hour on the phone with me. After I'd interviewed her, she asked how else she could help. Would it be useful to introduce me to other women? Did I have a book agent? Did I need anything else? Every woman I spoke to from the group was similarly encouraging, connecting me with other women who might make good interview subjects or offering to help with the proposal or with publicity.

These women weren't trying to sell me anything. They were genuinely trying to support me, volunteering to share their own experience and to help connect me with other people who could help me out. Over the coming years, I watched as the first woman, Susan, did the same for other women: hosting book-launch parties, connecting women with mentors and investors, and helping to spread the word about events or projects other women were working on via her large social media following. Along the way, she sent me notes when I hit meaningful milestones in my own career and continued to ask about the progress on my book and introduce me to other women with similar interests.

I had always been encouraged to network—all professional women have. But this was a whole different level of connection and support. At first I thought it was unique to this progressive and tight-knit group. But as I joined other networking groups and even a writing group with other women, I realized it wasn't. I'd just been fed this narrative that networking was mostly a means to leverage low-fidelity relationships to climb higher up the career ladder. That it was about making connections now that could lead to job and career-advancement opportunities later.

I guess that was a part of it. But the groups I belonged to also served as quasi-support groups. It wasn't just a one-off coffee or an autofilled congratulatory note to a LinkedIn connection for a new job or work anniversary; it was about making real connections with women who would offer advice and encouragement, social media amplification for projects you were working on, and sometimes just moral support and a sympathetic ear.

This was a complete shift in the way we are often told to think about networking—and certainly how we've been told to think about ambitious working women. For decades we've been fed this scarcity myth that there's room for just one woman at the table, and we're all competing against one another to snag that seat.

"Unfortunately, because of our conditioning—that there's a small piece of the pie available to women—we've been told we have to beat each other out, or compete in ways that are zero-sum. So women are still being conditioned to fear and compete with each other," says Terri, who runs the branding business. "It is going to take a while to uncondition ourselves."

"Lifting One Up Lifts Us All Up"

It was my experience with this networking group, and Susan in particular, that led me to question the fears I'd had about how competitive and antagonistic ambitious women could be. I realized a lot of those beliefs were based on what I'd been told—or even movies I'd seen, like *Working Girl* or *The Devil Wears Prada* that featured women vying with each other for roles and recognition. That's a convenient narrative for the men in power. If women are convinced we have to compete with and hold each other down in order to reach the top, we will never change the ratio. If we're too busy pushing one another out of the way to grab the sole seat at the table, we aren't in a position to bring in new chairs or question why so many of the seats are held by men.

Heidi, the land development executive in Colorado, recalls that earlier in her career it often did feel like women were competing with, rather than supporting, each other. But that is starting to change. "I think there is a general shift going on away from this feeling of scarcity to the idea that lifting one up lifts us all up," she told me. "I think it's a conscious choice that our generation is making that we are not going to perpetuate that. We're flipping the paradigm. We're creating more opportunities for other women."

When she was elected president of her industry association—the second woman ever to be in that position—she says she saw an opportunity to spotlight other highly qualified women. "I worked to put more women of merit on the ladder to leadership," she told me. She hired the first female CEO of the organization and advocated for more members of the executive committee to be women. By the end of her tenure, women held a majority of seats. "You have to reach out, you have to speak up and lift other women up. That's my focus right now. Who am I going to promote, get seen, get recognition for?"

Recently, she recalled, the law firm her company works with took out an ad announcing the promotion of a female managing partner. When she realized it was the first woman at that level ever, she offered to pay for another ad, congratulating her and noting she was the first female managing partner in the firm's nearly four-decade-long history. "If we don't use our platforms to point out these firsts, I feel like we're not doing our jobs," she told me. "I haven't always been strong enough to fight the fight, but I am using my voice now and my platform and position to help the culture shift."

The truth is, in order for us to succeed and to change the ratios, we *have* to work together and lift each other up.

"When you find women you work really well with and who have the confidence in themselves to bring the women around them up, it is magic," says Lisa Johnson, the VP of marketing at a healthcare startup. "Had I not had those kinds of female mentors and sponsors, I wouldn't be where I am today. It's so important for women to be each other's sponsors and supporters. I feel like it's my duty now to pass that on."

As I've witnessed in my own networking groups, there is a genuine admiration and respect for one another and a real desire to do just that. We share virtual high-fives and congratulate each other on promotions and new jobs, both privately on our listserv, WhatsApp groups, and Slack channels and publicly on our social networks. We share job openings and make connections. We recommend other qualified women for legal, accounting, PR, and other services. We amplify each other's posts and show up for one another's events. And we commiserate and strategize when someone shares an experience she's had in the office or with an investor or a boss that reeks of sexism or harassment or condescension.

"Women are often more apt to be candid about failures and setbacks, and that can help to keep us motivated to keep going in the face of countless obstacles," Bobbi Rebell, *How to Be a Financial Grownup* author, certified financial planner, and a member of one of my networking groups, told me. "It can help establish a mindset of success when you see that other women have excelled despite having so many other responsibilities competing for our attention."

Most important has been recognizing that there was nothing inherently wrong with any of us and our approaches. There was nothing that needed to be *fixed*. Sure, we could all grow and develop our talents and potential, and there are always adjustments to make to fit in with a company's culture. But we realized the feeling that we had to modulate our voices and emotions, soften our approach, and play down our ambitions and our families at work was just a simple survival technique for a workplace culture that wasn't designed to support women's advancement.

In fact, it was designed initially to exclude us from all but the supporting roles.

A Pocket Posse

At times, I'd wonder how I'd lasted so long without these other women in my life. They were like my pocket posse. Even when I was the only woman in the room, I knew now that I wasn't alone. I could slip out my phone and connect with one of them in an instant.

One morning before work, I sat on the edge of our bed, watching videos on my Marco Polo app from a ten-person group of women that had formed after we'd spent a weekend together at a writing retreat. I'd just posted a video about a series of interviews I had coming up for a potential new project. "That sounds big!" said one woman. "I can't wait to hear more. Of course, you'll knock 'em dead." The next chimed in with "Good luck! You'll be great!" in her twenty-second video. And they went on.

My husband was watching quietly from the other side of the bedroom. After I'd filmed a thank-you video in response, he looked at me. "I cannot imagine guys supporting each other like that," he said. "But maybe it would be nice if we did." It dawned on me: This is what networking can be for women. We have redefined and expanded what it means to be connected. And in a powerful way. I began to realize: *This* is how we will change the ratio. This is how we will close the gaps. This is how it happens. With all of us working together to lift each other up so that we can all ascend.

For months before the pandemic shut down our office last year, I'd spend some of each commute to and from work reading through the day's postings from women on my listserv who were often dealing with the same kinds of challenges I was, and we all commiserated, offering advice and support. Sometimes I watched new Marco Polo clips from my writing group on the subway or as I got ready for work and tapped a heart or a like or a high-five emoji in response if I wasn't in a place where I could shoot a video in response.

And once a month for the past two years, I've gathered in person or on Zoom with a "Core" group of eight other women in senior management across an array of industries who are part of Chief, a female networking group with clubhouses in New York and Chicago and plans to open more in Los Angeles, Boston, and San Francisco. As they shared experiences, I began to see myself in their stories, too. We had the chance to talk through potential solutions and approaches, dissecting what had worked for some and might work for others, or talking through the lessons learned. We gave each other support and sometimes the nudge we needed to leave a bad situation. We helped each other determine what was helpful feedback and what was biased. Without exception, every one of those morning meetings has left me feeling empowered and a part of something bigger—an amazing community of women, yes, but also part of a movement to transform our work culture into one in which everyone is heard and seen and has the opportunity to explore their full potential.

That LeanIn.org–McKinsey report found that identifying as an "only" (for example, the only woman in the room) often had "disastrous consequences for women's careers." Women who were surrounded by men in the office became 1.5 times more likely to consider quitting their jobs. They also experienced sexual harassment and microaggressions at a higher rate than women who were not the only ones at their level. "When women were 'onlies,' they needed to provide more evidence of their competence, were more likely to be addressed in a less-than-professional way, and were more likely to have their judgment questioned, compared to women who had other women at work." If I didn't have those groups—if I wasn't getting a different perspective and reassurance that I wasn't alone—there were times I might have quit, too.

That's one reason Lindsay Kaplan told me that she and Carolyn

Childers founded Chief in 2019. "We all know that there's a severe dearth of women—especially BIPOC women—in the C-suite. But what we don't talk about enough is how difficult it is for women to *stay* in positions of senior leadership once they get there. Attrition rates for women in the C-suite are going up, and we shouldn't be surprised—when you get to the top and you're surrounded by men who have had drastically different professional experiences, and who are experiencing different personal and professional challenges, you're going to feel isolated and unsupported," she told me. "Our vision was to create a small private network of women executives to help receive the support and mutual solidarity we rarely find within our own workplaces."

Having risen to senior executive roles in the New York startup scene, Lindsay and Carolyn quickly realized that not only was it lonely at the top, but also there were few resources directed at helping women in senior levels continue to grow. "We knew that to continue advancing and succeeding in our careers, we needed to surround ourselves with a diverse community of women executives who, even if they weren't experiencing the exact same challenges as we were, would understand and empathize with the unique experience of being a woman leader," Lindsay told me.

Building Your Breadwinning Squad

In short: *You want a squad.* No matter where you are in your career, you want to have close connections to people, especially other women, who are going to support you in your ambitions. This isn't about having people who can fill in for emergency childcare, though that's important too, but rather having peers who will be able to identify with your situation, be your sounding board about new career options, and cheer you on when you hit a new milestone. You need people who can lift you up and whom you can lift up in return.

And you want to find other women who are breadwinner-minded. If the women who surround you aren't thinking and living like breadwinners, you may quickly realize something's lacking in your conversations. That doesn't mean you can't be friends, of course. But you also want to talk about that life you're out to create with other people who get it, people who can talk about investing and real estate and negotiating that big deal or offer. When your social circle doesn't talk about wealth, you miss out. And just as important, when you're striving for more and the people around you are settling for less, it's tough to relate and it's easy to get discouraged. To start, you need only one person—a colleague, coach, or mentor—whom you admire and who can hold you accountable, provide guidance and support, and remind you where you're going.

I've been fortunate that I can talk to my mom, a retired accounting professor who has successfully managed her own investment portfolio for decades, about investing—in both stocks and bonds, and in real estate. I've shown her my portfolio, and we openly discuss different investing strategies. (I've also talked with my dad about his.)

But it's been equally important to have breadwinner-minded peers who are committed to building their wealth and living life on their terms. That includes Simran, who built up a sizable nest egg before launching her skincare startup at forty-nine and has walked me through some of her wealth-building strategies; and Laura, who runs her own PR business and has helped guide me through compensation negotiations and compared notes on other wealth-building strategies. And Mayumi, who consciously surrounded herself with people operating successful businesses larger than hers so she could learn from them and taught me to level up my game by seeking out people who were already successfully doing what I wanted to do. And Alia, who opened my eyes to the possibility of earning enough through investments and passive income to cover expenses and no longer be dependent on a paycheck. Peers like these have inspired me and taught me to expand the way I look at my own wealth-building potential and possibilities.

If you live in a big city, it's probably easier to get to know women who are thinking like breadwinners (whether or not they are the main earners) and looking at not just how to make money but how to grow it. They might not be in your line of work, and that's okay. It's smart to find people who are as driven as you are but who are building wealth in different ways. This gets you out of your professional bubble and provides you with new perspectives. Depending on where you live, though, finding a social circle of breadwinner-minded women might not be so easy. In that case, cultivating relationships with other like-minded women could mean joining a Meetup group or becoming a member of a virtual or local networking group. Trust me, they're out there. And growing.

More Ways to Connect

Chief, which has grown to more than three thousand members and five locations in two years, isn't the only organization committed to helping connect women and advance them professionally and financially. Others include the Seattle-based network the Riveter, which has thirty thousand online community members, and the Coven, a membership community with coworking spaces in the Twin Cities that's grown to one thousand members in three years. There's also Dreamers & Doers, a female-focused digital community with thousands of members; Luminary, a New York–based "collaboration hub for women to develop, network, and connect" that's attracted more than six hundred members in two years; and AllBright, a 2017-founded digital community for "smart-minded women of all ages and stages" with physical locations in London and L.A. and plans to expand further. ("The sisterhood works and I think we need it now more than ever," AllBright cofounder Debbie Wosskow told me.) There are also groups focused specifically on women of color like nFormation, which launched in 2020, and on working moms, like HeyMama, which has more than three thousand members. Most have digital memberships and offerings, so you can join regardless of where you live.

One of the first such organizations is the twenty-four-year-old Ellevate Network (formerly 85 Broads), which now has more than thirty-five thousand members—"a powerful coalition of ambitious and supportive women who believe there is strength in numbers," according to Ellevate CEO Kristy Wallace.

"There's no way to know what challenges you'll face, but one thing is certain: You don't need to face them alone," she told me. "Tapping into a community that understands what you are experiencing and wants to support you is incredibly valuable."

It's not just career-focused groups that are springing up. As the *New York Times* reported in 2020, "Across the country, women's investing groups, from Meetups to clubs organized by the nonprofit BetterInvesting, are helping some women to focus on their finances in ways, their members say, that Wall Street firms, fund companies and financial advisers have fallen short." The article spotlighted the Austin Women's Investing Group, which was founded in 2011 and has since grown to more than 2,000 members.

There are also groups like Ladies Who Launch, a nonprofit cofounded by two former executives at Square, Sarah Friar and Kelly McGonigle, that supports and educates female entrepreneurs (and aspiring entrepreneurs) throughout the world with online resources and events; and Savvy Ladies, a New York–based nonprofit that's provided financial education and planning resources to more than fifteen thousand women of varied backgrounds since Francis Financial CEO Stacy Francis founded it in 2003.

Of course, not everyone has access to these groups in person, but most provide online resources and opportunities to connect virtually, too. Female-focused networking groups, co-working spaces, and wealth-building communities are popping up throughout the country, and online options span the country and the globe. Whether you join an existing network or build an informal group yourself, it's important to connect with breadwinner-minded women with whom you can build relationships, exchange ideas and advice, and support each other as you work toward your future goals.

The Power of a Whisper Network

As a corollary, you also want to be frank when it comes to talking about money, with both women *and* men. Salary transparency is a hot topic in the media, but few people actually follow through on getting comfortable with it (one podcast host found that women were way more forthcoming about their favorite sexual position than their bank balance). That's got to change if we're going to close the gender wage and wealth gaps and reach our earning and wealth-building potential.

"We have to start talking about these things and holding each other accountable," Emma Johnson, the author of *The Kickass Single Mom* and founder of the popular website Wealthy Single Mommy, told me. "We can't dismiss it just because it's uncomfortable. We need louder voices from women calling each other out [saying] there is nothing wrong with making money for the sake of making money. Honestly, every time I talk to women, I ask, How much are you making? How much are you charging?"

Terri, who runs the branding business, talks with other women but said she also made a point of expanding beyond her female network to seek out "the most privileged, white, middle-aged men" she knew when she was pricing out different consulting services. "And nine times out of ten, they would tell me I wasn't charging enough," she told me.

That included male clients. She remembered one in particular in financial services. After she created the firm's new brand positioning, language, and content overnight and delivered it the next morning, the head of the firm pulled her aside. "He said, 'I'm going to tell you something, and I don't want you to hold this against me. I think you're undercharging, but I want to be grandfathered in,'" Terri said. "I more than doubled my rate after that conversation."

Stephanie, the doctor in Maryland, credits her informal "whisper" network of female friends and colleagues with helping her negotiate for higher pay and promotions—one friend even helped her craft an email asking for a raise. "It's been so important to have that network of strong female friends and colleagues. The friendship and support that we give each other has been crucial," she told me. "We build each other up."

Equally as important as talking about how to grow your salary and your rates is getting comfortable talking about how to grow your wealth.

Building Our Careers and Our Wealth

"I still feel like a lot of women don't realize how exciting it is to make your own wealth, to build your own wealth. It's so nice to have that cash and be able to grow it," Heather, the New York–based sales director, told me. "I talk about it all the time with my husband, but I still can't talk about it with many of my girlfriends, because they just aren't thinking about it."

Imagine if we gathered with other women to discuss and compare the best ways to build not just our careers but *our wealth*. I have—and I hope this book and the growing number of female-focused investing clubs and networking communities become the catalyst for more wealth-building conversations.

The truth is, it can still feel uncomfortable talking about money—whether it's the income or the investments you make. It *can* be lonely at the top if you're an only. And sometimes it still feels like we must perform ten times better than the white guy down the hall to get the same promotion or recognition.

But there are also millions of breadwinning women out there who are thinking about how to build their careers and their wealth, and how to be able to have a life (and maybe family) as well. It's just a matter of finding them. And there's a groundswell of women across the country and the world who are working to help bring us together, to change the cultural beliefs and biases that often hold us back, and to pave the way for the next generation of women to be able to have it all—however they define that.

People like Chief cofounders Lindsay and Carolyn. And Amy Nelson, mom of four girls and founder of the Riveter, who's been an outspoken advocate for equal pay. And Georgene Huang and Romy Newman, who cofounded the platform Fairygodboss for women to connect with other professional women and find relevant career-related resources, including anonymous employer reviews (that consider criteria like flexibility and whether women are promoted equally to men) and job listings (that include a rundown of benefits like paid leave and childcare), plus virtual recruiting events, webinars with various experts, and career-related content.

Women like Sallie Krawcheck, chair of the Ellevate Network and CEO and cofounder of Ellevest, a digital-first investment platform for women. And Lorine Pendleton, a member of Pipeline Angels, a network of women investors changing the face of angel investing and providing capital to women entrepreneurs, who recently co-launched the Portfolia Rising America Fund, which focuses its investments on female- and minority-led entrepreneurial companies.

And Women 2.0 CEO Kate Brodock (whom I met through Chief), who last year launched a VC fund called W to invest in companies with women and underrepresented founders with a goal of raising $48 million; she told me, "We're going to go big because this space needs it!" (In 2019, $6.1 billion was invested in female-founded companies, according to Crunchbase, representing *less than 3 percent* of all venture dollars invested. But in 2020, a growing number of VC funds pledged to direct more of their money into companies led by women and people of color, including SoftBank, which pledged $100 million.)

The bottom line is that if we want to change the ratio and create more opportunities, we need to invest in and lift up each other and make sure our voices are heard. We need to advocate loudly for new models and new approaches to workplace culture that support and celebrate us for who we are, instead of continuing to contort ourselves to fit an outdated model that doesn't serve us. And we need to speak up about inequities in pay, VC funding, and representation at the table (of all underrepresented groups). But we don't need to do it alone.

We are in this together. And as Lindsay Kaplan told me, "While women can make an incredible impact individually, we are far more powerful together."

CONCLUSION

Beyond Breadwinning

Creating the Life You Want

Real change, enduring change, happens one step at a time.
—Ruth Bader Ginsburg

As you've probably figured out by now, you're not alone on this journey. You're joining a rising tide of women who want more—more for themselves and more for each other. More money, more choices, more say, and more agency over their lives. Women who are starting to make conscious choices with their money and careers in order to ensure that they're set up to have the life they want, without having to depend on someone else for it. Women who are questioning the limitations of the conventional breadwinner model and the inequities we still face in the workplace and at home and wondering if there is a better way. One that will, ultimately, benefit women *and* men.

A growing number of women are already realizing the power and freedom that comes with embracing a breadwinner mindset and with having true agency over our lives. We're recognizing that if we're reliant on someone else to cover the bills and fund our future, we cede the power to determine our own destiny and can end up in a situation that doesn't serve us (or, worse, that actually harms us). When we can't support ourselves, how can we support others?

As you may have already found, becoming your own breadwinner allows you to expand your purview and the possibilities you see for your life. And as you rise up, you will be better positioned to bring those around and behind you forward, too. And to change the rules and challenge the conventions that have held us back, so the next waves of women who come up will have even more opportunities to achieve their potential and to have it all—however they define it.

But we are still in the early days of this revolution, and there are still obstacles and obsequiousness to overcome. In many ways, the system is still not set up for women to succeed. All along the way, we are encouraged to think *smaller*, to want less, to compromise. To just be satisfied with what we have and stop asking for more. Stop rocking the boat. Stop questioning convention. All along the way, we are tempted time and time again with the fantasy of being taken care of, as if drifting into dependency is like slipping into a warm bath. And we are simultaneously fed the idea that providing for ourselves is hard. That it's drudgery—difficult and exhausting, a burden. So we need to be reminded that ultimately it is the opposite of that.

The real promises of thinking like a breadwinner are:

- freedom
- agency over our own lives
- the power to choose our own paths
- the ability to live as we want
- the confidence to know that we can provide for ourselves and for others
- the relief of not being reliant on anyone else
- the discovery of whole new thresholds of possibility within ourselves
- the capability to lift others up as well

This is happening already.

We are starting to build our own wealth so that *we* can determine our own futures. And we are speaking up and banding together with other women (and men) in the workplace to advocate for change and policies that support us in our full lives with paid leave to care for kids or ailing loved ones, reasonable working hours, equal pay, and an environment that allows everyone to be seen and heard.

Take the seven female employees at Google who organized the Google Walkout for Real Change, in which more than twenty thousand men and women participated, including senior management and employees from Google offices around the world, demanding changes to what they deemed a toxic workplace culture. And the dozens of women who shared their experiences via email at Microsoft, which led to a major overhaul of company policies related to sexual harassment and discrimination. And in mid-2020, the dozens of women in the gaming industry who came forward with allegations of gender-based discrimination, harassment, and sexual assault, leading to resignations and several prominent companies vowing to stop sponsoring streamers who had faced accusations and to take actions to fight discrimination and harassment.

And there are women joining together to demand equity outside the office, too. Most of us are aware of the twenty-eight members of the U.S. women's national soccer team, which holds a record four World Cup championships and four Olympic gold medals, who banded together to fight for equal pay, eventually suing the U.S. Soccer Federation for gender and wage discrimination. Lesser known, perhaps, are the six female big-wave surfers—Andrea Moller, Bianca Valenti, Keala Kennelly, Paige Alms, Karen Tynan, and Sabrina Brennan—who founded the Commission for Equity in Women's Surfing in 2016. Three years later, surfing's governing body, World Surf League, agreed to start awarding equal prize money to male and female athletes in all its events.

It's not just women. A growing chorus of female *and* male voices are joining together to demand that companies wake up to the fact that in order to retain the best talent, they need to create environments that allow women to thrive more in every industry—and increasingly, they're being heard.

An array of companies already offer benefits and solutions to address some of the traditional barriers women face while trying to advance in the workplace. Johnson & Johnson, which won the top spot on *Working Mother*'s 2019 list of best companies for working moms (and was again among the top in 2020), offers assistance with fertility treatments and adoption, extended paid leave, and backup dependent care—and has a good representation of women at the senior management level. IBM, which is also near the top of the list, reimburses up to $50,000 per year for a child with mental, physical, or developmental special needs. Other companies include perks like reimbursement for prenatal classes, surrogacy, and egg freezing; the ability to buy extra vacation days at a discounted rate; and a four-day compressed workweek.

Many on the magazine's 2020 list offer the same amount of parental leave for both genders (including American Express, Dow Jones, and UBS, which offer a minimum of twenty weeks). Netflix, which has almost a fifty-fifty gender split among its workforce, now allows *unlimited* paid parental leave in the year after the birth or adoption of a child. And at least eighty companies have publicly stated that they have, or will, set targets for the number of women they hire to ensure a more equitable gender split (several have diversity efforts in place, too, to ensure better representation of all races and ethnicities).

Dell Technologies, which employs more than 150,000 worldwide, announced plans in late 2019 to have women make up at least 40 percent of management roles worldwide by 2030 and to increase African American and Latinx representation to at least a quarter of its workforce. In a report released last May, Intel, which employs more than one hundred thousand workers, said it plans to increase the number of women in technical roles to 40 percent and double the number of women and underrepresented minorities in senior roles by 2030. And in mid-2020, in the wake of widespread Black Lives Matter protests, Sundar Pichai, CEO of Google parent Alphabet, which also has more than one hundred thousand employees, vowed to increase the proportion of "leadership representation of underrepresented groups" in the company by 30 percent by 2025.

Bringing More Voices to the Table

Those women who are starting to move into positions of power are reimagining and redefining what that looks like—and helping bring more female voices to the table, too. In a recent report, Credit Suisse took a closer look at the so-called Queen Bee syndrome, the outdated argument that women in senior positions actively exclude other women from having a seat in top management. Their findings? "Female CEOs are actually much *more* likely to surround themselves with other women in senior roles. In fact, female CEOs are 50 percent more likely than male CEOs to have a female CFO, and 55 percent more likely to have women running business units."

That's not just good for women but good for business. Several studies have suggested that having women on the executive team improves company results, and that women-led companies outperform those led only by men. One analysis by Quantopian, a Boston-based trading firm, found that between 2002 and 2014, companies with women in control saw returns that were *226 percent higher* than those with no women in leadership. The analysis found that female chief revenue officers in Fortune 1000 companies delivered three times the returns of the S&P 500 firms run predominately by men.

Consulting firm McKinsey calculated in a 2019 analysis that companies in the top quartile of gender diversity on executive teams "were 25 percent more likely to experience above-average profitability" than companies in the bottom quartile. Peakon, an HR insights platform that works with hundreds of organizations around the world to collect and analyze employee feedback, also found that women-led organizations are more likely to have "engaged, inspired and satisfied employees." And the Credit Suisse report, which looked at twenty-seven thousand senior managers at over three thousand companies covered by the financial institution's analysts, concluded, "The higher the percentage of women in top management, the greater the excess returns for shareholders." In short, women-led companies perform better.

Female-founded startups are reporting similar results. When it comes to raising capital, male founders consistently outpace female founders; but when it comes to actually generating revenue, researchers have found that female-founded startups tend to come out ahead. In one study, Boston Consulting Group followed 350 startups over five years and discovered that those founded by women generated 78 cents for every dollar invested in their companies—*more than double* the 31 cents per dollar invested that male-founded startups generated, on average. Over the five-year period, the researchers calculated that companies founded or cofounded by women generated 10 percent more in cumulative revenue than companies founded just by men. Another analysis, by TechCrunch, found that female-founded and female-cofounded companies are actually overindexing for unicorn status—a term given to startups that are valued at over a billion dollars—despite the lack of investment money.

While there's more work to be done, especially in bringing greater diversity into the C-suite and board rooms—advancing more women of color into management and leadership roles and directing more investment into companies founded by women, and particularly women of color—a cultural reckoning is underway. There's a growing acknowledgment of the inequities women, and particularly women of color, have faced in the workplace and in getting funding for businesses and commitments to change. There's also a growing recognition of the importance of having more diverse representation not just in the private sector but in government. At least 141 women were set to serve in Congress in 2021, breaking the record of 127 set in 2019. (They include Ilhan Omar and Rashida Tlaib, the first Muslim women elected to Congress, and Sharice Davids and Deb Haaland, the first Native American women elected to Congress—though Haaland was up for a potential cabinet appointment at this writing.) And, of course, Kamala Harris became the first female, and first woman of color, to be Vice President.

As We Build Our Wealth, We Build Our Power

Of course, there's still a ways to go. The data show that women are still being paid less on average and offered fewer opportunities for development, advancement, and meaningful work at many companies. And even with the record growth, women still represent just over a quarter of all voting members in Congress. Changing all that will take time. But as we build our wealth, we build our power. And as we ascend in our careers, we can pull others forward as well. So that one day, women will no longer have to worry about practicing power poses, adjusting our wardrobes and makeup, or modulating the sound of our voices to command the attention of our male peers. We will no longer have to worry about the way we speak, dress, walk, or stand in order to be heard and taken seriously. Because we can finally make our own rules.

Already, trailblazing women have founded successful startups that support other women's advancement in the workplace—and founding incubators and funds that support women and minorities who are launching their own ventures. Take Danielle Weisberg and Carly Zakin, who in 2012 founded TheSkimm, a startup that's already profitable and has more than 7 million subscribers to its daily news roundup, plus guides and tools to help its mostly millennial female readership advance in their careers and successfully manage their money and their health. And Georgene Huang and Romy Newman, who founded Fairygodboss, the Glassdoor-like career site and social network for professional women that's raised $14 million and grown to more than 1.5 million registered users in five years. And former Goldman Sachs executive Edith Cooper and her daughter, Jordan Taylor, who raised $1 million to launch a career-development platform called Medley for women early in their careers. The pair, who are Black, wrote that the launch of their startup "broadens the definition of the possible." And Natalia Oberti Noguera, founder and CEO of Pipeline Angels, a network of women investors that's changing the face of angel investing and creating capital for female social entrepreneurs. New data from Duquesne University in Pittsburgh show that women invest in women at nearly three times the rate that men do, and there's a growing number of female-led VC firms doing just that, including Female Founders Fund, BBG Ventures, Halogen Ventures, Jane VC, Cleo Capital, and Kate Brodock's W Fund.

Not only are these female founders, leaders, and advocates badass breadwinners themselves, but they are paving the way for millions of other women to have the opportunity to build their own wealth (and their own businesses!) and tap their unlimited potential. Of course, you don't need to start or fund a business, organize a protest, or advance to the C-suite to be a part of this movement forward. But it helps to remember that we are not alone and that we cannot address the remaining inequities that hold women—and especially women of color—back unless we work together, speak up, and stand up for one another and, as we rise, remember to help others up, too.

Embracing a breadwinning mindset allows you to be in a position not just to support yourself but also to support others. When you ascend to new heights in your career, you are better positioned to sponsor, spotlight, and promote other talented women around you, too. When you are able to build enough wealth to support the future you want and the people you love, you are also better positioned to put your money behind candidates and causes you believe in. If you are financially secure, you are better positioned to share your knowledge and resources with those who aren't.

Ultimately, thinking like a breadwinner sets you up to have more wealth, more power, and more of a say in what the future looks like for you *and* for other women. Talk about winning.

Acknowledgments

ENORMOUS THANKS TO the dozens of women who trusted me with their stories and who gave generously of their time and insights for this book. Equally huge thanks to my agents, Richard Pine and Eliza Rothstein, for their advocacy, enthusiasm—and patience! And to my extraordinary editor at Putnam, Michelle Howry, for nurturing this book to fruition with her deft editing skills, insightful feedback, and thoughtful approach. Thanks to my copy editor, Maureen Klier, for her conscientious edits, sharp eye for redundancies, and kind comments. Thanks to my stepmom, Jane Barrett, who gave me a dog-eared copy of *The Cinderella Complex* and encouraged me to write an update. Thanks to Mayumi Young, one of my dearest friends, whose support, encouragement, and wisdom helped keep me going. Thanks to Caroline McCarthy, Paula Derrow, and Meghan Stevenson for your early edits and for helping to sharpen my prose in the proposal. And to Suzanne Kingsbury for helping to coax the book out of my head and heart and onto the page. Thanks to Jennifer Crews and the remarkable, breadwinning women of my Chief core group, who provided validation, inspiration, and the nudge to get this over the finish line. Thanks to Sally Kim, Elora Weil, Emily Mlynek, Ashley Di Dio, and the rest of the Putnam and Penguin Random House team, who believed in this book and worked hard (through a pandemic no less) to bring it out into the world. Thanks to Kennedy Reynolds, Lauren Vann, Jacob Welch, and Britney Glass for championing me and this book and helping me build a public presence and a website that felt true and authentic to who I am and what I believe.

And thanks to Joy Stephan, Stacie Appel, Laura Goldberg, and the rest of my friends and my family, who inspire and uplift me every day, for their unwavering love and support. I am so deeply grateful to all of you.

Notes

Chapter 1: The Breadwinner Next Door

16 **divorce rates were relatively low:** Francesca Frida, "More Americans Are Single Than Ever Before—and They're Healthier, Too," *The Observer*, January 16, 2018, https://observer.com/2018/01/more-americans-are-single-than-ever-before-and-theyre-healthier-too/.

16 **marriage rate has been on the decline:** Ana Swanson, "144 Years of Marriage and Divorce in the United States, in One Chart," *Washington Post*, June 23, 2015, https://www.washingtonpost.com/news/wonk/wp/2015/06/23/144-years-of-marriage-and-divorce-in-the-united-states-in-one-chart/.

16 **outnumbered married ones for the first time in history:** *The World*, "Singles Now Outnumber Married People in America—and That's a Good Thing," Public Radio International, September 14, 2014, https://www.pri.org/stories/2014-09-14/singles-now-outnumber-married-people-america-and-thats-good-thing.

16 **More than half of Americans between eighteen and thirty-four today:** Anna Orso, "Forever Alone? More Than Half of Young Americans Don't Have a 'Steady Partner,' a Record High," *Philadelphia Inquirer*, https://www.inquirer.com/news/dating-match-millennials-marriage-study-single-half-20190322.html.

16 **The average age of first-time mothers . . . in the United States has also risen:** T. J. Mathews and Brady E. Hamilton, "Mean Age of Mother, 1970–2000," *National Vital Statistics Reports* 51, no. 1 (December 11, 2002), Centers for Disease Control, https://www.cdc.gov/nchs/data/nvsr/nvsr51/nvsr51_01.pdf; and National Center for Health Statistics, "Births and Natality," January 20, 2017, Centers for Disease Control, https://www.cdc.gov/nchs/fastats/births.htm.

16 **And more of us are raising those kids *by ourselves*:** Rebecca Lake, "What Is the Average Age of Marriage in the U.S.?," The Balance, June 27, 2020, https://

www.thebalance.com/what-is-the-average-age-to-have-a-baby-in-the-u-s-4582455.

16   **one in four kids in this country is growing up with a single mom:** United States Census Bureau, "The Majority of Children Live with Two Parents, Census Bureau Reports," press release, November 16, 2016, https://www.census.gov/newsroom/press-releases/2016/cb16-192.html.

16   **more single millennial moms than married ones:** Belinda Luscombe, "More Millennial Mothers Are Single Than Married," *Time*, June 17, 2014, https://time.com/2889816/more-millennial-mothers-are-single-than-married/.

17   **the birth rate for unmarried teens and single moms:** Sally C. Curtin, Stephanie J. Ventura, and Gladys M. Martinez, "Recent Declines in Nonmarital Childbearing in the United States," National Center for Health Statistics data brief, no. 162 (August 2014), Centers for Disease Control and Prevention, https://www.cdc.gov/nchs/data/databriefs/db162.pdf.

17   **Isabel Sawhill, a senior fellow at the Brookings Institution:** Claire Cain Miller, "Single Motherhood, in Decline over All, Rises for Women 35 and Older," *New York Times*, May 8, 2015, https://www.nytimes.com/2015/05/09/upshot/out-of-wedlock-births-are-falling-except-among-older-women.html.

18   **the majority of men *and* women still said they prefer**: Catherine H. Tinsley, Taeya M. Howell, and Emily T. Amanatullah, "Who Should Bring Home the Bacon? How Deterministic Views of Gender Constrain Spousal Wage Preferences," *Organizational Behavior and Human Decision Processes* 126 (January 2015): 37–48, https://www.sciencedirect.com/science/article/abs/pii/S0749597814000685.

18   **nearly half of all marriages end in divorce:** American Psychological Association, "Marriage and Divorce," https://www.apa.org/topics/divorce/.

19   **women's household income fell by 41 percent after a divorce:** United States Government Accountability Office, *Retirement Security: Women Still Face Challenges*, Special Committee on Aging, report to the chairman, no. 12-699, July 2012, https://www.aging.senate.gov/imo/media/doc/hr250gao.pdf.

20   **the percentage of families in which only a father works:** Sarah Jane Glynn, "An Unequal Division of Labor," Center for American Progress, May 18, 2018, https://www.americanprogress.org/issues/women/reports/2018/05/18/450972/unequal-division-labor/.

20   **6.5 million unmarried women in cohabiting opposite- or same-sex couples:** Wendy Wang, "The Happiness Penalty for Breadwinning Moms," Institute for Family Studies, June 4, 2019, https://ifstudies.org/blog/the-happiness-penalty-for-breadwinning-moms.

20   **49 percent of employed women in the United States:** Carrie Dann, "Poll: Workplace Equality Stalls for Women Even as Perceptions Improve," NBC News, March 22, 2018, https://www.nbcnews.com/politics/first-read/poll-workplace-equality-stalls-women-even-perceptions-improve-n859206.

20   **moms were still contributing at least 40 percent of household earnings:** Elyse Shaw, C. Nicole Mason, Valerie Lacarte, and Erika Jauregui, "Holding Up Half the Sky: Mothers as Workers, Primary Caregivers, and Breadwinners During COVID-19," Institute for Women's Policy Research, https://iwpr.org

/iwpr-issues/employment-and-earnings/holding-up-half-the-sky-mothers-as-workers-primary-caregivers-breadwinners-during-covid-19-2/.

21 **Some of those jobs never came back:** Rakesh Kochhar, "Two Years of Economic Recovery: Women Lose Jobs, Men Find Them," Pew Research Center, July 6, 2011, https://www.pewsocialtrends.org/2011/07/06/two-years-of-economic-recovery-women-lose-jobs-men-find-them/.

21 **The percentage of men working today is actually lower:** "Civilian Labor Force Participation Rate by Age, Sex, Race, and Ethnicity," U.S. Bureau of Labor Statistics, last modified September 1, 2020, https://www.bls.gov/emp/tables/civilian-labor-force-participation-rate.htm.

21 **At the end of 2019 . . . more women than men were in the workforce:** Amara Omeokwe, "Women Overtake Men as Majority of U.S. Workforce," *Wall Street Journal*, January 10, 2020, https://www.wsj.com/articles/women-overtake-men-as-majority-of-u-s-workforce-11578670615.

21 **Even in the pandemic, women's earnings continued to account:** "Employment Status of the Civilian Population by Sex and Age," United States Bureau of Labor Statistics, last modified August 7, 2020, https://www.bls.gov/news.release/empsit.t01.htm.

Chapter 2: What's Been Baked into Us

25 **"bad message to send to anybody . . . especially to girls":** Stephen J. Dubner, "Does Hollywood Still Have a Princess Problem," *Freakonomics*, October 23, 2019, https://freakonomics.com/podcast/princess/.

25 **women in the United States still earn just 82 cents for every dollar that men do:** "America's Women and the Wage Gap," National Partnership for Women and Families Fact Sheet, September 2020, https://www.nationalpartnership.org/our-work/resources/economic-justice/fair-pay/americas-women-and-the-wage-gap.pdf.

25 **Black and Latina women earn even less:** Robin Bleiweis, "Quick Facts About the Gender Wage Gap," Center for American Progress, March 24, 2020, https://www.americanprogress.org/issues/women/reports/2020/03/24/482141/quick-facts-gender-wage-gap/.

26 **they weren't confident they'd be able to retire comfortably:** Transamerica Center for Retirement Studies, "Nineteen Facts That Illuminate Women's Retirement Risks," news release, November 14, 2019, https://www.transamericacenter.org/docs/default-source/women-and-retirement/tcrs2019_pr_women_and_retirement_press-release.pdf.

26 **by the time they reach retirement age:** Merrill Lynch and Age Wave, "Women and Financial Wellness: Beyond the Bottom Line," https://www.bofaml.com/content/dam/boamlimages/documents/articles/ID18_0244/ml_womens_study.pdf.

27 **GiftCards.com survey found that girls even get less money:** GiftCards.com, "Adolescent Income and Financial Literacy," September 2018, https://www.giftcards.com/adolescent-income-and-financial-literacy.

27 **Bri Godwin, a media relations associate:** Jared Lindzon, "How Parents Talk

About Money Differently to Their Sons and Daughters," *Fast Company*, January 14, 2019, https://www.fastcompany.com/90283344/how-parents-talk-about-money-differently-to-their-sons-and-daughters.

27 **twice as many boys as girls reported having access to credit cards:** T. Rowe Price, "Parents, Kids and Money Survey," 2019, https://www.slideshare.net/TRowePrice/t-rowe-prices-11th-annual-parents-kids-money-survey.

28 **"Did I inadvertently favor my son over my daughter?":** Judith Ward, "Parents: Are You Favoring Boys over Girls?," *Huffington Post*, September 3, 2014, https://www.huffpost.com/entry/parents-are-you-favoring-_b_5761448.

28 **research firm Age Wave analyzed the money coverage:** Merrill Lynch, "Women and Financial Wellness."

28 *90 percent* **of money articles aimed at women:** Anne Boden, "Why We Need to #MakeMoneyEqual," Starling Bank, March 13, 2018, https://www.starlingbank.com/blog/make-money-equal/.

29 **"With men, money is all about power suits and investing":** Kristen Wong, "The Myth of the Frivolous Female Spender," *New York Times*, October 4, 2019, https://www.nytimes.com/2019/10/04/us/myth-frivolous-female-spender.html.

30 **"From the very beginning, we train children to have unconscious gender bias":** Homa Khaleeli, "Geena Davis: 'The More TV a Girl Watches, the Fewer Options She Thinks She Has in Life,'" *The Guardian*, February 29, 2016, https://www.theguardian.com/lifeandstyle/2016/feb/29/geena-davis-tv-girl-gender-equality-thelma-louise-women.

30 **female characters are far less likely to even be** *employed***:** Stacy Smith, Marc Choueti, Ashley Prescott, and Katherine Pieper, "Gender Role and Occupations: A Look at Character Attributes and Job-Related Aspirations in Film and Television," 2013, Geena Davis Institute on Gender in Media, https://seejane.org/wp-content/uploads/key-findings-gender-roles-2013.pdf.

30 *81 percent* **of jobs depicted in family shows are held by men:** Maria Aspen, "Geena Davis Talks Tracking Hollywood's Diversity Data, Advocating for Women in STEM, and Not Playing Role Models," *Inc.*, https://www.inc.com/maria-aspan/geena-davis-women-in-stem.html.

31 **ads continue to promote sexism and distorted female body images:** Stacy Landreth Grau and Yorgos C. Zotos, "Gender Stereotypes in Advertising: A Review of Current Research," *International Journal on Advertising* 35, no. 5 (Gender Issue in Advertising, 2016): 761–70, https://www.tandfonline.com/doi/abs/10.1080/02650487.2016.1203556.

31 **In another study funded by the Institute on Gender in Media:** https://seejane.org/research-informs-empowers/diversity-inclusivity-report-gender-in-youtube-advertising/.

31 **Sarah Moshman . . .** *Forbes* **interview:** Kathy Caprino, "What's Wrong with the Media's Portrayal of Women Today, and How to Reverse It," *Forbes*, November 21, 2014, https://www.forbes.com/sites/kathycaprino/2014/11/21/whats-wrong-with-the-medias-portrayal-of-women-today-and-how-to-reverse-it/#360f5bf044c2.

31 **engagement with Disney princess products and movies:** Sarah Coyne, Jennifer Ruh Linder, Eric E. Rasmussen, David A. Nelson, and Victoria Birkbeck, "Pretty as a Princess: Longitudinal Effects of Engagement with

Disney Princesses on Gender Stereotypes, Body Esteem, and Prosocial Behavior in Children," *Child Development* 87, no. 6 (June 2016), https://www .researchgate.net/publication/304071159_Pretty_as_a_Princess_Longitudinal _Effects_of_Engagement_With_Disney_Princesses_on_Gender_Stereotypes _Body_Esteem_and_Prosocial_Behavior_in_Children.

34 **One study by the Girl Scouts found that nearly half of girls:** Girl Scout Research Institute, "Having It All: Girls and Financial Literacy," April 2013, https://www.girlscouts.org/content/dam/girlscouts-gsusa/forms-and -documents/about-girl-scouts/research/GSRI_Having_It_All_report.pdf.

34 **financial planning "is too difficult to even think about":** Merrill Lynch, "Women and Financial Wellness."

34 **58 percent of women leave those crucial choices:** Christy Rakoczy, "Americans Are (Sort of) Confident About Money and Finances, Survey Says," Student Loan Hero, December 3, 2018, https://studentloanhero.com/featured /financial_confidence_survey/.

34 **Younger women between ages twenty and thirty-four were actually the *most* likely to defer:** Emily Zulz, "Many Women Defer to Men for Financial Decisions," ThinkAdvisor, March 7, 2019, https://www.thinkadvisor.com /2019/03/07/many-women-defer-to-spouses-on-big-financial-decisions-ubs/.

34 **Only 36 percent of millennial women:** Shelley Schwartz, "Women Lagging in Retirement Saving: Survey," CNBC, March 4, 2015, https://www.cnbc.com /2015/03/04/women-lagging-in-retirement-saving-survey.html.

35 **single women are less likely than any other demographic group:** Fidelity Investments, "Single Women on the Rise," press release, November 21, 2017, https://www.fidelity.com/about-fidelity/individual-investing/single-women-on -the-rise.

35 **men have nearly twice as much stashed in an emergency fund:** BMO Harris, "Majority of Americans Are Saving, but Most Lack a Financial Plan," news release, May 28, 2015, https://newsroom.bmoharris.com/2015-05-28-BMO -Harris-Premier-Services-Majority-of-Americans-Are-Saving-But-Most-Lack-a -Financial-Plan.

35 **Over the course of their lifetimes, men save more than three times:** TurboTax, "He Saves, She Saves: Men vs. Women's View on Savings," infographic, July 12, 2013, https://blog.turbotax.intuit.com/income-and -investments/he-saves-she-saves-men-vs-womens-view-on-savings -infographic-14898/.

35 **single women have more debt, higher credit card usage:** Geng Li, "Gender-Related Differences in Credit Use and Credit Scores," June 22, 2018, Board of Governors of the Federal Reserve System, https://www.federalreserve.gov /econres/notes/feds-notes/gender-related-differences-in-credit-use-and-credit -scores-20180622.htm.

Chapter 3: The Joy of Breadwinning

37 **often *less* likely to be in the workforce once her income matched his:** Marianne Bertrand and Emir Kamenica, "Gender Identity and Relative

Income within Households," *The Quarterly Journal of Economics* 130, no. 2 (2015): 571–614, accessed at: https://econpapers.repec.org/article/oupqjecon /v_3a130_3ay_3a2015_3ai_3a2_3ap_3a571-614.htm.

38   **"Men with Breadwinning Wives More Likely to Cheat":** Kelly Wallace, "Men with Breadwinning Wives More Likely to Cheat," CNN, October 7, 2016, https://www.cnn.com/2016/10/07/health/infidelity-breadwinners-cheat -husband-wife/index.html.

38   **"Men Stress Out if They're Not the Breadwinner":** Nicole Lyn Pesce, "Men Stress Out if They're Not the Breadwinner," *New York Post*, November 20, 2019, https://nypost.com/2019/11/20/men-stress-out-if-theyre-not-the -breadwinner-study/.

38   **"Can a Female Breadwinner Have a Happy Marriage?"** Minda Zetlin, "Can a Female Breadwinner Have a Happy Marriage?" *Inc.*, December 18, 2015, https://www.inc.com/minda-zetlin/can-a-female-breadwinner-have-a-happy -marriage.html

38   **"Super-Successful Women Struggle in Love":** Suzanne Venker, "Super-Successful Women Struggle in Love," *Washington Examiner*, October 9, 2019, https://www.washingtonexaminer.com/opinion/why-super-successful-women -struggle-in-love.

38   **"Dating Successful Women Makes Men Uneasy":** Shana Lebowitz, "Dating Successful Women Makes Men Uneasy," *Business Insider*, March 2, 2018, https://www.businessinsider.com/dating-successful-women-makes-many-men -uneasy-2018-3.

38   **"A Sociologist Explains Why Wealthy Women Are Doomed to Be Miserable":** Rachel Sherman, "A Sociologist Explains Why Wealthy Women Are Doomed to Be Miserable," *Quartz*, November 9, 2017, https://qz.com /1124298/a-sociologist-explains-why-wealthy-women-are-doomed-to-be -miserable/.

38   **"If you want to be successful in your career, don't have children":** Kristen Houghton, "Most Successful Women Are Childless," *Huffington Post*, April 15, 2013, https://www.huffpost.com/entry/childless_b_2630389.

38   **Even the *Harvard Business Review* warned:** Marianne Cooper, "For Women Leaders, Likability and Success Hardly Go Hand in Hand," *Harvard Business Review*, April 30, 2013, https://hbr.org/2013/04/for-women-leaders-likability-a.

38   **it went viral, landing her on all the morning shows:** Jessica Knoll, "I Want to Be Rich and I'm Not Sorry," *New York Times*, April 28, 2014, https://www .nytimes.com/2018/04/28/opinion/sunday/women-want-to-be-rich.html.

39   **Reading *those* headlines, you might think that breadwinning wives:** Mona Chalabi, "How Many Women Earn More Than Their Husbands?," FiveThirty-Eight, February 5, 2015, https://fivethirtyeight.com/features/how-many-women -earn-more-than-their-husbands/.

39   **husbands not being willing to do their fair share of household work is the bigger factor:** Kate Irby, "Wife the Breadwinner? You're More Likely to Get Divorced Unless Husbands Do This," *Miami Herald*, May 4, 2017, https:// www.miamiherald.com/news/nation-world/national/article148558804.html.

40   *USA Today* **ran a story headlined:** Aimee Picchi, "More Women Are Now Outearning Their Husbands—and Emotions Can Be Big," *USA Today*, March 3,

2020, https://www.usatoday.com/story/money/2020/03/03/gender-wage-gap
-more-women-out-earning-husbands/4933666002/.

40   **the majority of men seemed to be just fine:** TD Ameritrade, "Breadwinners
Survey," March 2020, https://s2.q4cdn.com/437609071/files/doc_news
/research/2020/breadwinners-survey.pdf.

40   **"For both men and women, economic dependency is associated":** Christin L.
Munsch, "Her Support, His Support: Money, Masculinity, and Marital
Infidelity," *American Sociological Review* 80, no. 3 (May 31, 2015), https://
journals.sagepub.com/doi/abs/10.1177/0003122415579989.

40   **splitting the division of housework equitably:** Alexandra Killewald,
"Money, Work, and Marital Stability: Assessing Change in the Gendered
Determinants of Divorce," *Sociological Review* 81, no. 4 (2016), 696–719,
https://www.asanet.org/sites/default/files/attach/journals/aug16asrfeature.pdf?
mod=article_inline.

41   **This has been echoed by several other studies:** Maddy Savage, "Why
Promoted Women Are More Likely to Divorce," BBC Worklife, January 22,
2020, https://www.bbc.com/worklife/article/20200121-why-promoted-women
-are-more-likely-to-divorce.

41   **About half of women now say they outearn or make around the same
amount:** TD Ameritrade, "Breadwinners Survey."

41   **less than 4 percent of women earned more than their husbands in 1960:**
Wendy Wang, Kim Parker, and Paul Taylor, *Breadwinner Moms: Mothers Are
the Sole or Primary Provider in Four-in-Ten Households with Children; Public
Conflicted About the Growing Trend*, Pew Research Center, May 29, 2013,
https://www.pewsocialtrends.org/wp-content/uploads/sites/3/2013/05
/Breadwinner_moms_final.pdf.

42   **despite growing evidence that we often perform better as investors:** Fidelity
Investments, "Fidelity Investments Survey Reveals Only Nine Percent of
Women Think They Make Better Investors Than Men, Despite Growing
Evidence to the Contrary," press release, May 18, 2017, https://www.fidelity
.com/about-fidelity/individual-investing/better-investor-men-or-women.

50   **same-sex couples "are far more likely to each take on some traditionally
'feminine' and some 'masculine' chores":** Stephanie Coontz, "How to Make
Your Marriage Gayer," *New York Times*, February 13, 2020, https://www
.nytimes.com/2020/02/13/opinion/sunday/marriage-housework-gender
-happiness.html.

50   **researchers found, they're happier for it:** Abbie E. Goldberg and Maureen
Perry-Jenkins, "The Division of Labor and Perceptions of Parental Roles:
Lesbian Couples Across the Transition to Parenthood," *Journal of Social and
Personal Relationships*, 24 (2007), https://wordpress.clarku.edu/agoldberg/files
/2012/03/Goldberg-PerryJenkins-JSPR-2007.pdf.

50   **lesbians tend to earn more than their heterosexual counterparts:** 2016 report
by the Treasury Department, https://www.treasury.gov/resource-center/
tax-policy/tax-analysis/Documents/WP-108.pdf; Marieka Klawitter, "Meta-
Analysis of the Effects of Sexual Orientation on Earnings," *Industrial Relations*
54, no. 1 (January 2015), 4–32, https://onlinelibrary.wiley.com/doi/abs/10.1111
/irel.12075.

50 **female same-sex couples report more total household income:** Danielle Paquette, "The Surprising Reason Why Lesbians Get Paid More Than Straight Women," *Washington Post*, February 25, 2016, https://www.washingtonpost .com/news/wonk/wp/2016/02/25/the-surprising-reason-why-lesbians-get-paid -more-than-straight-women/.

Chapter 4: Dream Bigger

55 **effects of mental imagery on the brain:** Tim Blankert and Melvyn R. W. Hamstra, "Imagining Success: Multiple Achievement Goals and the Effectiveness of Imagery," *Basic and Applied Sociology* 39, no. 1 (2017), https:// www.tandfonline.com/doi/full/10.1080/01973533.2016.1255947.

55 **increasingly accepted psychological technique to help accelerate learning:** Corina Schuster, Roger Hilfiker, Oliver Amft, et al., "Best Practice for Motor Imagery: A Systematic Literature Review on Motor Imagery Training Elements in Five Different Disciplines," *BMC Medicine* 9, article no. 75 (2011), http://bmcmedicine.biomedcentral.com/articles/10.1186/1741-7015-9-75.

55 **improved soldiers' cognitive and physical abilities:** David Vergun, "Mental Skills Training Improving Soldier Performance," Army News Service, August 5, 2015, https://www.army.mil/article/153231/mental_skills_training_improving _soldier_performance.

55 **students who simulated a successful performance:** Lien B. Pham and Shelley E. Taylor, "From Thought to Action: Effects of Process- Versus Outcome-Based Mental Simulations on Performance," *Personality and Social Psychology Bulletin*, February 1, 1999, https://journals.sagepub.com/doi/10.1177/01461672990 25002010.

56 **"when you create an image that is crisp and has color":** Richard Feloni, "A Sports Psychologist Shares the Visualization Technique That's Helped Super Bowl Champions and Olympic Gold-Medalists," *Business Insider*, August 21, 2017, https://www.businessinsider.com/sports-visualization-technique-2017-8.

56 **those who visualize achieving their financial goals:** TD Bank, "Visualizing Goals Influences Financial Health and Happiness, Study Finds," January 20, 2016, https://newscenter.td.com/us/en/news/2016/visualizing-goals-influences -financial-health-and-happiness-study-finds.

60 **"Studies have shown it takes more compelling evidence to change beliefs":** Amy Morin, "Why It's So Hard to Change the Self-Limiting Beliefs You Learned During Childhood," *Forbes*, October 5, 2017, https://www.forbes .com/sites/amymorin/2017/10/05/why-its-so-hard-to-change-the-self -limiting-beliefs-you-learned-during-childhood/#6c870f322185.

60 **Nina Cooke, a business coach certified in neuro-linguistic programming:** Joy Burnford, "Limiting Beliefs: What Are They and How Can You Overcome Them?," *Forbes*, January 30, 2019, https://www.forbes.com/sites/joyburnford /2019/01/30/limiting-beliefs-what-are-they-and-how-can-you-overcome-them /#3aa076376303.

62 **A 2016 survey by Weight Watchers:** "Average Woman Criticizes Herself at Least Eight Times a Day" January 3, 2016, Weight Watchers U.K., https://

www.swnsdigital.com/2016/01/average-woman-criticises-herself-at-least-eight
-times-a-day/.

63 **participants boosted their performance:** "Self-Affirmations May Calm
Jitters, Boost Performance," *Personality and Social Psychology Bulletin,* April 17,
2015, https://www.sciencedaily.com/releases/2015/04/150417085408.htm.

Chapter 5: More Savings = More Choices

73 **"How many of them have secrets like the one you're about to keep?":** Paulette
Perhach, "A Story of a Fuck Off Fund," *The Billfold,* January 20, 2016, https://
www.thebillfold.com/2016/01/a-story-of-a-fuck-off-fund/.

75 **money as a "significant source of stress":** American Psychological
Association, "Stress in America—2020," October 2020, https://www.apa.org
/news/press/releases/stress/2020/report-october.

78 **fewer than half of women were regularly saving:** Katie Bryan, "Less Than
Half of U.S. Households Report Good Savings Progress, According to 9th
Annual America Saves Week," February 22, 2016, America Saves Week,
https://americasavesweek.org/less-than-half-of-u-s-households-report-good
-savings-progress-according-to-9th-annual-america-saves-week-survey/.

79 **nearly one in four women had less than $100 saved:** Cameron Huddleston,
"Most Americans Lack Savings to Pay for These Huge Emergencies," February 8,
2018, https://www.chicagotribune.com/business/ct-biz-emergency-savings
-personal-finance-20180208-story.html.

79 **nearly one-third of women said they had more credit card debt:** Amanda
Dixon, "Nearly Half of Americans Say Boosting Emergency Savings Trumps
the Need to Reduce Debt," Bankrate, February 20, 2020, https://www.bankrate
.com/banking/savings/financial-security-february-2020/.

86 **"chasing something that we don't even want":** Jessica Dore, "Personal Values
vs. Cultural Conditioning: Helping Patients Tell the Difference," Psych
Central, May 4, 2018, https://pro.psychcentral.com/personal-values-vs-cultural
-conditioning-helping-patients-tell-the-difference/.

Chapter 6: Give Yourself Some Credit

90 **credit card debt in the United States topped *$1 trillion*:** Board of Governors
of the Federal Reserve System, "Consumer Credit–G.19," June 2020, last
updated August 7, 2020, https://www.federalreserve.gov/releases/g19/current/.

90 **one survey found nearly twice as many women as men:** Abby Hayes, "The
Debt Gender Gap: How Women Can Close It," *U.S. News and World Report,*
June 26, 2015, https://money.usnews.com/money/blogs/my-money/2015/06
/26/the-debt-gender-gap-how-women-can-close-it.

90 **We also carry higher balances:** Nitro, "Debt Regret," https://www.nitrocollege
.com/research/debt-regret.

90 **women are more likely than men to make only minimum:** Gary R. Mottola,
"In Our Best Interest: Women, Financial Literacy, and Credit Card Behavior,"

Numeracy 6, no. 2 (2013): Article 4, https://scholarcommons.usf.edu/cgi/view content.cgi?article=1134&context=numeracy.

90 **single women tend to use their credit cards more:** Li, "Gender-Related Differences in Credit Use and Credit Scores."

90 **men are much more likely than women to say they pay their bill on time:** "Fewer Americans Are Paying Their Credit Card Balances in Full—Especially Women," CompareCards, August 22, 2019, https://www.prnewswire.com /news-releases/fewer-americans-are-paying-their-credit-card-balances-in-full— especially-women-according-to-comparecards-report-300905830.html.

91 **the *average* interest rate was over 20 percent:** Sienna Kossman, "Average Credit Card Interest Rate Is 20.19%," The Balance, accessed on October 1, 2020, https://www.thebalance.com/average-credit-card-interest-rate-4772408.

91 **new card offers carried more than 16 percent in interest:** Kelly Dilworth, "Average Credit Card Interest Rates," Creditcards.com, accessed on October 2, 2020, https://www.creditcards.com/credit-card-news/rate-report.php.

91 **more women than men end up filing for bankruptcy:** Li, "Gender-Related Differences in Credit Use and Credit Scores."

91 **a process that helps wipe out most debts:** Leslie E. Linfield, "2010 Annual Consumer Bankruptcy Demographics Report: A Five Year Perspective of the American Debtor," Institute for Financial Literacy, September 2011, https:// papers.ssrn.com/sol3/papers.cfm?abstract_id=1925006.

91 **filing for bankruptcy can send a good credit score:** Lucy Lazarony, "What Happens to Your Credit Score After Bankruptcy?," Credit.com, March 10, 2020, https://www.credit.com/credit-scores/3-things-bankruptcy-does-to-your -credit-score/.

91 **subprime credit cards can carry interest rates of more than 25 percent:** Josh Smith, "What Is a Prime vs. Subprime Credit Score?," Credit.com, https:// www.credit.com/blog/what-is-a-prime-vs-subprime-credit-score-189867/.

92 **Other research by Credit Sesame found similar trends:** Credit Sesame, "The Closing Credit Score Gender Gap: 4 Takeaways for International Women's Day," March 8, 2020, https://www.creditsesame.com/blog/credit/international -womens-day/.

92 **parents are more likely to teach their sons how to build credit:** GiftCards.com, "Adolescent Income and Financial Literacy."

92 **women generally have lower levels of financial literacy:** Mottola, "In Our Best Interest."

93 **going from a "fair" credit score to a "very good" score:** Kali McFadden, "Raising a 'Fair' Credit Score to 'Very Good' Could Save Over $56,000," LendingTree, January 7, 2020, https://www.lendingtree.com/personal/study -raising-credit-score-saves-money/.

95 **with nearly $1.7 trillion in outstanding student loan debt:** Federal Reserve Bank of St. Louis, "Student Loans Owned and Securitized, Outstanding (SLOAS)," https://fred.stlouisfed.org/series/SLOAS.

95 **That translates to almost $1.1 trillion in student debt that women owe:** American Association of University Women, *Deeper in Debt: Women and Student Loans* (Washington, DC: AAUW, May 2017), https://www.aauw.org /app/uploads/2020/03/DeeperinDebt-nsa.pdf.

96 **"If total debt is less than annual income":** Susan Tompor, "Black Women Bear Largest Burden in Student Debt Crisis," *Detroit Free-Press*, October 14, 2019, https://www.freep.com/in-depth/money/personal-finance/susan -tompor/2019/10/10/student-debt-crisis-us-black-women/2233035001/.

96 **it can take student borrowers with a bachelor's degree:** One Wisconsin Institute, "The Impact of Student Loan Debt on the National Economy," June 13, 2013, https://drive.google.com/file/d/0B8LurBVUNQZfQVhYZWZ vamlfd00/view.

96 **If you have federal student loans:** Federal Student Aid, "Income-Driven Repayment Plans," United States Department of Education, https://studentaid .gov/manage-loans/repayment/plans/income-driven.

97 **To qualify for the best rates:** Ryan Lane, "Should You Refinance Federal Student Loans?," NerdWallet, July 14, 2020, https://www.nerdwallet.com /blog/loans/student-loans/should-you-refinance-federal-student-loans/.

98 **68 percent of the median U.S. household's wealth:** B. Ravikumar, "Staff Pick: Who Has Equity in Their Homes? Who Doesn't?," Federal Reserve Bank of St. Louis, May 21, 2019, https://www.stlouisfed.org/on-the-economy/2019 /may/staff-pick-who-equity-their-homes-who-doesn't.

98 **homeowners' median net worth was *eighty times* larger:** Jonathan Eggleston and Donald Hays, "Many U.S. Households Do Not Have Biggest Contributors to Wealth: Home Equity and Retirement Accounts," United States Census Bureau, August 27, 2019, https://www.census.gov/library /stories/2019/08/gaps-in-wealth-americans-by-household-type.html.

101 **Nearly 57 percent of Americans have a FICO score of 700:** The Ascent, "Here's What Americans' FICO Scores Look Like—How Do You Compare?," July 29, 2020, https://www.fool.com/the-ascent/credit-cards/articles/heres-what -americans-fico-scores-look-like-how-do/.

102 **submit all the applications in a two-week period:** Kendall Little, "How Can Shopping Loan Rates Affect Your Credit?," December 6, 2019, Bankrate.com, https://www.bankrate.com/finance/credit-cards/rate-shopping-loans-credit -score/.

103 **among those with a score below 680:** Kate Gibson, "A Credit Bump for Those Paying Wireless Bills on Time," December 18, 2018, https://www.cbsnews .com/news/experian-offers-credit-bump-for-paying-utility-wireless-bills-on -time/.

104 **need a score of at least 690 for the best offers:** Claire Tsosie, "What Is a Balance Transfer, and Should I Do One?," NerdWallet, accessed on October 3, 2020, https://www.nerdwallet.com/article/credit-cards/balance-transfer-3.

105 **54 percent of men:** Matt Schulz, "CompareCards.com 2018 Balance Transfer Credit Card Report," December 12, 2018, https://www.comparecards.com /blog/balance-transfer-credit-card-report/.

106 **it's important to be aware of what you're actually spending:** Lu-Hai Liang, "Does e-Money Make You Spend More?," BBC, December 5, 2019, https:// www.bbc.com/future/article/20191204-does-e-money-make-you-spend-more.

107 **That alone was worth $520 based on valuations:** Points Guy, "What Are Points and Miles Worth? August 2020 Monthly Valuations," accessed in August 2020, https://thepointsguy.com/guide/monthly-valuations/.

107   **equal to a 7.8 percent return on airline-related spending:** Points Guy, "What Are Points and Miles Worth?"

108   **you can earn literally thousands:** Erica Sandberg, "How Much Can You Really Make with a Cash Back Card?," Creditcards.com, April 17, 2020, https://www.creditcards.com/credit-card-news/how-much-money-make-with -cash-back-cards.php.

Chapter 7: Invest in Your Future

109   **parents are more likely to teach girls how to track their spending and budget:** Lindzon, "How Parents Talk About Money Differently to Their Sons and Daughters."

109   **men are much more likely to take finance and business courses:** Andrea Hasler and Annamaria Lusardi, *The Gender Gap in Financial Literacy: A Global Perspective*, Global Financial Literacy Excellence Center, George Washington University School of Business, July 2017, https://gflec.org/wp-content/uploads /2017/07/The-Gender-Gap-in-Financial-Literacy-A-Global-Perspective -Report.pdf?x87657.

109   **as women, we tend to feel less knowledgeable:** Merrill Lynch and Age Wave, "Women and Financial Wellness: Beyond the Bottom Line." https://www .bofaml.com/content/dam/boamlimages/documents/articles/ID18_0244 /ml_womens_study.pdf.

110   **less than half of the women surveyed:** Fidelity, "Money Fit Women Study: Executive Summary," https://www.fidelity.com/bin-public/060_www_fidelity _com/documents/women-fit-money-study.pdf.

110   **men continue to be much more confident:** Merrill Lynch and Age Wave, "Women and Financial Wellness: Beyond the Bottom Line." https://www .bofaml.com/content/dam/boamlimages/documents/articles/ID18_0244 /ml_womens_study.pdf.

110   **many of us end up waiting too long:** Business Wire, "Women Demand More from Their Money: 7-in-10 to Take Steps in the Next Six Months to Make Their Money Work Harder and Grow," November 15, 2018, https://www .businesswire.com/news/home/20181115005114/en/Women-Demand-Money -7-in-10-Steps-Months-Money.

111   **among those with 401(k) balances below $5,000:** Retirement Clearinghouse, "Manual Portability and the Mobile Workforce," http://info.rch1.com/mobile workforce.

111   **only a quarter of women:** Financial Finesse, "Gender Gap in Financial Wellness," January 1, 2017, https://www.financialfinesse.com/2017/01/01 /special-report-roi-of-improving-employee-retirement-preparedness-2/.

111   **one in five women:** Laura Wronski, "CNBC-SurveyMonkey Poll: International Women's Day 2020," CNBC, https://www.surveymonkey.com /curiosity/cnbc-international-womens-day-2020/.

113   **women still make up just 9 percent of traders:** Intercontinental Exchange, "Women on Wall Street," 2020, https://www.intercontinentalexchange.com /about/corporate-responsibility/diverse-leadership/women-on-wall-street.

113   **women still end up deferring to their male partners:** UBS, "Women Put Financial Security at Risk by Deferring Long-Term Financial Decisions to Spouses, UBS Research Reveals," March 6, 2019, https://www.ubs.com /global/en/media/display-page-ndp/en-20190306-financial-security.html.

114   **For men, investing for retirement was number one:** Willis Towers Watson, "Gender Differences in Saving for Retirement Linked to Financial Needs, Willis Towers Watson Survey Finds," press release, March 28, 2018, https:// www.willistowerswatson.com/en-US/news/2018/03/gender-differences -on-saving-for-retirement-linked-to-financial-needs.

115   **"Women are afraid of losing money":** Jean Chatzky, "Why Women Invest 40 Percent Less than Most Men (and How We Can Change It)," NBC, September 25, 2018, https://www.nbcnews.com/better/business/why-women -invest-40-percent-less-men-how-we-can-ncna912956.

118   **a small fraction of the thousands of companies that trade publicly:** Editorial Board, "Where Have All the Public Companies Gone?," Bloomberg, April 2, 2018, https://www.bloomberg.com/opinion/articles/2018-04-09/where-have -all-the-u-s-public-companies-gone.

119   **women actually *do* tend to outperform men in the returns:** Brad M. Barber and Terrance Odean, "Boys Will Be Boys: Gender, Overconfidence, and Common Stock Investment," *Quarterly Journal of Economics*, February 2001: 261–92, http://faculty.haas.berkeley.edu/odean/papers%20current%20versions /boyswillbeboys.pdf.

119   **Women today have retirement balances:** Galina Young and Jean A. Young, "Women Versus Men in DC Plans," Vanguard Center for Investor Research, January 2019, https://institutional.vanguard.com/iam/pdf/GENDRESP.pdf.

119   **women are 80 percent more likely than men:** National Institute on Retirement Security, "Women 80% More Likely to Be Impoverished in Retirement," press release March 1, 2016, https://www.nirsonline.org/2016/03 /women-80-more-likely-to-be-impoverished-in-retirement/.

123   **you want to contribute the max allowed under law:** Internal Revenue Service, "401(K) Contribution Limit Increases to $19,500 for 2020; Catch-Up Limit Rises to $6,500," last updated November 10, 2020, https://www.irs.gov /retirement-plans/plan-participant-employee/retirement-topics-401k-and -profit-sharing-plan-contribution-limits.

125   **if you earned $139,000 or more:** Internal Revenue Service, "Amount of Roth IRA Contributions That You Can Make for 2020," last updated November 10, 2020, https://www.irs.gov/retirement-plans/amount-of-roth-ira-contributions -that-you-can-make-for-2021.

127   **analysts are usually talking about how much the S&P 500 Index has grown:** Michael Santoli, "The S&P 500 Has Already Met Its Average Return for a Full Year, But Don't Expect It to Stay Here," CBNC, June 18, 2017, https:// www.cnbc.com/2017/06/18/the-sp-500-has-already-met-its-average-return -for-a-full-year.html.

129   **average index fund had an expense ratio of just 0.07 percent:** Investment Company Institute, "Trends in the Expenses and Fees of Funds, 2019," *ICI Research Perspective* 26, no. 1 (March 2020), https://www.ici.org/pdf /per26-01.pdf.

129   **total return of more than 240 percent over a decade:** Anna-Louise Jackson, "How Much $500 Invested 5 Different Ways 10 Years Ago Would Be Worth Now," Grow, December 10, 2019, https://grow.acorns.com/what-500-dollars -invested-different-ways-10-years-ago-would-be-worth-now/.

138   **1 percent rule:** Carol M. Kopp, "One Percent Rule," November 11, 2020, Investopedia, https://www.investopedia.com/terms/o/one-percent-rule.asp.

139   **housing values in New York City had dropped:** Jeff Andrews, "NYC Home Prices Nearly Doubled in the 2010s. What Do the 2020s Hold?," CurbedNY, December 13, 2019, https://ny.curbed.com/2019/12/13/21009872/nyc-home -value-2010s-manhattan-apartments.

Chapter 8: Getting the Dough You Deserve

144   **nearly 20 percent wage gap:** National Partnership for Women and Families, "America's Women and the Wage Gap," March 2020, https://www.national partnership.org/our-work/resources/economic-justice/fair-pay/americas-women -and-the-wage-gap.pdf.

144   **we earn less than men in nearly *every, single occupation*:** Lea Woods, "Despite Increased Labor Force Participation Among Women, Gender Wage Gap Persists, Even in the Occupations They Dominate," Institute for Women's Policy Research, March 24, 2020, https://iwpr.org/media/press-releases/despite -increased-labor-force-participation-gender-wage-gap-persists/.

144   **men outearn women at every level of educational attainment:** Anthony Carnevale, Nicole Smith, and Artem Gulish, *Women Can't Win: Despite Making Educational Gains and Pursuing High-Wage Majors, Women Still Earn Less Than Men*, Georgetown University Center on Education and the Workforce, https://1gyhoq479ufd3yna29x7ubjn-wpengine.netdna-ssl.com/wp -content/uploads/Women_ES_Web.pdf.

144   **the gender wage gap is often *even wider*:** American Association of University Women, "The Simple Truth About the Gender Pay Gap," https://www.aauw.org /research/the-simple-truth-about-the-gender-pay-gap/.

145   **between *$1 million* and *$1.5 million*:** Jennifer Ludden, "Ask for a Raise? Most Women Hesitate," *All Things Considered*, February 8, 2011, https://www.npr.org /2011/02/14/133599768/ask-for-a-raise-most-women-hesitate.

146   **lost out on more than half a million dollars:** Jianyi Nie, "Johns Hopkins Faculty Data Shows How a Gender Pay Gap Adds Up over a Lifetime," Johns Hopkins University School of Medicine, January 30, 2019, https://hub.jhu.edu /2019/01/30/gender-pay-gap-hopkins-faculty/.

147   **staying at a company for longer than two years:** Cameron Keng, "Employees Who Stay in Companies Longer Than Two Years Get Paid 50% Less," *Forbes*, June 22, 2014, https://www.forbes.com/sites/cameronkeng/2014/06/22 /employees-that-stay-in-companies-longer-than-2-years-get-paid-50-less /#c9b2572e07fa.

148   **employees who stick with the same company:** PayScale, "2020 Compensation Best Practices: Winning the Juggling Act," https://www.payscale.com/cbpr.

148   **expect a 3 percent annual raise:** *2017 Human Capital Benchmarking Report*,

Society for Human Resource Management, December 2017, https://www
.shrm.org/hr-today/trends-and-forecasting/research-and-surveys/Documents
/2017-Human-Capital-Benchmarking.pdf.

148   **10 to 20 percent increase in your salary:** Adam Hayes, "Salary Secrets: What
Is Considered a Big Raise?," Investopedia, February 8, 2020, https://www
.investopedia.com/articles/personal-finance/090415/salary-secrets-what
-considered-big-raise.asp.

148   **estimates average recruiting fees:** Matt Deutsch, "The Biggest Recruitment
Fees," Top Echelon, February 20, 2019, https://www.topechelon.com/blog
/placement-process/typical-placement-recruitment-fees-average/.

148   **the cost of replacing an employee:** Shane McFeely and Ben Wigert, "This
Fixable Problem Costs U.S. Businesses \$1 Trillion," Gallup, https://www
.gallup.com/workplace/247391/fixable-problem-costs-businesses-trillion.aspx.

148   **average time it takes to fill any given position:** *2016 Human Capital
Benchmarking Report*, Society for Human Resource Management, November
2016, https://www.shrm.org/hr-today/trends-and-forecasting/research-and
-surveys/Documents/2016-Human-Capital-Report.pdf.

148   **typical mid-level managers require:** Joe Mullich, "They're Hired, Now the
Real Recruiting Begins," Workforce.com, January 5, 2004, https://www
.workforce.com/news/theyre-hired-now-the-real-recruiting-begins.

150   **when we negotiate on behalf of others:** Tel Aviv University, "Study Finds
Women Achieve Better Results When Negotiating on Behalf of Friends,"
September 7, 2016, Phys.org, https://phys.org/news/2016-09-women-results
-behalf-friends.html.

152   **though women were more likely than men to be considered "top performers"
at work:** Visier, "Visier Insights' Equal Pay Day Brief Finds Younger Female
Workers Lost Ground in 2017," news release, April 10, 2018, https://www
.visier.com/press-release/visier-insights-equal-pay-day-brief-finds-younger
-female-workers-lost-ground-in-2017/.

152   **men are *40 percent* more likely than women:** Engage Employee, "Men 40
Percent More Likely Than Women to Be Promoted in Management Roles,"
August 25, 2016, https://engageemployee.com/men-40-percent-likely-women
-promoted-management-roles/.

152   **the gap widens as you advance up each rung:** Lean In, "Women in the
Workplace," October 1, 2020, https://wiw-report.s3.amazonaws.com/Women
_in_the_Workplace_2020.pdf.

152   **more than one-third of companies had just one female C-level executive:**
Lean In, "The 'Broken Rung' Is the Biggest Obstacle Women Face," https://
leanin.org/women-in-the-workplace-2019.

152   **women are less likely to *even ask* for a raise:** Jingcong Zhao, "New Research:
Men Promote Men and Women Promote Women," PayScale, May 3, 2018,
https://www.payscale.com/career-news/2018/05/new-research-promotion
-gap.

152   **women applied for a promotion only when they met 100 percent:** Tara
Sophia Mohr, "Why Women Don't Apply for Jobs Unless They're 100%
Qualified," *Harvard Business Review*, August 25, 2014, https://hbr.org/2014
/08/why-women-dont-apply-for-jobs-unless-theyre-100-qualified.

153   **The average man with a bachelor's degree earns $34,000 more annually:** Carnevale, Smith, and Gulish, *Women Can't Win.*

153   **potential earnings capacities of different career choices:** Carnevale, Smith, and Gulish, *Women Can't Win.*

153   **a woman with a bachelor's degree will see only a 51 percent increase:** Carnevale, Smith, and Gulish, *Women Can't Win.*

155   **women account for 32 percent of chief marketing officers:** Korn Ferry, "Korn Ferry Analysis of Largest U.S. Companies Shows Percentage of Women in Most C-Suite Roles Dramatically Lagging Male Counterparts," December 17, 2017, https://www.kornferry.com/about-us/press/korn-ferry-analysis-of-largest -us-companies-shows-percentage-of-women-in-most-c-suite-roles-dramatically -lagging-male-counterparts.

155   **women currently hold just thirty:** Catalyst, "List: Women CEOs of the S&P 500," August 3, 2020, https://www.catalyst.org/research/women-ceos-of -the-sp-500/.

155   **even women who are in the same C-level:** Comparably, "Study: What the C-Suite Earns (a Look at Executive Pay in Tech)," July 11, 2018, https://www .comparably.com/blog/what-the-c-suite-earns-a-look-at-executive-pay -in-tech/.

155   **only about *6 percent* of women are employed:** Elise Gould, Jessica Schieder, and Kathleen Geier, "What Is the Gender Pay Gap and Is It Real? The Complete Guide to How Women Are Paid Less Than Men and Why It Can't Be Explained Away," Economic Policy Institute, October 20, 2016, https:// www.epi.org/publication/what-is-the-gender-pay-gap-and-is-it-real/#epi -toc-18.

155   **nearly half the overall gender wage gap:** Francine D. Blau and Lawrence M. Kahn, "The Gender Wage Gap: Extent, Trends, and Explanations," National Bureau of Economic Research, Working Paper Series, no. 21913, January 2016, https://www.nber.org/papers/w21913.pdf.

156   **About 42 percent of working mothers have cut:** Kim Parker, "Women More Than Men Adjust Their Careers for Family Life," Pew Research Center, October 1, 2015, https://www.pewresearch.org/fact-tank/2015/10/01/women -more-than-men-adjust-their-careers-for-family-life/; https://www.american progress.org/issues/women/reports/2020/10/30/492582/covid-19-sent-womens -workforce-progress-backward/.

156   **suffer up to a 7 percent pay penalty upon their return:** PayScale, "Here Is How Much It Costs to Leave the Workforce," September 21, 2018, https:// www.payscale.com/career-news/2018/09/heres-how-much-it-costs-to-leave -the-workforce.

161   **men's earnings increased by more than 6 percent:** Third Way, "The Fatherhood Bonus and the Motherhood Penalty: Parenthood and the Gender Gap in Pay," September 2, 2014, https://www.thirdway.org/report/the -fatherhood-bonus-and-the-motherhood-penalty-parenthood-and-the-gender -gap-in-pay.

161   **studies have indicated mothers are *more* productive:** Matthias Krapf, Heinrich W. Ursprung, and Christian Zimmermann, "Parenthood and Productivity of Highly Skilled Labor: Evidence from the Groves of Academe,"

Federal Reserve Bank of St. Louis Research Division, Working Paper 2014–
001A, January 2014, https://s3.amazonaws.com/real.stlouisfed.org/wp/2014
/2014-001.pdf.

Chapter 9: Do Less, Achieve More

165 **It follows that women have to do *better* than a man:** Elizabeth H. Gorman and
Julie A. Kmec, "We (Have to) Try Harder: Gender and Required Work Effort in
Britain and the United States," *Gender and Society* 21, no. 6 (December 1, 2007):
828–56, https://journals.sagepub.com/doi/10.1177/0891243207309900.

165 **women consistently reported having to work harder:** Anne E. Bromley,
"Surveys of British and American Employees Conclude Women Must Work
Harder," UVA Today, November 27, 2007, https://news.virginia.edu/content
/surveys-british-and-american-employees-conclude-women-must-work-harder.

166 **"age detracts more from physical appearance for women than for men":** David
Neumark, Ian Burn, Patrick Button, "Is It Harder for Older Workers to Find
Jobs? New and Improved Evidence from a Field Experiment," *National Bureau
of Economic Research,* November 2017, https://www.nber.org/papers/w21669.

166 **studies confirming that housework is still considered women's work:** Claire
Cain Miller, "Why Women, but Not Men, Are Judged for a Messy House,"
New York Times, June 11, 2019, https://www.nytimes.com/2019/06/11/upshot
/why-women-but-not-men-are-judged-for-a-messy-house.html.

166 **women who are slim and wear makeup:** Nancy L. Etcoff, Shannon Stock,
Lauren E. Haley, Sarah A. Vickery, and David M. House, "Cosmetics as a
Feature of the Extended Human Phenotype: Modulation of the Perception of
Biologically Important Facial Signal," *PLoS One* 6, no. 10 (October 3, 2011),
shttp://www.plosone.org/article/info:doi%2F10.1371%2Fjournal.pone
.0025656.

166 **perceived to be more competent than . . . overweight counterparts:** Stuart
W. Flint, Martin Čadeck, Sonia C. Codreanu, et al., "Obesity Discrimination
in the Recruitment Process: 'You're Not Hired!,'" *Frontiers in Psychology* 7
(2016), https://www.ncbi.nlm.nih.gov/pmc/articles/PMC4853419/.

166 **come across as sexy, the effect is reversed:** Melissa L. Wookey, Nell A.
Graves, and J. Corey Butler, "Effects of a Sexy Appearance on Perceived
Competence of Women," *Journal of Social Psychology* 149, no. 1 (2009): 116–18,
https://pubmed.ncbi.nlm.nih.gov/19245051/.

167 **"considerably higher and more inflexible":** Kate Fox, "Mirror, Mirror: A
Summary of Research Findings on Body Image," Social Issues Research
Center, 1997, http://www.sirc.org/publik/mirror.html.

167 **hold just 38 percent of managerial positions:** Lean In, "Women in the
Workplace."

168 **"women volunteer for these non-promotable tasks more than men":** Linda
Babcock, Maria P. Recalde, and Lise Vesterlund, "Why Women Volunteer for
Tasks That Don't Lead to Promotions," *Harvard Business Review*, July 16,
2018, https://hbr.org/2018/07/why-women-volunteer-for-tasks-that-dont-lead
-to-promotions.

168 **"how we can make better choices for ourselves":** Chris Fleisher, "Women's Work? Why Female Employees Take on Thankless Tasks Shunned by Men . . . and How That May Hurt Women's Careers," American Economic Association, March 15, 2017, https://www.aeaweb.org/research/women-men-promotable -task-differences.

169 **"much more likely to ask women because we knew that they would say yes":** Linda Babcock, Marie P. Recalde, Lise Vesterlund, and Laurie Weingart, "Gender Differences in Accepting and Receiving Requests for Tasks with Low Promotability," *American Economic Review* 107, no. 3, 714–47, https://gap .hks.harvard.edu/breaking-glass-ceiling-%E2%80%9Cno%E2%80%9D -gender-differences-declining-requests-non%E2%80%90promotable -tasks.

169 **they are assigned 55 percent of all work:** Hive, "State of the Workplace: Part 1—Gender," https://hive.com/state-of-the-workplace/gender-2018/.

170 **still often designated as the default support staff in the corporate world:** Joan C. Williams, "Sticking Women with the Office Housework," *Washington Post*, April 14, 2014, https://www.washingtonpost.com/news/on-leadership/wp /2014/04/16/sticking-women-with-the-office-housework/

171 **if she turns down a request, she may be penalized:** M. E. Heilman and J. J. Chen, "Same Behavior, Different Consequences: Reactions to Men's and Women's Altruistic Citizenship Behavior," *Journal of Applied Psychology* 90, no. 3 (2005): 431–41, http://psycnet.apa.org/journals/apl/90 /3/431/.

172 **whereas when men help out, it tends to be in more visible:** A. H. Eagly and M. Crowley, "Gender and Helping Behavior: A Meta-Analytic Review of the Social Psychological Literature," *Psychological Bulletin* 100, no. 3 (1986): 283–308, https://psycnet.apa.org/record/1987-10139-001.

179 **they were actually *less* productive:** Modupe Akinola, A. Martin, and Katherine Phillips, "To Delegate or Not to Delegate: Gender Differences in Affective Associations and Behavioral Responses to Delegation," *Academy of Management Journal* 61, no. 4 (2018): 1476–491, https://www8.gsb.columbia .edu/researcharchive/articles/25937.

179 **"Get things off your plate so that you can take on new challenges and innovate":** Jeffrey A. Tucker, "Why Women Workers Might Be Less Willing to Delegate," American Institute for Economic Research, October 13, 2019, https://www.aier.org/article/why-women-workers-might-be-less-willing-to -delegate/.

181 **one-third of Americans work on the weekend:** Daniel S. Hamermesh and Elena Stancanelli, "Long Workweeks and Strange Hours," National Bureau of Economic Research, Working Paper Series 20449, September 2014, https:// www.nber.org/papers/w20449.

181 **after about forty-eight hours a week:** John Pencavel, "The Productivity of Working Hours," Institute for the Study of Labor, Discussion Paper no. 8129, http://ftp.iza.org/dp8129.pdf.

181 **actually lead to a 1 percent *decrease* in wages:** Jeffrey T. Denning, Brian Jacob, Lars Lefgren, and Christian vom Lehn, "The Return to Hours Worked Within and Across Occupations: Implications for the Gender Wage Gap,"

National Bureau of Economic Research, Working Paper no. 25739, April 2019, https://www.nber.org/papers/w25739.

182 **"daughters, on the other hand, may miss the chance to gain confidence":** Lisa Damour, "Why Girls Beat Boys at School and Lose to Them at the Office," *New York Times*, February 7, 2019, https://www.nytimes.com/2019/02 /07/opinion/sunday/girls-school-confidence.html.

Chapter 10: Beyond Passion

189 **"But, let's be real. None of this guarantees wealth, or even financial success."** Leonard A. Schlesinger, Charles F. Kiefer, and Paul B. Brown, "Choosing Between Making Money and Doing What You Love," *Harvard Business Review*, March 29, 2012, https://hbr.org/2012/03/choosing-between -making-money.

Chapter 11: Now What?

211 **two paychecks are often necessary:** Pew Research Center, "The Rise in Dual Income Households," June 18, 2015, https://www.pewresearch.org/ft_dual -income-households-1960-2012-2/.

211 **nearly half of all households with kids:** Cynthia Hess et al., *The Status of Women in the States*, Institute for Women's Policy Research, June 2015, http:// statusofwomendata.org/wp-content/uploads/2015/02/IWPR-Final-Report-6 -5-2015.pdf and Elyse Shaw et al., *Mothers as Workers, Primary Caregivers, and Breadwinners During COVID-19*, Institute for Women's Policy Research, May 2020, https://iwpr.org/wp-content/uploads/2020/06/Holding-Up-Half-the -Sky-Mothers-as-Breadwinners.pdf.

212 **in order to stay home with their kids:** Lisa Belkin, "The Opt-Out Revolution," *New York Times Magazine*, October 26, 2003, https://www.nytimes.com/2003 /10/26/magazine/the-opt-out-revolution.html.

212 **a follow-up article that included many of the same women:** Judith Warner, "The Opt-Out Generation Wants Back In," *New York Times*, August 11, 2013, https://www.nytimes.com/2013/08/11/magazine/the-opt-out-generation-wants -back-in.html.

212 **a quarter of the women surveyed took jobs with fewer management responsibilities:** Laura Sherbin, and Diana Forster, "Off-Ramps and On-Ramps Revisited," *Harvard Business Review*, June 2010, https://hbr.org/2010 /06/off-ramps-and-on-ramps-revisited.

218 **Women *are* still the ones most likely to put their careers on hold:** Liz Elting, "Why Women Quit," *Forbes*, August 21, 2019, https://www.forbes.com/sites /lizelting/2019/08/21/why-women-quit/; https://www.marketplace .org/2020/07/16/moms-are-reducing-work-hours-4-5-times-more-than -dads-during-pandemic/.

218 **Fewer than a third of different-sex couples in a 2016 study:** Daniel L. Carlson, Amanda J. Miller, Sharon Sassler, and Sarah Hanson, "The Gendered

Division of Housework and Couples' Sexual Relationships: A Reexamination," *Journal of Marriage and Family* 78, no. 4 (2016): 975–95, https://onlinelibrary .wiley.com/doi/pdf/10.1111/jomf.12313.

218   **women still spend two hours more** *each day* **cleaning:** Cynthia Hess, Tanima Ahmed, and Jeff Hayes, "Providing Unpaid Household and Care Work in the United States: Uncovering Inequality," Institute for Women's Policy Research and Oxfam America, Briefing Paper, January 2020, https://iwpr.org/wp -content/uploads/2020/01/IWPR-Providing-Unpaid-Household-and-Care -Work-in-the-United-States-Uncovering-Inequality.pdf.

218   **married mothers actually spend** *more* **time on housework:** Joanna R. Pepin, Liana C. Sayer, and Lynne Casper, "Marital Status and Mothers' Time Use: Childcare, Housework, Leisure, and Sleep," SocArXiv, January 17, 2018, https://osf.io/preprints/socarxiv/4xz8q/.

219   **women across the country who work full-time spend 22 percent more time:** American Time Use Survey, U.S. Bureau of Labor Statistics, https://www.bls .gov/tus/.

219   **women who earn more than their husbands actually take on even more:** Kim Parker and Wendy Wang, "Time in Work and Leisure: Patterns by Gender and Family Structure," chap. 6 in *Modern Parenthood: Roles of Moms and Dads Converge as They Balance Work and Family* (Washington, DC: Pew Research Center, March 14, 2013), https://www.pewsocialtrends.org/2013/03/14 /chapter-6-time-in-work-and-leisure-patterns-by-gender-and-family -structure/.

Chapter 12: Letting Go

222   **men between eighteen and thirty-four years old in opposite-sex relationships:** Claire Cain Miller, "The Household Work Men and Women Do, and Why," *New York Times*, February 12, 2020, https://www.nytimes .com/2020/02/12/us/the-household-work-men-and-women-do-and-why.html.

222   **In marriages formed before 1992:** Sabino Kornrich, Julie Brines, and Katrina Leupp, "Egalitarianism, Housework, and Sexual Frequency in Marriage," *American Sociological Review* 78, no. 1 (February 2013): 26–50, https:// journals.sagepub.com/doi/abs/10.1177/0003122412472340.

222   **later studies that looked at marriage data from 2006:** Council on Contemporary Families, "A Reversal in Predictors of Sexual Frequency and Satisfaction in Marriage," June 20, 2016, https://contemporaryfamilies.org/sex -equalmarriages/.

222   **those who divided housework and childcare:** Daniel L. Carlson, Sarah Hanson, and Andrea Fitzroy, "The Division of Child Care, Sexual Intimacy, and Relationship Quality in Couples," *Gender and Society* 30, no. 3 (2016), 442–66, https://journals.sagepub.com/doi/pdf/10.1177/0891243215626709.

222   **Women still do about two hours more:** Kim Parker and Wendy Wang, "Americans' Time at Paid Work, Housework, Child Care, 1965 to 2011," chap. 5 in *Modern Parenthood: Roles of Moms and Dads Converge as They Balance Work and Family* (Washington, DC: Pew Research Center, March 14, 2013), https://

www.pewsocialtrends.org/2013/03/14/chapter-5-americans-time-at-paid-work
-housework-child-care-1965-to-2011/

222 **working women are more than three times:** Pew Research Center, "Raising
Kids and Running a Household: How Working Parents Share the Load,"
November 4, 2015, https://www.pewsocialtrends.org/2015/11/04/raising
-kids-and-running-a-household-how-working-parents-share-the-load/.

223 **data show boys are assigned fewer chores than girls:** Claire Cain Miller, "A
'Generationally Perpetuated' Pattern: Daughters Do More Chores," *New York
Times*, August 8, 2018, https://www.nytimes.com/2018/08/08/upshot/chores
-girls-research-social-science.html.

223 **get paid more for them:** Renee Morad, "The Gender Pay Gap Starts Earlier
Than You Think," NBC News, October 29, 2018, https://www.nbcnews.com
/know-your-value/feature/gender-pay-gap-starts-earlier-you-think-ncna
925696.

228 **women get caught between two incompatible beliefs:** Alison Escalante,
"Should Storm: Parents and the Culture of Criticism," *Psychology Today*,
October 28, 2018, https://www.psychologytoday.com/us/blog/shouldstorm
/201810/shouldstorm.

228 **Working mothers spend as much time doing activities:** Claire Cain Miller,
"The Relentlessness of Modern Parenting," *New York Times*, December 25,
2018, https://www.nytimes.com/2018/12/25/upshot/the-relentlessness-of
-modern-parenting.html.

229 **"the cultural ideal of motherhood":** Alison Escalante, "Drowning in
Parenting Stress? Here's What to Do About It," *Psychology Today*, March 18,
2019, https://www.psychologytoday.com/us/blog/shouldstorm/201903
/drowning-in-parenting-stress-heres-what-do-about-it.

229 **moms bore the burden across Western cultures:** Loes Meeussen and Colette
van Laar, "Feeling Pressure to Be a Perfect Mother Relates to Parental
Burnout and Career Ambitions," *Frontiers in Psychology* 9 (2018), https://www
.ncbi.nlm.nih.gov/pmc/articles/PMC6230657/.

232 **data show women are no better at it than men:** Leah Ruppanner, "Women
Are Not Better at Multitasking. They Just Do More Work, Studies Show,"
Science Alert, August 15, 2019, https://www.sciencealert.com/women-aren
-t-better-multitaskers-than-men-they-re-just-doing-more-work.

232 **human brains actually cannot manage multiple activities:** John Hamilton,
"Think You're Multitasking? Think Again," *Morning Edition*, NPR, October 2,
2008, https://www.npr.org/templates/story/story.php?storyId=95256794.

232 **both parents report feeling more rushed:** Leah Ruppanner, Francisco Perales,
and Janeen Baxter, "Harried and Unhealthy? Parenthood, Time Pressure, and
Mental Health," *Journal of Marriage and Family* 81, no. 2 (2019): 308–26,
https://onlinelibrary.wiley.com/doi/abs/10.1111/jomf.12531.

235 **suffered *no* negative consequences:** Rachel G. Lucas-Thompson, Wendy A.
Goldberg, and JoAnn Prause, "Maternal Work Early in the Lives of Children
and Its Distal Associations with Achievement and Behavior Problems: A
Meta-Analysis," *Psychological Bulletin* 136, no. 6: 915–42, https://www.apa
.org/pubs/journals/releases/bul-136-6-915.pdf.

236 **"Kids of working moms grow into happy adults":** Kathleen L. McGinn,

Mayra Ruiz Castro, and Elizabeth Long Lingo, "Learning from Mum: Cross-National Evidence Linking Maternal Employment and Adult Children's Outcomes," *Work, Employment and Society* 33, no. 3 (2019): 374–400, http://journals.sagepub.com/eprint/DQzHJAJMUYWQevh577wr /full.

236 **improved cognitive development:** Amy Hsin and Christina Felfe, "When Does Time Matter? Maternal Employment, Children's Time with Parents, and Child Development," *Demography* 51, no. 5 (2014): 1867–94, https://www .ncbi.nlm.nih.gov/pmc/articles/PMC4860719/.

237 **the more engaged dads are in a positive way:** Anna Sarkadi, Robert Kristiansson, Frank Oberklaid, and Sven Bremberg, "Fathers' Involvement and Children's Developmental Outcomes: A Systematic Review of Longitudinal Studies," *Acta Pædiatrica* 97, no. 2 (2008): 153–58, https://onlinelibrary.wiley .com/doi/abs/10.1111/j.1651-2227.2007.00572.x.

237 **healthier and happier than moms who stay at home:** American Psychological Association, "Working Moms Feel Better Than Stay-at-Home Moms, Study Finds," *ScienceDaily*, December 12, 2011, https://www.sciencedaily.com/releases /2011/12/111212124520.htm

239 **"parenting network" of the brain:** Eyal Abraham, Talma Hendler, Irit Shapira-Lichter, et al., "Father's Brain Is Sensitive to Childcare Experiences," *Proceedings of the National Academy of Sciences* 111, no. 27 (May 2014): 9792–97, https://www.pnas.org/content/early/2014/05/22/1402569111.

239 **"we're all born with the circuitry to help us be sensitive caregivers":** Elizabeth Norton, "Parenting Rewires the Male Brain," *Science*, May 27, 2014, https://www.sciencemag.org/news/2014/05/parenting-rewires-male-brain.

239 **As we earn more, Munsch found:** American Sociological Association, "Being the Primary Breadwinner Is Bad for Men's Psychological Well-Being and Health," *ScienceDaily*, August 19, 2016, https://www.sciencedaily.com/releases /2016/08/160819084356.htm.

Chapter 13: Beyond "Having It All"

244 **"practical" tips for working moms:** Joyce Gabriel and Bettye Baldwin, *Having It All: A Practical Guide to Managing a Home and a Career* (New York: Warner Books, 1980).

245 **"I never, so to speak, had it all":** Claudia Luther, "Helen Gurley Brown, Longtime Cosmopolitan Editor, Dies at 90," *Los Angeles Times*, August 14, 2012, https://www.latimes.com/local/obituaries/la-me-helen-gurley-brown -20120814-story.html.

248 **women weren't held back because of trouble balancing the competing demands:** Robin J. Ely and Irene Padavic, "What's Really Holding Women Back?," *Harvard Business Review* (March–April 2020), https://hbr.org/2020/03 /whats-really-holding-women-back.

249 **valorizing long work hours and an on-demand culture:** Sarah Green Carmichael, "The Research Is Clear: Long Hours Backfire for People and for Companies," *Harvard Business Review*, August 19, 2015, https://hbr.org

/2015/08/the-research-is-clear-long-hours-backfire-for-people-and-for
-companies.

249 **leads to more employee health problems and turnover:** Bronwyn Fryer, "Are
You Working Too Hard?" *Harvard Business Review*, November 2005, https://
hbr.org/2005/11/are-you-working-too-hard.

250 **most working dads say they wish they had more time:** Gretchen Livingston,
"Most Dads Say They Spend Too Little Time with Their Children; About a
Quarter Live Apart from Them," Pew Research Center, January 8, 2018,
https://www.pewresearch.org/fact-tank/2018/01/08/most-dads-say-they
-spend-too-little-time-with-their-children-about-a-quarter-live-apart-from
-them/.

250 **They're still feeling pressure to be the main earner:** National Parents'
Organization, "Survey: Fathers Experience Greater Work-Family Conflict
Than Ever Before," blog, https://nationalparentsorganization.org/blog/17056
-survey-fathers-expe.

251 **nearly six in ten male breadwinners with children:** Shireen Kanji, "Men
Want to Spend More Time at Home—Even If It Means Taking a Pay Cut,"
The Conversation, September 11, 2015, https://theconversation.com/men
-want-to-spend-more-time-at-home-even-if-it-means-taking-a-pay-cut
-47333.

252 **The average cost for daycare:** Editorial staff, "Child Care Costs More in 2020,
and the Pandemic Has Parents Scrambling for Solutions," Care.com, June 15,
2020, https://www.care.com/c/stories/2423/how-much-does-child-care-cost/.

252 **percentage of companies that actually offer them now:** Care.com, press
release, "Care.com Survey Finds One in Three Families Spend 20% or More of
Household Income on Child Care," July 17, 2018, https://www.care.com
/press-release-1-in-3-families-spend-20-of-income-on-child-care-p1186
-q92524253.html.

252 **moms were 40 percent more likely than dads:** Leila Schochet, "The Child
Care Crisis Is Keeping Women out of the Workforce," Center for American
Progress, March 28, 2019, https://www.americanprogress.org/issues/early
-childhood/reports/2019/03/28/467488/child-care-crisis-keeping-women
-workforce/.

253 **U.S. companies lose an estimated $12.7 billion annually:** Sandra Bishop-
Josef, Chris Beakey, Sara Watson, and Tom Garrett, *Want to Grow the
Economy? Fix the Child Care Crisis* (New York: Council for a Strong America
and Ready Nation, January 2019), https://strongnation.s3.amazonaws.com
/documents/602/83bb2275-ce07-4d74-bcee-ff6178daf6bd.pdf?1547054862
&inline;%20filename=%22Want%20to%20Grow%20the%20Economy
?%20Fix%20the%20Child%20Care%20Crisis.pdf%22.

253 *45 percent* **of working parents experienced childcare issues:** Annabelle Timsit
and Lila MacLellan, "How the Biggest Names in Tech Stack Up on Backup
Childcare Benefits," Quartz, March 13, 2019, https://qz.com/work
/1568480/amazon-competitors-with-backup-childcare-google-facebook-apple
-microsoft/.

253 **childcare services can decrease employee absences:** Early Care and Learning
Council, "Why Should Employers Care? Relationship Between Productivity

and Working Parents," https://childcarecouncil.com/wp-content/uploads/2014 /07/Why-Should-Employers-Care-ECLC.pdf.

253 **It has since opened one at its four-hundred-employee:** Rose Marcario, "Our Company Policies for Families," Patagonia, https://www.patagonia.com/stories /family-business-weighing-the-business-case/story-32958.html.

253 **The outdoor clothing company reported recently that 100 percent:** Dean Carter, "Why Strong Families Build Strong Businesses," Medium, March 9, 2016, https://medium.com/@patagonia/why-strong-families-build-strong -businesses-e20ac8928767.

253 **only 4 percent of U.S. companies now offer free on-site childcare:** Society for Human Resource Management, "2019 Employee Benefits Survey," https:// www.shrm.org/hr-today/trends-and-forecasting/research-and-surveys/pages /benefits19.aspx.

253 **employers who've provided paid or subsidized care:** Alameda County Early Care and Education Program, "Overview of Federal and State Child Care Related Tax Credits," Child Care Law Center, June 2002, https://www.acgov .org/ece/credits.htm.

254 **another 5 percent of employers overall:** Kenneth Matos, Ellen Galinsky, and James T. Bond, *2016 National Study of Employers* (Society for Human Resource Management, 2017), https://www.shrm.org/hr-today/trends-and-forecasting /research-and-surveys/Documents/National%20Study%20of%20Employers .pdf.

254 **Starbucks captured headlines:** Meera Jaganathan, "Starbucks Will Offer Its Employees Backup Child Care for Just $1 Per Hour," MarketWatch, October 10, 2018, https://www.marketwatch.com/story/starbucks-will-offer -its-employees-backup-child-care-for-just-1-per-hour-2018-10-10-1288327.

254 **Bright Horizons . . . said it has seen a 70 percent increase:** Jena McGregor, "Amazon Moms Are Every Working Mom, Calling for Backup Day-Care Benefits," *Washington Post*, March 6, 2019, https://www.washingtonpost.com /business/2019/03/06/amazon-moms-are-every-working-mom-calling-backup -day-care-benefits/.

254 **nearly 40 percent of U.S. jobs:** Jonathan I. Dingel and Brent Neiman, "How Many Jobs Can Be Done at Home?," Becker Friedman Institute for Economics at the University of Chicago, June 2020, https://bfi.uchicago.edu/wp-content /uploads/BFI_White-Paper_Dingel_Neiman_3.2020.pdf.

254 **before the pandemic, only around 8 percent of all employees:** U.S. Bureau of Labor Statistics, "Table 3. Workers Who Worked at Home and How Often They Worked Exclusively at Home by Selected Characteristics, Averages for the Period 2017–2018," Economic News Release, last modified September 24, 2019, https://www.bls.gov/news.release/flex2.t03.htm.

254 **60 percent of U.S. employees:** Megan Brenan, "U.S. Workers Discovering Affinity for Remote Work," Gallup, April 3, 2020, https://news.gallup.com /poll/306695/workers-discovering-affinity-remote-work.aspx.

255 **nearly half of those working remotely:** Peyton Shelburne, "The Pandemic Is Exposing More Americans to Remote Work, and Many Are Latching On to the Practice," Morning Consult, July 1, 2020, https://morningconsult.com /form/pandemic-remote-work-preferences/.

255   **headline last year: "Is the Five-Day Office Week Over?"** Claire Cain Miller, "Is the Five-Day Office Week Over?," *New York Times*, July 2, 2020, https://www.nytimes.com/2020/07/02/upshot/is-the-five-day-office-week-over.html.

255   **both workers and their employers found that productivity:** Vala Afshar, "Majority of Remote Workers Are More Productive and Communicative," ZDNet, May 12, 2020, https://www.zdnet.com/article/majority-of-workers-are-more-productive-and-communicative-at-home/.

255   **found they were 13 percent more efficient:** Nicholas A. Bloom, James Liang, John Roberts, and Zhichun Jenny Ying, "Does Working from Home Work? Evidence from a Chinese Experiment," *Quarterly Journal of Economics* (2015), 165–218, https://www.gsb.stanford.edu/faculty-research/publications/does-working-home-work-evidence-chinese-experiment.

255   **expected remote-work arrangements would remain:** Alexander W. Bartik, Zoe B. Cullen, Edward L. Glaeser, et al., "What Jobs Are Being Done at Home During the Covid-19 Crisis? Evidence from Firm-Level Surveys," National Bureau of Economic Research, Working Paper no. 27422, June 2020, https://www.nber.org/papers/w27422.

255   **43 percent of employees in business services:** David Altig, Jose Maria Barrero, Nick Bloom, et al., "Firms Expect Working from Home to Triple," *Macroblog*, Federal Reserve Bank of Atlanta, https://www.frbatlanta.org/blogs/macroblog/2020/05/28/firms-expect-working-from-home-to-triple.

255   **72 percent of employers say remote work:** Human Capital Advisory Group, "The Rise of the Remote Workforce: Benefits, Behaviors and Best Practices," March 17, 2020, Global Workplace Analytics, https://bhcagroup.com/remote-workforce#:~:text=According%20to%20Global%20Workplace%20Analytics,work%20arrangements%20increase%20employee%20morale.

256   **nearly half of the 246 employers it surveyed:** Alight Solutions, "How Employers Are Responding to COVID-19: Paid Time Off," March 18, 2020, https://alight.com/research-insights/employers-responding-covid-19-paid-time-off.

256   **It extended the duration of paid family-leave benefits from six to eight weeks starting in July 2020:** Employee Development Department, State of California, "FAQS: Paid Family Leave Eligibility," accessed on October 3, 2020, https://edd.ca.gov/Disability/FAQ_PFL_Eligibility.htm.

256   **Paid family leave is (as of this writing) now mandated:** Lisa Nagele-Piazza and Allen Smith, "Paid Leave May Be 2020's Biggest Workplace News," Society for Human Resource Management, January 2, 2020, https://www.shrm.org/resourcesandtools/legal-and-compliance/employment-law/pages/2020-workplace-trends.aspx.

257   **nearly 30 percent of working women nationwide:** Kelly Jones and Britni Wilcher, "Reducing Maternal Labor Market Detachment: A Role for Paid Family Leave," Working Paper, American University of Economics, EconPapers, 2019, https://econpapers.repec.org/paper/amuwpaper/2019-07.htm.

257   **up to a 50 percent reduction after five years:** March of Dimes, "New Study Reveals Paid Family Leave Policies Lead to 20% Fewer Women Leaving the Workforce," January 3, 2020, https://www.marchofdimes.org/news/new-study

-reveals-paid-family-leave-policies-lead-to-20-fewer-women-leaving-the
-workforce.aspx.

257   **paid time off nearly closed the gap in workforce participation:** Institute for
Women's Policy Research, "Fact Sheet: Paid Family Leave Increases Mothers'
Labor Market Attachment," January 2020, https://www.marchofdimes.org
/materials/B383-Paid-Leave-Fact-Sheet.pdf.

257   **the program had actually generated cost** *savings***:** Eileen Appelbaum and
Ruth Milkman, *Leaves That Pay: Employer and Worker Experiences with Paid
Family Leave in California*, Center for Economic and Policy Research, January
2011, https://www.cepr.net/documents/publications/paid-family-leave-1
-2011.pdf.

257   **paternity leave can improve outcomes:** Petra Persson and Maya Rossin-
Slater, "When Dad Can Stay Home: Fathers' Workplace Flexibility and
Maternal Health," National Bureau of Economic Research, Working Paper no.
25902, October 2019, https://www.nber.org/papers/w25902.

257   **"significantly increase the personal and economic well-being of their
families":** U.S. Department of Labor, "Paternity Leave: Why Parental Leave
for Fathers Is So Important for Working Families," policy brief, 2016, https://
digitalcommons.ilr.cornell.edu/cgi/viewcontent.cgi?article=2604&context=
key_workplace.

258   **more than 80 percent of U.S. employees:** Stephen Miller, "Paid Family Leave,
on the Rise, Helps Women Stay in the Workforce," Society for Human
Resource Management, January 15, 2020, https://www.shrm.org/resourcesand
tools/hr-topics/benefits/pages/paid-family-leave-helps-women-stay-in-the
-workforce.aspx.

258   **Nearly two hundred well-known companies now offer:** Fairygodboss, "Paid
Maternity Leave: 180 Companies Who Offer the Most Paid Leave," https://
fairygodboss.com/articles/paid-maternity-leave-companies-who-offer-the
-most-paid-leave.

258   **more than a dozen major companies:** Yusuf George, "The 14 Companies
Taking the Lead on Parental Leave," Just Capital, June 20, 2019, https://
justcapital.com/news/companies-taking-the-lead-on-parental-leave/.

259   **schools are closed 80 percent longer:** Casey Quinlan, "Our Outdated School
Schedules Are Hurting Working Parents," Center for American Progress,
October 12, 2016, https://archive.thinkprogress.org/our-outdated-school
-schedules-are-hurting-working-parents-6d8c0f3dca5a/.

259   **only one of every three students:** Afterschool Alliance, "This Is Afterschool,"
March 2020, http://afterschoolalliance.org/documents/National-One-Pager
-2020.pdf.

260   **about 1.5 million kids participated nationwide:** Emily Parker, Louisa Diffey,
Bruce Atchison, *How States Fund Pre-K: A Primer for Policymakers,* Education
Commission of the States, 2018, https://www.ecs.org/wp-content/uploads
/How-States-Fund-Pre-K_A-Primer-for-Policymakers.pdf#page=5.

260   **offer truly universal free pre-K:** Parker, Diffey, and Atchison, *How States
Fund Pre-K: A Primer for Policymakers,* 5.

260   **several cities have also taken initiatives:** CityHealth and the National
Institute for Early Education Research, *Pre-K in American Cities: Quality and*

Access Grow, but Cities Are Missing Opportunities to Create Lasting Benefits for Their Youngest Learners, 12, http://nieer.org/wp-content/uploads/2019/01/CH_Pre-K_H.1.23.19pdf.pdf#page=12.

260   **return on investment for high-quality pre-K programs:** James J. Heckman, "13% ROI Research Toolkit," Heckman, https://heckmanequation.org/resource/13-roi-toolbox/.

260   **United States would see a net benefit of $83.3 billion:** Cristina Novoa and Katie Hamm, "The Cost of Inaction on Universal Preschool," Center for American Progress, October 31, 2007, https://www.americanprogress.org/issues/early-childhood/news/2017/10/31/441825/the-cost-of-inaction-on-universal-preschool/.

Chapter 14: Find Your Allies

272   **researchers noted a . . . "broken rung":** Lean In, "The 'Broken Rung' Is the Biggest Obstacle Women Face," https://womenintheworkplace.com/2019.

286   **The article spotlighted the Austin Women's Investing Group:** Joshua Brockman, "Women Are 'Claiming Their Power' in Investment Clubs of Their Own," *New York Times*, April 24, 2020, https://www.nytimes.com/2020/04/24/business/women-investing-clubs-retirement.html.

287   **one podcast host found that women were way more forthcoming:** Gaby Dun, "Why We'd Rather Talk About Sex Than Money—and How I Plan to Change It," *The Guardian*, November 2, 2016, https://www.theguardian.com/money/2016/nov/02/bad-with-money-talking-about-finances-gaby-dunn-podcast.

289   **Amy Nelson, mom of four girls and founder of the Riveter:** Amy Nelson, "The Riveter's Amy Nelson: For Mother's Day, Let's Give Women Equal Pay," NBC News, May 6, 2020, https://www.nbcnews.com/know-your-value/feature/riveter-s-amy-nelson-mother-s-day-let-s-give-ncna1201516.

289   **In 2019, $6.1 billion was invested:** Gené Teare, "EoY 2019 Diversity Report: 20 Percent of Newly Funded Startups in 2019 Have a Female Founder," Crunchbase News, January 21, 2020, https://news.crunchbase.com/news/eoy-2019-diversity-report-20-percent-of-newly-funded-startups-in-2019-have-a-female-founder/.

Conclusion

293   **shared their experiences via email at Microsoft:** Dave Gershgorn, "Amid Employee Uproar, Microsoft Is Investigating Sexual Harassment Claims Overlooked by HR," Quartz, April 4, 2019, https://qz.com/1587477/microsoft-investigating-sexual-harassment-claims-overlooked-by-hr/.

293   **several prominent companies vowing to stop sponsoring:** Dean Takahasi, "Sexual Abuse Allegations Rock the Game Industry Again," Venture Beat, June 24, 2020, https://venturebeat.com/2020/06/24/sexual-abuse-allegations-rock-the-game-industry-again/.

293   **six female big-wave surfers:** Ruchika Tulshyan, "7 Lessons from the U.S. Women's Soccer Team's Fight for Equal Pay," *Harvard Business Review*, September 25, 2019, https://hbr.org/2019/09/7-lessons-from-the-u-s-womens -soccer-teams-fight-for-equal-pay.

294   **now allows *unlimited* paid parental leave:** Amy Watson, "Netflix: Global Gender Distribution of Employees, 2019–2020," Statista, June 8, 2020, https://www.statista.com/statistics/1000377/netflix-employees-gender/.

294   **increase African American and Latinx representation:** Dell Technologies, *Our Social Impact Plan for 2030: Progress Made Real*, https://corporate.delltech nologies.com/content/dam/delltechnologies/assets/corporate/pdf/dell -technologies-progress-made-real-2030-plan.pdf.

294   **double the number of women and underrepresented minorities:** Intel, *Corporate Responsibility at Intel, 2019–20*, http://csrreportbuilder.intel.com /pdfbuilder/pdfs/CSR-2019-20-Full-Report.pdf.

294   **proportion of "leadership representation of underrepresented groups":** Mike Murphy, "Google Promises to Improve Diversity at Senior Levels, Commits $175 Million for Black Businesses," MarketWatch, June 17, 2020, https://www.marketwatch.com/story/google-promises-to-improve -diversity-at-senior-levels-commits-175-million-for-black-businesses-2020 -06-17?.

295   **female CEOs are 50 percent more likely:** Mark Misercola, "Higher Returns with Women in Decision-Making Positions," Credit Suisse, March 10, 2016, https://www.credit-suisse.com/corporate/en/articles/news-and-expertise /higher-returns-with-women-in-decision-making-positions-201610.html.

295   **returns that were *226 percent higher*:** Karen Rubin, "Research: Investing in Women-Led Fortune 1000 Companies," Quantopian, February 11, 2015, https://www.quantopian.com/posts/research-investing-in-women-led -fortune-1000-companies.

295   **female chief revenue officers in Fortune 1000:** R. Kress, "Numbers Show Women-Led Companies Outperform Competitors," Ivy Exec, https://www .ivyexec.com/career-advice/2017/women-led-companies-outperform -competitors/.

295   **"were 25 percent more likely to experience above-average profitability":** Sundiatu Dixon-Fyle, Kevin Dolan, Vivian Hunt, and Sara Prince, "Diversity Wins: How Inclusion Matters," McKinsey and Company, May 19, 2020, https://www.mckinsey.com/featured-insights/diversity-and-inclusion/diversity -wins-how-inclusion-matters.

295   **"engaged, inspired and satisfied employees":** Heartbeat, "The XX Factor: The Strategic Benefits of Women in Leadership," Peakon, https://peakon.com /heartbeat/reports/the-strategic-benefits-of-women-in-leadership/.

296   **"The higher the percentage of women in top management":** Misercola, "Higher Returns with Women in Decision-Making Positions."

296   **female-founded startups tend to come out ahead:** Emma Hinchliffe, "Funding for Female Founders Stalled at 2.2% of VC Dollars in 2018," *Fortune*, January 28, 2019, https://fortune.com/2019/01/28/funding-female -founders-2018/.

296   **companies founded or cofounded by women:** Katie Abouzahr, Matt Krentz,

John Harthorne, and Frances Brooks Taplett, "Why Women-Owned Startups Are a Better Bet," Boston Consulting Group, June 6, 2018, https://www.bcg .com/publications/2018/why-women-owned-startups-are-better-bet.

296   **female-founded and female-cofounded companies:** Claire Diaz-Ortiz, "The Rise of the Great Winged Unicorn," TechCrunch, February 20, 2020, https:// techcrunch.com/2020/02/20/the-rise-of-the-winged-pink-unicorn/.

297   **TheSkimm, a startup that's already profitable:** Pennsylvania Conference for Women, "TheSkimm Co-founders: Progress Comes When Hearing 'No' Starts to Lose Its Meaning," November 11, 2020, https://www .paconferenceforwomen.org/theskimm-co-founders-progress-comes-when -hearing-no-starts-to-lose-its-meaning/.

297   **Glassdoor-like career site and social network:** Fairygodboss, "Fairygodboss Raises $10M to Become Daily Habit for Career-Minded Women," Fairygodboss, https://fairygodboss.com/articles/fairygodboss-raises-series-a.

297   **Edith Cooper and her daughter:** Emma Hinchliffe, "Slack Board Member and Former Goldman Sachs Executive Launches a Career Development Startup with Her Daughter," *Fortune*, July 21, 2020, https://fortune.com/2020/07/21 /medley-career-development-edith-cooper-jordan-taylor-mother-daughter -business/?.

298   **women invest in women at nearly three times the rate:** Seth Oranburg and Mark Geiger, "Do Female Investors Support Female Entrepreneurs? An Empirical Analysis of Angel Investor Behavior," Duquesne University School of Law, Research Paper no. 2019-06, https://papers.ssrn.com/sol3/papers.cfm ?abstract_id=3429077.

Index